Encyclopedia of the Undead

A
FIELD GUIDE
TO CREATURES
THAT CANNOT
REST IN PEACE

Dr. Bob Curran

New Page Books
A division of The Career Press, Inc.
Franklin Lakes, NJ

Encyclopedia of the Undead

Edited by Gina Talucci

Typeset by Eileen Dow Munson

Cover design by Lu Rossman/DigiDog Design

Cover illustration by Ian Daniels

Printed in the U.S.A. by Book-mart Press

To order this title, please call toll-free 1-800-CAREER-1 (NJ and Canada: 201-848-0310) to order using VISA or MasterCard, or for further information on books from Career Press.

The Career Press, Inc., 3 Tice Road, PO Box 687,
Franklin Lakes, NJ 07417
www.careerpress.com
www.newpagebooks.com

Library of Congress Cataloging-in-Publication Data

Curran, Bob.
Encyclopedia of the undead : a field guide to creatures that cannot rest in peace / by Bob Curran.
p. cm.
Includes index.
ISBN 1-56414-841-6 (pbk.)
1. Vampires. 2. Werewolves. 3. Zombies. 4. Ghouls and ogres. I. Title.

GR830.V3C87 2006
398′.45—dc22

2005056184

To my wife, Mary,

and my children, Michael and Jennifer,

for all their help, support, and tolerance during

the writing of this book.

Acknowledgments

To the staff at New Page Books for all their help with this book.

Contents

Preface

The purpose of this book is to explore both the history and perceptions of the Undead, and whether legends concerning them have in their roots some form of reality. It also looks at how these perceptions have developed and deeply ingrained themselves within the human psyche. Through the years, both aspects have often become so inextricably intertwined that it is sometimes difficult to delineate the various strands that make up the beliefs and treat them separately. The concept of the Undead must be viewed as a cohesive whole. An understanding of such interconnected historical detail and perceptual development does not, therefore, readily lend itself to the piecemeal and fragmented entry system, which means that the reader has to "refer back" to other entries in order to understand the topic. So that full justice can be done to the areas considered, it has been decided not to follow what might be considered as the standard procedures for encyclopaedias or directories. Rather, the book follows a more "flowing" approach, so that the topic in question can be fully explored, but under a series of general subject headings that will guide the reader to the specific area which is being considered. In this way, we can get a much better picture of how perceptions of the Undead and supernatural creatures have grown and changed over the years. In this way, we feel that we can do the subjects covered a proper justice.

I am, nevertheless, well aware that some readers may require some form of listing in order to pick up on specialisms and topics of particular interest. To this end, I have placed a full A–Z listing at the back of the book. This approach, I hope, will give an ordered, comprehensive, and readable text whilst also providing specific points to which the reader can refer. I realize, of course, that this may not be the "normal approach" to such works but then, the subjects with which we are dealing are not "normal" either.

The concept of the Undead, and of the beings that haunt the deepest recesses of our minds, continue to both alternately terrify and fascinate us. They are complex, shifting entities, deriving their character and substance from a number of sources, both ancient and modern. I hope that, in both content and structure, this book has done them a frightening justice.

Introduction

A Carnival of Terrors

We see Agencies above the reach of our comprehension and things performed by Bodies seemingly Aerial, which surpass the strength, power, and capacity of the most robust Mortal.

—Richard Bovet, *Pandaemonium*

Stories concerning the Undead have always been with us. From out of the primal darkness of Mankind's earliest years, come whispers of eerie creatures, not quite alive (or alive in a way which we can understand), yet not quite dead either. These may have been ancient and primitive deities who dwelt deep in the surrounding forests and in remote places, or simply those deceased who refused to remain in their tombs and who wandered about the countryside, physically tormenting and frightening those who were still alive. Mostly they were ill-defined—strange sounds in the night beyond the comforting glow of the fire, or a shape, half-glimpsed in the twilight along the edge of an encampment. They were vague and indistinct, but they were always there with the power to terrify and disturb. They had the power to touch the minds of our early ancestors and to fill them with dread. Such fear formed the basis of the earliest tales although the source and exact nature of such terrors still remained very vague.

And as Mankind became more sophisticated, leaving the gloom of their caves and forming themselves into recognizable communities—towns, cities, whole cultures—so the Undead travelled with them, inhabiting their folklore just as they had in former times. Now they began to take on more definite shapes. They became walking cadavers; the physical embodiment of former deities and things which had existed alongside Man since the Creation. Some still remained vague and ill-defined but, as Mankind strove to explain the horror which it felt towards them, such creatures emerged more readily into the light.

In order to confirm their abnormal status, many of the Undead were often accorded attributes, which defied the natural order of things—the power to transform themselves into other shapes, the ability to sustain themselves by drinking human blood, and the ability to influence human minds across a distance. Such powers—described as supernatural—only leant an added dimension to the terror that humans felt regarding them.

And it was only natural, too, that the Undead should become connected with the practice of magic. From very early times, Shamans and witchdoctors had claimed at least some power and control over the spirits of departed ancestors, and this has continued down into more "civilized" times. Formerly, the invisible spirits and forces that thronged around men's earliest encampments, had spoken "through" the tribal Shamans but now, as entities in their own right, they were subject to magical control and could be physically summoned by a competent sorcerer. However, the relationship between the magician and an Undead creature was often a very tenuous and uncertain one. Some sorcerers might have even *become* Undead entities once they died, but they might also have been susceptible to the powers of other magicians when they did.

From the Middle ages and into the Age of Enlightenment, theories of the Undead continued to grow and develop. Their names became more familiar—werewolf, vampire, ghoul—each one certain to strike fear into the hearts of ordinary humans. They were no less fearsome than the vague, shapeless entities that had circled the fires of ancient people—only now they had a form and a definition. Now, they were set within a context of fear. And they reflected some of the cultural attributes of those who believed in them—the Semite, the European, the African, and later the West Indian. Thus, golems, afreets, zombies, djinni, and draugr wandered by night (and sometimes by day) causing fear wherever they passed. As in earlier times, they may have been seen as the physical manifestations of old gods and powers or the walking dead—those who lay in the churchyards. They also included demons—beings that had never been truly born but yet included elements of both the living and the dead. Is it any wonder, therefore, that such a caravan of horrors traversed the world on a daily and nightly basis? Such undead beings appeared everywhere and in all cultures.

The purpose of this book is to detail at least some of the entities previously mentioned and to examine their possible origins. It is not meant to dismiss them as fearsome beings, nor to explain them away, nor to deny the horror that they generate. Rather it attempts to present a picture of terrible entities that have frightened Mankind across the years, that have shaped common nightmares, and have inspired the darker elements of the literary imagination. It seeks to celebrate that which lurks in the shadows or which gazes from the darkness at the solitary passerby with a frenzied and hungry eye

Look behind you down the darkened street! Is that a movement beyond the furthest streetlight? Peer out of your window into the gloom! Was that something, half-glimpsed, that moved away as you did so? Listen! Was that a cry or a voice speaking from amongst the shadows of the hallway? The ancient horrors of the Undead are perhaps far nearer than we would care to imagine. Turn the pages of this book, if you dare, and discover just what might be lurking out there in the gathering darkness.

Vampires

Robert the younger died and was buried in the churchyard, but used to go forth from the grave at night and disturb and frighten the villagers, and the village dogs would follow him, barking mightily.

—M. R. James,
Twelve Medieval Ghost Stories

Arguably no monster has imbedded itself so deeply in the human psyche than the vampire. The very word has the power to conjure up visions of ruined castles, perched on a crag somewhere amongst the Carpathian Mountains of Eastern Europe; of tall and saturnine Romanian noblemen, swathed in dark cloaks; and of terrified peasantry huddled in forest-bound huts and villages holding crucifixes or adorning themselves with garlic. The term is also suggestive of ruined churches, opened coffins, and wooden stakes. All this is, of course, the stock Hollywood image of the vampire that has been fed to us through the years by various celluloid representations. But how much of it is true? Just how accurate is our idea of this most familiar of monsters?

The idea of the vampire most probably has part of its origins in the ancient perceptions of the restless dead. These have been blended with stories of other night terrors to form the vampire motif with which we are all so familiar. Coupled with this are notions of how the dead conducted themselves and conduct how they interact with and react to the living.

Greece

During the Classical Greek Homeric period, (8th–7th centuries B.C.), the spirits of those who died in bed or who were slain in battle went flittering away like bats to some unspecified and hazy afterlife, usually known as Hades, to remain there forever. They spent their time murmuring quietly to each other in the eternal darkness, perhaps arguing over family pedigrees, giving endless descriptions of famous battles, complaining about unresolved wrongs in their former life, or simply making comments on the place in which they found themselves. They took little or no interest in the everyday world in which the living existed. Indeed, some perceptions from this period concerning the dead claimed that they actually *forgot* their existence in the world of the living and spent eternity drifting listlessly about along the shores of underground rivers—namely the Styx and the Lethe, murmuring and complaining to themselves.

RiverLethe

It is said that as soon as the dead inhaled the fumes of the River Lethe, they forgot their former lives and became torpid and sluggish—giving us the words *lethargy* and *lethargic* today. This fits with the concepts of the Afterlife in some other ancient cultures. For instance, the early Semites believed that Sheol (the Hebrew Afterworld) was a dank and misty place through which the spirits of the dead wandered aimlessly, only dimly able to recall any aspect of their former lives. They were largely harmless, ineffectual entities about whom the living were not terribly bothered and who, in general did not interact at all with the material world. They might be called back through magical rites in order to pronounce on some aspect of their former world, such as when the spirit of Samuel was summoned to prophesy for King Saul by the Witch of Endor, a medium who dwelt in the country between Mount Tabor and the Hill of Moreh—but generally they were left to their own dark existence.

However, by the time Socrates was forced by the Athenian authorities to drink the hemlock that killed him in 399 B.C., the perception of the dead had changed dramatically, at least in Classical Greece. No longer were they the compliant, ineffective spirits; they were now robust and active, wandering about burial grounds late at night and making their presence known. They shouted abuse, they tormented and terrorized passersby, and they sometimes attacked the living and even killed them. They could threaten their descendants and maim former neighbours. Rather than ignoring the spirits as they had done in former years, the living now feared them. These returning spectres were not the insubstantial, wafting shades of Victorian melodrama with which we are familiar; rather these were the corporeal, substantial figures that they had been in real life. They crossed between the world of the dead and the world of the living for various reasons: to harangue their descendants for some misdemeanour (real or imagined); to claim conjugal rights; to complete unfinished business left over from their time in the living world; to offer often unwanted advice, to take revenge on those whom they disliked, despised, or who had done them wrong; or simply to cause trouble amongst those who survived them. Such a trouble did these returning phantoms present that the officials in some of the Greek city states viewed with intense suspicion the Cults of the Dead and the Cults of ancient Heroes who worshipped the honoured dead within their precincts.

Not only did these phantoms appear during the hours of darkness (although this was their favoured time in order to terrify people) but they also revealed themselves during the day, particularly at mid-day, which was an especially auspicious time as morning passed into afternoon. And as the years passed, such appearances often became more dangerous and malevolent as perceptions of the dead amongst the Classical cultures gradually began to change.

Coupled with the returning dead, there were other terrors that made the blood of the Greeks run cold. Many of them also ventured out during the hours of darkness and many of them maliciously attacked the living or sought to do them some harm. One of these horrors was Hecate.

Hecate

Hecate enjoys something of an ambivalent and confusing position because it is not extremely clear as to whether she was considered a night-demon or a dark goddess. Although some Greeks referred to her as Hecate, others knew her as Aragriope, meaning "savage face" hinting at a far older entity. She was the daughter of the Titans (giants) Perses and Asteria, although others record her parents as Zeus and Scylla (a nymph who was turned into a sea-monster by the enchantress Circe, devouring all mariners who passed by her rock). She was also considered to be the dark side of the goddesses Artemis, Selene (the moon goddess), and Diana and was regarded as the Queen of the Ghostworld and matriarch of all witches; the mistress of chthonic rites and black magic. As soon as it was dark, she emerged from the Underworld to do harm to those against whom she had taken spite against. In this she was accompanied by many other foul and dangerous creatures, denizens of the Phantom world over which she ruled. These were simply known to the Greeks as "The Companions" but they comprised a legion of hideous goblins and "watchers of the night"—ill-defined terrors, some of which may have had an appetite for human blood. As she passed their houses, Hecate induced nightmares and night fevers, which sapped the strength of many sleepers, leaving them tired and listless in the morning.

Mormo

Amongst her "Companions" were Mormo, terrible shadowy entity who was frequently used by Greek mothers to frighten unruly children, and the Empusas, hideous and terrifying beings that exhibited many of the characteristics that we now associate with vampires. Whilst Hecate passed by, these horrific entities would often enter the houses of the living in order to attack the sleepers, particularly small children and the old and frail. This phantom could take a thousand different shapes, each one, the Greeks believed, more horrid and loathlsome than the last. The writer Aristophanes declared that such a creature was "clothed all about with blood and boils and blisters" and described it as "a foul vampire."

Lamia

Besides Hecate and her hellish entourage, there were other creatures that stalked the Grecian night, terrifying sleepers and harming them as they rested. Such a being was the Lamia, who usually killed small children and attacked sleeping men. Similar to Hecate, the Lamia had her origins in Classical folklore and legend. She was, according to tradition, the daughter of Belus and Libya and was a beautiful queen of the Libyan country. She was in fact so beautiful that the god Zeus fell in love with her and visited her nightly. She bore him a number of children, angering Zeus's wife, the goddess Hera. In anger Hera slew all her children, driving Lamia mad and sending her to live in the caves of the desert. Soon her fabled beauty had drained away and she became an old and monstrous woman who preyed on small children, in retaliation for the loss of her own. Under cover of darkness she travelled between the Greek houses, killing whatever infants she could find and devouring their flesh. She had become almost similar to a wild animal and the mere mention of her name struck terror into the heart of every mother. The Lamia attacked the old who were unlikely to defend themselves and, in the guise of a beautiful woman (which she was magically able to generate), she copulated with men as they slept. The Lamia, it was said, was actually fuelled by unholy lusts. She drew the semen and bodily fluids, upon which she subsisted, from male sleepers, leaving them tired and exhausted in the morning.

Cercopes

The Greeks also believed that the darkness brought out beings known as Cercopes. These were malicious and malignant goblins that followed in the wake of both Hecate and the Lamia with the intent of doing harm. Plunder and thievery were their speciality, but they were also known to drink the blood of young children, which they drank from the arms and legs of sleeping infants. They were small, squat, and swift, and were incredibly dangerous if cornered. They went in and out of the Greek houses at will. With all of these monsters and the continual threat of the returning, antagonistic dead, it is a wonder that the Greek people got any sleep at all!

Rome

Many of these terrors transferred themselves to the later Roman culture. There were, however, certain additions to the carnival of monsters that emerged after the sun had gone down. For example, there were the Roman Striges.

Striges

The name Striges came from a Latin word meaning "screech-owl," and would later come to mean a "witch or evil sorceress." It was also a term of abuse for an ugly old woman. However, in their original form, the Striges were horrors that sometimes visited humans after dark. They had the faces of ancient women but the bodies of vultures, with large and ungainly breasts that were full of poisonous milk. Their claws dripped filth and were poisonous to the touch. Most interestingly, some traditions said that these creatures subsisted upon blood, whether it was the blood of animals or humans, and this was the reason for visiting humans as they rested. The idea of the blood-drinking night visitor or vampire was already starting to take shape. Not only did the Striges attack sleepers, they also spread plague and disease through the filth on their claws—the spreading of sickness would also become a characteristic of early vampirism and would remain a belief in some Western cultures to this day.

Incubi/Succubi

Other horrific night visitors that might also prey on Roman sleepers were the incubi and succubi In some cases, these two were said to be differing aspects of the same demon. But it was generally held that the incubi was male whilst the other, much more prolific and dangerous succubus, was female. The name *succubus* probably comes from the Latin *succubare,* meaning "to lie under" and it is possible that the demon was a variant of the Greek Mormo, who was sometimes considered to be both female and sexually voracious. Indeed, it was a sexually voracious appetite that characterised both the incubus and the succubus. Both demons (or various aspects of the one demon) had sexual intercourse with men and women as they slept. The succubus in particular drew the seed from sleeping men, sexually exhausting them, and might have even done so to do them harm. Although initially a terror in ancient Rome, the succubus was to assume greater attention in the early Christian period right through to the Middle Ages, when the demon was thought to plague monks in order to distract them from their holy vows. Monks often experienced erotic dreams and nocturnal emissions, which were credited to the attentions of the succubus during the night. In his *Compendium Malificarum,* written some time in the 16th century, the Milanese monk and demonologist Francesco Maria Guazzo details succubi in his list of demons that torment the righteous. He states that these dreams are in fact real and the experiences of the monks, in the throes of their eroticism, were due to a completely physical manifestation of the demon whose desire was not only to break their vows of chastity but to do them actual harm. Guazzo was following the categories of demons, which had been established by the Byzantine thinker, Michael Psellus the Younger. It is thought that Psellus was born around 1018 in the city of Nicodema (now Izmit on the Gulf of Astacus) and that, as a child, he had been exposed to both Greek and Roman culture. Although more associated with the Platonist school of thought, Psellus did outline certain categories of demons, one of which was "terrors of the night" which included beings that both extracted semen and drank blood. This would undoubtedly prove the inspiration for Guazzo many centuries later.

Sumeria

The notion of the predatory spirit, especially a female spirit, found echoes in other cultures, especially the early Sumerian. Here there was a widespread belief in the demoness Lilith, who had allegedly been the first wife of Adam.

Lilith

During the 3rd century B.C. in Sumer, Lilith was known as Lil, the winged storm spirit, or spirit of vengeance. As such, she was greatly feared. This terror seems to have percolated down from ancient Sumeria into the early Hebrew tradition. The Semitic *Zohar,* or Book of Splendour (part of the *Kabbalah* and written around the 13th century allegedly using extremely ancient sources), states that she was born out of the k'lifah, "the membrane for the marrow"

which in turn had been born out of the Primordial Light. It was the first century Talmudic scholar Jerimia ben Eleazar who linked Lilith with Adam, claiming that when he had been expelled from the Garden of Eden, he got on with the demoness in the wilderness and had "begot many ghosts and demons" who were called liln or lilm. These creatures accompanied Lilith on her nightly travels, just as "The Companions" had accompanied Hecate in ancient Greece, entering houses and attacking those within. Also in the second century, Rabbi Hanina ben Dosa stated: "One may not sleep alone in a house, for whoever sleeps alone in a house is seized by Lilith." The entity then, was strongly associated with attacks on the lonely and the vulnerable. There was a strong sexual element here as well, as the demon also sought intercourse with whoever it attacked—very much in the style of the succubus. In the morning, victims were found, exhausted and drained—some were even dead—setting the tone for later vampiric entities that absorbed energy, semen, or blood.

Ancient Slavic

Further notions of predatory nocturnal creatures were to be found in ancient Slavic beliefs. At night, sleeping men were visited by the rusalka, a water spirit that sometimes mated with humans. Although largely benign, this being was driven by powerful erotic impulses and was an insatiable lover. She physically drained those whom she encountered, sapping their youth and vitality and leaving them as old and withered husks.

Draugr

As the centuries passed, these ancient terrors began to merge with perceptions of the angry and volatile dead from other cultures. Viking belief, for instance, maintained the notion of a draugr, a corporeal revenant who wandered about the countryside, performing acts of great violence against former associates or against those whom it encountered. Many of these dead lay within tomb-like barrows which were scattered across the Scandinavian landscape. These resembled houses in which the dead might "live" and from which they would venture forth, during the hours of darkness, to engage in wicked acts.

Although many of the tales concerning draugr are thought to have originated in Iceland, they soon became known across the Nordic world and even further afield. There are accounts of them from Britain and France, recounted in both Latin and Anglo-Saxon script. From these coffin mounds, the spectres hurled abuse at passers-by and often pelted them with stones. And they attached themselves to any house that had been erected nearby, terrorising the inhabitants by appearing in front of them as soon as it was dark. The Icelandic *Laxdoela Saga,* written around the 13th century (although the contents reflect much earlier fragmentary writings), includes the story of one Hrapp, who wandered from his howe (tomb) each night, to create mayhem in the district and even to kill several of his former servants. The *Eyrbyggia Saga,* written at the monastery of Helgalfel, around the middle of the 14th century, recounts the story of the vicious ghost of Thorolf Halt-foot who, together with a group of Undead companions, terrorized and devastated the country round about his burial chamber. Many of the stories concerning them reflected the earlier tales of the unquiet dead of Greece and Rome. However, a certain Christian element, asserting the superiority of the Church, was now beginning to creep into Western stories of the restless dead.

For example, around 500 A.D., there is a record of a famous encounter in a haunted house by Bishop Germanus—a place frequented by a spectre who was especially violent. The account of this is given by Constantineus, a near contemporary of Germanus that hints back to the malicious ghosts of ancient Greece and Rome. The Bishop of Auxerre in France, whilst on an important journey with his retinue, was overtaken by darkness and sought shelter in a rather disreputable hovel, which locals said was haunted. As the party settled down for the night, they were suddenly disturbed by a horrific and malevolent apparition that rose up out of the ground in front of them and proceeded to pelt them with stones. The Bishop begged the ghost to desist but it hurled abuse at them and began to pummel them with handfuls of earth. Germanus called on the ghost to stop in the Name of God and, at the mention of the holy name, it ceased its violence and became very humble. It revealed its true form: the spirit of an evil man who had been buried there without the proper rites of the Church. The Bishop asked it to show where its bones were buried and instructed a grave to be dug. The bones were interred; the Bishop said special prayers and the hovel was no longer haunted. In this tale, the Church showed its power over the unquiet dead.

In fact, subsequent Christian folklore concerning the dead now increasingly emphasised the triumph of the forces of virtue over wandering cadavers. Those who died within the bosom of the Church were especially blessed, even though they were deceased and did not experience the anger or violence which beset those who had passed away unshriven. Much was made of a popular tale recounted by the early Christian writer Evagrius Ponticus (345–399 A.D.). The story concerns a certain holy Anchorite named Thomas who died in a suburb of the city of Antioch. Being destitute and having no possessions, the hermit was buried in a portion of the city's burying-grounds reserved for beggars and paupers. The following morning, however, it was found that the corpse had clawed its way through the earth and made its way to a mausoleum in the richest part of the cemetery. There it had laid itself down to rest. It was immediately removed and re-interred but the same thing happened on the following morning and it was noted that there were disturbances in several other graves around the area. The people summoned the patriarch Ephriam, who recommended that the body be carried in triumph to the city and placed in a shrine, with a special service to be held in honour of the Anchorite in the local church. Whether this was designed to exalt the hermit and to prevent him from walking about or to keep other cadavers in their graves is unclear. Similar stories exist concerning the lives of other hermits, monks, bishops, and saints. St. Macarius of Egypt, for instance, is said to have raised a man from his grave to testify to the innocence of a monk accused of killing him. The *History of the Franks,* speculated to be written by a group of monks, states how St. Injurieux, a notable senator of Clermont in Auvergne, rose from his tomb and went to lie with his wife Scholastica in an adjoining grave.

Celtic

Ancient stories of the restless dead and of the night terrors that wandered about as soon as darkness settled over the land gradually fused together to create legends of hostile cadavers who left their tombs in order to attack the living. In many of these legends, blood played a significant part. Blood, after all, had been recognized since the time of the Roman physician Galen as one of the central "humours" of the body—the life force without which none could live. It was also a source of heat which warmed the body—fevers, Galen taught, were brought about by a surplus of blood, which is why ancient and some early modern physicians bled their patients or applied leeches to suck the blood from them. After a time in the cold earth of the grave, it was suggested that corpses were in need of the warmth of blood to restore them to a semblance of vitality. Moreover, because their veins and arteries were seemingly withered and shrivelled after death, they needed blood coursing through their dead bodies to restore even a semblance of life. Initially it was perceived that such cadavers might take the blood of animals that they encountered, but later it was thought that they might look towards nearby humans for some form of vile sustenance.

The Yorkshire churchman and writer, William of Newburgh (1136–98 A.D.), tells of a revenant in Buckinghamshire, England, that created much restlessness amongst a cowherd, despite the attentions of several watchmen. It returned night after night, unsettling the animals in the byre in which they were kept and around a nearby house. Although not stated, the implication was that the revenant was trying to drink the blood of these cattle. It further entered the house where it had once lived and attempted to lie in bed with its former wife whom William describes as "an honourable woman." The matter was eventually placed in front of the Bishop, whose advisors suggested exhuming the body and cremating it. The Bishop himself, however, was opposed to this—it sounded too much like sacrilege—and instead advised opening the grave and placing a scroll of absolution on the chest of the corpse. This appeared to have the desired effect and the dead man walked no more.

William goes on to recount similar stories—such as that of the ghost in Berwrick on the Scottish borders, which (with the help of Satan himself, says William) wandered nightly from its tomb, attacking those who slept in the town beyond. At daybreak, the cadaver would return to its tomb to rest before rising to recommence its nocturnal attacks. In addition to the attacks, the wandering corpse spread disease and sickness throughout the entire countryside. In the end, ten sturdy men dug up the body, which was then dismembered and burned.

Later, however, a greater part of the population of Berwick was carried off by a great pestilence, which it was assumed, was Satan wreaking revenge on the town for its destruction of his agent.

William's tale may have given rise to a later legend that purportedly comes from Annandale, also in southern Scotland, and dates from the early 14th century. In this, the Scottish king, Robert the Bruce (Robert I) visited a local lord and whilst he was there, a wretched man was brought before the lord for poaching. The lord sentenced him to death, but the king, being in a good mood, commuted the sentence and pardoned the poacher. Robert then left the area and the local lord, in violation of the king's wishes, had the man rearrested and executed. From then on, the region was troubled by the man's walking corpse. This cadaver not only drank the blood of those whom it savaged but spread a virulent plague in its wake. Churchmen were brought in to lay the body to rest but to no avail. In the end, the matter reached the ears of King Robert, who returned to the area and punished the local lord for his disobedience of his Majesty's commands. On King Robert's instructions, the cadaver of the executed man was exhumed from its grave, cut to pieces, and burned. The village was not troubled again. The site where these events occurred was said to have been very close to Berwick and it is possible that one tale may have influenced the other.

Some variants of the story, however, state that it was the Bruces' themselves who were the perpetrators of the heinous act and place responsibility fore the hanging of the unfortunate man on Robert I's father—also named Robert but known as "The Competitor." This occurrence is said to have taken place in the village of Annan in Dumfries and Galloway, and was carried out in 1138 A.D. against the wishes of a visiting saint—St. Malachy O'More, Bishop of Armagh, in the north of Ireland. When he found out what had happened, the saint cursed the Bruces in anger and the dead man rose from his grave and wandered the countryside, drinking the blood of cattle and spreading plague and disease wherever he went. In the end, he was pinned down by two knights who, intriguingly, drove a javelin through his heart before they burned him. The curse of St. Malachy—"the finger of God"—lingered with the Bruces in the shape of a disease. Robert I's father suffered from leprosy and spent the last years of his life as a virtual recluse.

Leanan Shee

The story may also have had some connection with an ancient Celtic fairy belief. Stories of blood-drinking or energy-sapping fairies (usually female) had existed in both Scotland and Ireland since the earliest times. In Ireland one such being was known as the Leanan Shee (the fairy mistress), a creature with a special affinity for humans. She was drawn to warriors and poets and often magically provided prowess for the former and inspiration for the latter. But her attentions came at a price. As she made love to the warrior or poet whose mistress she inevitably became, she drew both the strength and life from them in the manner of the ancient Roman succubus. In the end, they were little more than an empty husk, which the fairy then discarded in favour of another lover. Although the Leanan Shee did not actually drink blood, there were other Irish fairies that were said to do so. Some were said to dwell in the Magillycuddy Reeks in County Kerry in the very south of Ireland. In a lecture given at Trinity College in Dublin in 1963, the former Archivist of the Irish Folklore Commission (a Government-sponsored body set up to preserve Irish tradition), Sean O'Sullivan, (himself a Kerryman) stated that he'd heard of a castle guarding a mountain pass, high in the Reeks, that was inhabited by blood-drinking fairy creatures. The name of this place was Dun Dreach-fhoula, significantly pronounced *Drac-ola*, and meaning "the fort of evil blood," sometimes translated as "the fort of the blood visage." Unfortunately, O'Sullivan did not make any further reference to the location of the place either in his lectures or books. For instance, it does not appear in his most famous book, *Irish Wake Amusements*—and he died without ever revealing where it might be. Several academics have tried to locate it but even the most minute examination of the sites of the Barony of Kilkerron in which the Reeks lie reveals nothing. And yet tales of blood drinking and flesh eating persisted in the region well into the 20th century. In the 1930s, a collector for the Irish Folklore Commission, Tim Murphy, detailed a story from the remote mountain parish of Sneem in County Kerry that contained vampiric references. A farmer in the area had married a woman who was said to have fairy connections, who refused to eat any food that was cooked in the house but at night, would rise from her bed and go to the local cemetery where she dug up the bodies, drank the blood, and consumed the flesh. The husband followed her to the churchyard where he confronted her as a vampire. "You would not eat the good meat or drink the good beer at your own table but you would come here at night to eat this foul dinner," he told her. At this point, Murphy's story became confusing and mixed with another tale and the fate of this vampire was unclear. However, it was apparently representative of a number of stories from that isolated upland parish and from the region in general.

Abhartach

An even older tale, supposedly dating from the 5th or 6th centuries, also comes from Ireland. This is the legend of Abhartach, which comes from what is now County Derry in the north of the country. Abhartach was allegedly an ancient ruler of a small kingdom that bordered upon what is now the town of Garvagh. He was small (possibly deformed) but said to be a mighty magician and a tyrannical monarch. He was hated by his subjects who wished to be rid of him, but were too frightened to kill him themselves because of his alleged magic powers. They brought another chieftain named Cathain from a neighbouring kingdom to do the job for them. Cathain killed the tyrant and buried him standing up as befitted a Celtic chieftain. But the next day, Abhartach was back, demanding a bowl of blood from the wrists of his subjects in order, says the tale, to "sustain his vile corpse." Cathain came again, killed him, and reburied him, but the next day the dreadful cadaver was back, demanding the same gory tribute. Cathain then consulted with either the druids (Pagan holy men) or an early Christian saint (depending on what version of the story is told) as to why this should be. He was told that Abhartach wasn't completely dead, nor could he be killed, because of his magic powers. He was one of the marbh bheo (walking dead) who would torment his people unless he was suspended. Cathain could do this by killing him with a sword made of yew wood, burying him upside down, placing thorns around his grace, and a great stone directly on top of him. Cathain did all this, even going so far as to build a leacht or sepulchre over the gravesite. This monument gave the townland outside Garvagh its name—Slaghtaverty (Abhartach's leacht). Today, the sepulchre is gone, although it is said that one massive capstone remains over the actual burial site. A tree has grown there, too—supposedly from the original thorns, although this growth is much younger. The land around is considered "bad ground" and has changed ownership several times and few locals will approach the place after dark, even today. In the region they still talk about "the man who was buried three times."

The previous story was at one time extremely well known throughout Ireland. Although most probably a folk legend, it was written down as actual history in Dr. Geoffrey Keating's *Foras Feasa ar Eireann (A General History of Ireland)* between 1620 and 1631, perhaps making it the oldest written vampire story in Western Europe. It was later reprinted in 1880 in *A History of Ireland* by Patrick Weston Joyce and, it has been suggested, the Celtic chieftain Abhartach may have been the prototype for Bram Stoker's classic vampire figure, Dracula. It should be borne in mind that the two most famous vampire stories—Dracula and Carmilla, were both written by Irishmen, Bram Stoker and Sheridan Le Fanu respectively.

Glestigs

Tales of blood-drinking fairies and cadaverous Celtic chieftains have made their way into Scottish folklore as well. Stories from the Western Isles of the Hebrides spoke of fairies that drank both the milk and the blood of cattle. These ancient sprites were often attached to ancient tumuli—the graves of prehistoric peoples with whom they were often associated. Creatures known as glestigs often inhabited such places or the ruins of former castles and abbeys, luring in passers-by by calling out to them and then attacking them. In some cases they were also known to drink the blood of passing wayfarers.

Banshee

Also in the Highlands, beings known as the Baobhan Sith annoyed, tormented, and sometimes killed shepherds and herders as they tended their flocks in their shielings (shelters) on the high moors. The name simply means "spirit woman" and refers to a type of fairy whose roots go back into the mists of antiquity. She (and the fairy always appeared to be female) was the last representative of a goat-footed race that had lived in the Highlands before the time of true men and she had a passion for human blood. The Baobhan

Sith was also a shapeshifter and could approach her victims, usually lonely herders, in the guise of their wives or sweethearts whom they had left behind. When alone, the creature revealed its true nature and drank their blood. In her book, *The Supernatural Highlands,* Francis Thompson recounts a tale of three hunters who were beset by these vampires in the hills around Kintail. Having had a disappointing day during which they had caught nothing, they passed the night in a lonely hut, high up in a glen. Whilst one of them played on a trump (Jews harp) to pass the time, another languidly wished aloud that their wives and sweethearts could be with them in these desolate hills. Almost at once, the door of the hut opened and three women came in who, in the dim light, resembled those women, and who sat down with two of them beside the fire. The musician, very uncertain, kept to his own side of the blaze. The other two sat with the women, talking softly with their sweethearts whispering into their ears. In the uncertain light, the musician saw to his horror a stream of blood snaking across the floor. And as he squinted more closely in the murky light, he saw that the feet of the women on the other side of the fire resembled those of a goat or deer. With a cry, he leapt to his feet and dashed from the hut. Running across the hills, he heard the women pursue him. One said: "Dhith sibha'ur curhaich fain ach dh'thag mo curhaich fein mise" ("You ate your own victims, but mine escaped from me"). At last he made it to the door of a mountain cottage and was taken in. The following morning, he returned with some other men to the hut where he found the bodies of his two companions, strangled, broken, and drained of blood. It was well-known, he was told, that the gloomy glens of Kintail were home to vampires and blood-drinking fairies.

Fairies, it was believed in many parts of the Celtic world, could also sometimes reanimate dead bodies and use them for their own purposes—often to torment the living. For this reason, the bier upon which a body was borne to the graveyard was sometimes ritually smashed before the mourners left the churchyard. In this way, it was thought malefic spirits were prevented from taking over the corpse of the recently interred. There are stories of this being done, right up until the early 20th century, in places such as Islay in the Western Isles of Scotland and in Counties Roscommon and Carlow in Ireland.

Italy

It was not only in the Celtic world that tales of animated corpses were told. In Italy, there were, in some areas, legends of people who quite simply, "refused to die," although their bodily functions were deemed to have stopped. A popular Roman tale tells that in 1583, the fourteen-year-old son of a prince of the city, Fabrizio Massimo, died of an unexplained fever. However, after he'd been buried, the boy was seen again but his appearance seemed to be accompanied by a bout of sickness or plague that swept through certain sectors of the city. Although the apparition did not drink blood, death accompanied each of its visitations. The Roman people became seriously alarmed and the boy's family summoned a holy man, St. Philip Neri, to investigate the appearance. The holy man went straight to the boy's tomb and opened it, finding the child's corpse in a perfect state of preservation although he had been dead for some time. St. Philip, laid a hand on the cadaver's forehead, and immediately the boy sat up and opened his eyes. "Are you unwilling to die?" asked the saint. "No," replied the youth. "Are you resigned to yield up your soul?" continued the holy man. "I am," came the answer. "Then go!" commanded St. Philip and he blessed the body whereupon the youth fell back with a serene look upon his face and expired for a second time. The city was troubled no more, either by the apparition or by the plague.

A similar, earlier story is told regarding the 6th century Byzantine saint, Theodosius the Cenobite, as recounted by Theodore of Petra. One of the Brethren at Theodosius's monastery, a monk named Basil, died and was laid in his tomb. But from time to time, several of the other Brothers saw him at prayer in the chapel. Some even heard the sound of his voice as he prayed, whilst others saw him in his accustomed place among the choir stalls. Coupled with these visions, periodic sicknesses swept through the holy house. The monks consulted with St. Theodosius, who suggested prayer and fasting. He himself prayed earnestly and continually that the apparition might be relieved and, according to the legend, on one evening during a service, all the monks saw the vision of Basil. The phantom advised them that, because of their prayers (especially those of the saint himself), that it would now depart from them to the Afterlife and that forthwith, the illnesses that had raged amongst them would cease. He offered them the blessing "God be with, my father and my Brethren" and he vanished from their sight. Shortly afterwards the sicknesses passed and the monastery was not troubled again.

Eastern Europe

It is, perhaps, amongst the Slavic and East European peoples that the notion of the vampire seems to have gained hold. Indeed, the word itself may come from an ancient Turkish word, *oubir,* that meant "a witch or malignant sorcerer." Others have argued that it comes from an obscure Greek word meaning "to drink."

It is thought that belief in the walking dead—cadavers who did not necessarily drink blood but may have done so—was fairly widespread. There was also a belief that for every vampire that was created, there was also someone born who could slay it. Thus in the late 13th century, vampire hunters flourished in various parts of central and Eastern Europe adding to the myth. In fact, the situation grew so bad that during the reign of Wenceslaus III, King of Hungary (1301–1305) and King of Bohemia (1305–1306), an edict was issued forbidding the digging up of graveyards in order to "slay" malefic corpses. Bohemia was a country that occupied most of what is now the Central and Western Czech Republic.

The Shoemaker of Silesia

One of the earliest tales from the region concerns "The Shoemaker of Silesia" and is dated from around the year 1591. Silesia is now to be found within the borders of present-day Poland and was inhabited by Slavic peoples. The shoemaker dwelt in one of its major towns and sometime in September 1591, he committed suicide in a neighbour's garden by cutting his throat with his shoemaker's knife. Because the sin was so grievous, his wife and family put it about the locality that he had died from some unknown disease. All the same, a number of busybodies put it about that there was more to the shoemaker's death than first appeared and the authorities decided to investigate.

Spectrum

Whilst these deliberations were going on, the shoemaker himself appeared, or at least some shape, (called a "Spectrum" in the account) resembling him did. And it did not only appear at night but in the middle of the day as well. It wandered about the town, visiting houses when it pleased. Those who were sleeping were tormented by terrible dreams in which the figure of the shoemaker was featured prominently and those who were waking did so to find what seemed to be a heavy weight upon them, which was taken to be the shoemaker, albeit in an invisible state. There were perpetual complaints resonating all through the town. Of course, these appearances and experiences highlighted the memory of the shoemaker and raised further questions about his death, which his widow, family, and friends sought to suppress. So great did the horror become that the town officials considered digging up the shoemaker's corpse in order to inspect it. Terrified that it would now be disclosed as to how he met his end, his widow and sons begged the Council not to proceed, adding that they intended to apply to the Emperor's court for a ruling on the matter. However, the apparition became bolder—appearing by people's bedsides as soon as they lay down, or else lying down beside them and seeking to suffocate them with its attentions. It also struck them and pinched at their skin, drawing blood on some occasions. In the morning, the bruises and cuts and sometimes the marks of fingers about their throats were plain to see. The authorities could no longer ignore this situation and the Magistrate gave instructions that the body should be exhumed.

By this time, he had been in the ground for about eight months—from 22nd September 1591 to 18th April 1592. Yet when he was exhumed, his body was found to be "uncorrupted and not at all putrid" even though his burial clothes had already rotted. Not only this, but his hair, fingernails, and toenails had continued to grow whilst in the grave. Examining the body, a local Magistrate found what appeared to be a magical mark on the big toe of his right foot in the shape of a rose. The wound on his throat still gaped but had not become infected and his limbs and joints were as supple as the day he was buried.

His body was not reburied but was kept lying in the open from the 18th to the 24th of April and was inspected daily by the townspeople. His nightly wanderings did not cease, however, and many were still troubled by his nightly visitations. Nor did the corpse appear to decay in any way. In consternation, the people of the town buried him once more, this time under the local gallows in the hope that this would in some way restrain him, but it didn't. Neighbours were even more disturbed by the visitations of the Spectrum, which pinched them and tried to crush them, leaving them with blue and black marks all over their bodies. In the end, the shoemaker's wife went to a local magistrate and told him to do whatever was necessary to lay her husband's unquiet spirit to rest. The body was once again dug up from beneath the gallows and its head and legs were struck off with the blade of a spade (it was noted that it had grown even fleshier and seemed to have put on a little weight), its back was ripped open, and its heart was pulled out. To the horror of those around, the heart seemed very fresh and full of blood and appeared to pulse slightly, similar to the heart of a living man. All this, together with the rest of the body was placed on a pile of wood and was burned to ashes, which were then placed in a sack and dumped in a nearby river. This, the local people hoped, would be the end of the matter. But there were still more horrors to come.

A girl from the same town had died shortly after the shoemaker, after allegedly being visited by the Spectrum. Eight days afterward, she appeared to a fellow servant as she lay in bed and lay across her in an attempt to crush her. She then attacked an infant lying in its cot, and would have made off with it had a nurse not arrived at an opportune moment and saved it by calling out in the Name of Jesus, whereupon the spectre vanished. However, she continued to appear in various guises, including that of a hen. When one of the other maids decided to follow her back to the grave and see if it was indeed their former colleague, the hen grew to a monstrous size and grabbed her by the throat. The dead girl continued to terrorize the town for a whole month in various shapes: a dog, a goat, a cat, and an old woman. It was assumed by the local magistrates that the scourge of the Undead had been passed on from her encounter with the shoemaker's Spectrum. Her body was also dug up and burned and the spectral occurrences ceased.

The shoemaker of Silesia was only one of the alleged vampiric cases that began to manifest themselves into the culture of Central and Eastern Europe.

As the 17th century wore on, there were a number of further instances scattered across the towns and villages of Hungary and what is now the Czech Republic. Wandering ghosts, sometimes in the shapes of animals, and those who had died without the Sacraments, or who had died having committed some sin, roamed abroad, tormenting their neighbours and attacking their livestock. And in the dawn of the Enlightened 18th century, men of learning began to turn their attention in the direction of vampires, considering whether or not they in fact existed, just as they did with the notion of witches.

Magia Posthuma

One of the first considered reports on these apparitions was the treatise *Magia posthuma,* written in 1706 by Charles Ferdinand de Shertz. It was published in the town of Olmutz in Moravia and was dedicated to Prince Charles Joseph of Lorraine, Bishop of Olmutz and Osnabruk. Shertz, who was an eminent lawyer of his day, argued his case from a legalistic point of view. Concentrating on a number of cases, he came to the conclusion that so many trustworthy people had suffered from vampiric attentions that it was reasonable to assume that such creatures actually existed. In one of these cases—that of a herdsman—he noted that the ghost of the dead herder seemed able to exhaust his neighbours simply by loudly calling their name, suggesting that even the *voice* of the vampire had energy-sapping qualities. He also considered whether the body should be burned, and how the injuries which they inflicted upon the living should be dealt with.

Dissertatio de Uamparis Seruiensibus

Perhaps in response to Shertz's book (which was widely circulated), the number of instances of vampirism seemed to increase in Hungary and in surrounding districts. Indeed, during the early to mid-1700s, there was almost an epidemic, reminiscent of the days of Wenceslaus III. Such an epidemic appeared to reach its height in both Greater Serbia and in Hungary during the 1730s, prompting the thinker John Heinrich Zopfius to publish a further work on vampirism. The was in the form of a dissertation—*Dissertatio de Uamparis Seruiensibus* (published in 1733)—in which he painted lurid pictures of the dead rising from their graves to attack the living. Zopfus's work was only one of a plethora of such works issued from Germany, Italy, and England, as men of education turned their thoughts to a supposed vampire menace in Central and Eastern Europe. Such learned works included John Christian Stock's *Dissetatio de cadaueribus sanguisgus* (1732); Philip Rohr's *De masticatione mortuorum* (published in Leipzig in 1679) and John Christian Harenberg's *Von Vampyren* (1739). There were also many more. This corpus of vampire literature further included Cardinal Guieseppe Davenzatti, the Archbishop of Trani, whose work *Dissertazione sopra I vampiri* (1744) is regarded as the first major work by a churchman on the subject. The affairs and occurrences in Hungary and Moravia were now drawing the attention of the Vatican authorities, particularly that of Pope Benedict XIV. In 1746, the pontiff commissioned an enquiry into what was going on in Eastern Europe. The man he chose to conduct this investigation was a Frenchman by the name of Benedictine Dom Antoine Augustin Calmet (1672-1757). Calmet had a reputation both as a theologian and as a writer and his exegetical works had earned him a reputation far beyond the confines of the Catholic Church, although they have subsequently failed to stand the test of time. At the time of his appointment, he was a lecturer in theology at the abbey of Moyen-Moutier.

Calmet's brief was to investigate a number of occurrences in Hungary, Serbia, Bohemia, and Moravia; test their validity; and write a report, which would be forwarded to the Vatican. This report, presented in the form a treatise—*Dissertation sur les Apparitions, anges des demons et les Espirits, et sur les revenants et Vampires de Hungarie, de Boheme, de Moravia et de Silese* was received and subsequently printed in 1746.

Arnold Paole

There were a number of cases for Calmet to consider—particularly two rather famous stories that had been widely circulated. The first was the affair of one Arnold Paole, an ex-soldier from the district of Medvegia, in Serbia which was at that time part of the Austrian Empire. Paole had been a likeable, good-natured character who had gone off to serve in the Emperor's army in Turkish Serbia, returning home in 1727. He settled down as a farmer and became engaged to a local girl. However, his neighbours noticed that, since his return from the Army, his character had subtly changed. Although still extremely pleasant, he had become almost brooding and fearful, ready to jump at any shadow. He privately told his fiancée a strange story as an explanation. When stationed in Turkish Serbia, his regiment had been subject to the nightly attentions of a vampire. A group of men including Paole himself had been sent out to find the creature and destroy it. It was Paole who had located the creature's grave and who had dug it up, killing it after a brief struggle. However, in its death throes, the thing covered the young soldier in blood and grave earth. He had washed it away but ever after he still felt contaminated. He felt as though some unclean shadow was hanging over him and that something was watching him as he went about his work. His fiancée told him not to be foolish, but Paole's gloomy attitude continued. A week after the confession, he was killed in a fall from a cart and was quickly buried in the local cemetery.

Three weeks later, a number of people complained of seeing Arnold Paole about the town and several said that he had come into their bedrooms at night for some unspecified purpose. Shortly after, four of these complainants died from an unknown disease. The ghost of Arnold Paole was blamed for these deaths and the word "vampire" began to circulate in the district—people now heard of the curious story that he had told his fiancée. Even so, nothing was done immediately. Arnold Paole's grave was opened forty days after his death. To the alarm of everyone present, his body was found to be undecayed—and it got worse. Fresh blood had oozed from his eyes, nose, and ears and the front of his shirt, all across his chest, was found to be soaked in it. His fingernails had fallen off but had been replaced by new growths and his hair appeared to have grown considerably. For the locals, this was a sure sign that Arnold Paole had become a vampire, so a wooden whitethorn stake was driven into the corpse's heart in accordance with local custom. In response, the dead man gave a loud groan, which was heard by everyone present. The body was left in the open and surgeons were brought from Belgrade in order to examine it. They announced that Paole had been a vampire, and the four people who had died after reputedly seeing his ghost, were also exhumed and staked. However, the danger had not passed.

Four years afterwards, in 1731, seventeen people reputedly died, due to some sort of vampiric activity, evoking memories of Arnold Paole. A twenty year-old woman by the name of Stana had suddenly and inexplicably died after an illness which had lasted three days and which came directly after her confinement. On her deathbed, she confessed that she had secretly anointed herself with the blood of an alleged vampire in order to protect herself from its attentions whilst pregnant. (This, apparently, was a common belief in that part of Serbia.) Nevertheless, both she and her baby died. Both were rather carelessly buried and the body of the infant was subsequently dug up and devoured by a wolf pack. The body of the woman, however, was left untouched by the wolves and seemed to be in an undecayed state. When her grave was opened, it was found that her chest cavity was full of fresh blood and that she looked as fresh as when she had been alive. Both her finger and toenails were loose and came away when touched, revealing new ones growing underneath. The body was adjudged to be in "the vampire condition" and was burned. Another body, that of a sixteen year-old boy that had been buried for ninety days, was also exhumed and found to be as perfectly fresh as it had been when he was alive. The body of his companion was also unearthed and found to be in a similar condition. Another young girl was dug up some time after being interred, and her body was also found to be fresh and supple and when a stake was thrust into her, she disgorged a large amount of blood. These, and a number of others, provoked yet another vampire scare. Soon the name of Arnold Paole was circulating far and wide, adding to the debate on vampires.

Peter Plogojowitz

Another case that had excited some interest in the local area was that of a farmer from the village of Kisilova in the Rhum Province of Serbia named Peter Plogojowitz. The case had been investigated by an Army enquiry sitting at Belgrade. There was nothing unusual about Plogojowitz, he was a simple, sixty-two year old farmer who owned some land around Kisilova. He seemed extremely hale and hearty. Despite his apparent good health, Peter Plogojowitz suddenly sickened and died. Three nights after his interment, there were sounds from the kitchen of his house, and upon entering, his son, found the likeness of Plogojowitz standing there. The apparition asked him for food. When a meal was set down before him, he ate it, then rose and left the room, presumably going back to the grave. The next day, the son (who was very alarmed at his experience), told neighbours what had happened. He waited up the following night but the apparition of his father didn't appear. Yet the next night, he was back and asking for more food. This time, the son refused and Plogojowitz gave him a malevolent and threatening look before leaving. The next day Plogojowitz's son suddenly died. His death was only the first of six in the village, all of whom seemed to die within hours of each other. The cause of their deaths seemed to be due to exhaustion and excessive blood loss. Before dying, each of them had complained that they had seen the shape of Peter Plogojowitz either in their bedrooms or in a dream. In these dreams, he seemed to glide toward them and catch them by the throat, then lowered his head to bite and draw their blood from the wound. He was believed to have killed nine persons in this way within the space of a week. Despite the best efforts of the local apothecary, all those who had seen or dreamed of Plogojowitz died extremely quickly.

The local magistrates were determined to put an end to what was happening before a full-scale vampire hysteria broke out. They contacted a local Army commander who happened to be staying nearby, asking him to investigate. The commander arrived in Kislova, bringing with him two other officers, and proceeded to order the immediate exhumation of the body of Peter Plogojowitz. They actually opened all the graves of those who had died subsequent to the farmer's death, but paid close attention to the corpse that had been Plogojowitz. They found it almost undecayed and lying as if in a trance. In fact, it even appeared to be breathing almost imperceptibly. To the absolute terror of the examiners, the eyes were wide open, and several of those who observed them swore that they moved a little, following the movements of those around the body. His hair and nails had grown, a number of old wounds were now encased in freshly grown skin, and the joints remained supple and moved easily. The farmer's mouth was smeared with fresh blood, and his complexion was extremely florid, as though gorged with the substance. The commander and his assistants concluded that this was indeed the vampire who had been terrorizing the district and they should put an end to it. In accordance with local custom, a sharp wooden stake was driven into the cadaver's heart, resulting in great quantities of fresh blood pouring forth from every part of the body. Wood was subsequently gathered and formed into a pyre upon which the corpse was then burned. No evidence of vampirism was found upon any of the other bodies that were exhumed along with Plogojowitz. Their copses were replaced in caskets and reburied. After this the dreams and apparitions ceased, as did the deaths in the village.

Returning to Belgrade, the commander and his officers formally convened again and made a report, concluding that Peter Plogojowitz had indeed been a vampire. Because of the military involvement, this was one of the best attested cases of its time, and placed Central and Eastern Europe firmly at the centre of vampire lore.

Grando

Whilst the cases of Arnold Paole and Peter Plogojowitz were undoubtedly extremely famous and widely discussed, there were nevertheless other reasonably famous vampire cases as well. Erasmus Franciscus in his commentary on the Baron Valvasor's work *Die Ehre des Herzogthums Krain* (1698), mentions an interesting and famous instance from the district of Kranj in Carniola in Slovenia. A relatively wealthy landowner named Grando had always been a hard worker and was well-liked around the various villages and in the neighbouring city. However, around his 60th year, he was suddenly taken with a strange disease and subsequently died. About two weeks or so after his death, people were wakened from a sound sleep by a heavy weight landing on their chest and by pricking and pinching pains around their throats. There was no doubt in their minds that these had been caused by Grando, as several of them had dreamed about the landowner at the same time. The ecclesiastical authorities were approached and decreed that his grave should be opened, even though he'd been buried for several months. When this was done, it was found that the body was extremely fresh and flaccid and with a ruddy complexion. In fact, he looked as though he was simply sleeping. And as they gazed at the body, it appeared that the dead man's lips quivered and he smiled or bared his teeth.

He even parted his lips as if to breathe. And to add to their horror, the eyes of the corpse suddenly opened, whereupon all those present fell to their knees and began to recite sacred litanies against evil. A priest then raised a crucifix above his face and intoned "Raise thine eyes and look upon Jesus Christ who hath redeemed us from the pains of hell by His most Holy Passion and His precious Death upon the Rood." At first, the dead man looked confused, then an expression of intense sadness crossed his face and tears began to flow down his cheeks. After a solemn commendation of his soul and at a sign from the priest, the head of the vampire was struck from the body with a spade. The headless body jerked and convulsed as if it had been alive. After that, his former neighbours were no longer troubled in their sleep.

The Bad Lord Soulis and Robin Redcap

Although the majority of recorded cases which excited the scholarly minds of the 16th and 17th centuries occured in Central and Eastern Europe, other countries seemed to have certain instances of vampirism as well. Along the Scottish Borders, Hermitage Castle in Roxboroughshire enjoys a particularly sinister reputation as the home of an evil man who was believed to exhibit vampiric tendencies. This was "the bad Lord Soulis," a member of the de Soulis family who occupied the land from the mid-13th to the mid-14th century. Which Lord Soulis is being referred to is unclear, but it is certain that he was a tyrant and that he trafficked with dark powers. Together with a blood-drinking familiar or imp, whom he called "Robin Redcap," the Lord Souls kidnapped many people, including children who were tortured and murdered in lonely Hermitage Castle. Tradition also states that both he and the imp used their blood in diabolical rites and may have drunk it as well. Realizing what was happening, local people stormed the castle and overpowered the Lord, boiling him in lead—in some versions they wrapped the body in a sheet of lead to prevent his master, the Devil, from getting him, and to stop the corpse from rising and terrorizing the countryside once more.

Alexander Stewart, the Wolf of Badenoch

In the Scottish Highlands, the infamous Alexander Stewart, the 14th century Wolf of Badenoch, brother to King Robert III of Scotland, was supposed to drink blood amongst his Highland ceterans (outlaw soldiers) in his fortress at Lochindorb above Kingussie in the Spey Valley. Alexander was supposed to have sold his soul to the devil and to have a copy in his possession of the notorious *Book of Black Earth,* a terrible volume of reputedly prehistoric magic that he had partly copied down from the lips of Highland chailleachs (witches). This would form the basis of the equally infamous *Red Book of Appin* (called the Wicked Bible by the Covenanters), which was supposedly used by Stewart sorcerers right up until 1745 when it disappeared. Some of the spells contained therein were said to involve the shedding and drinking of human blood. The Wolf, of course, held his court in a massive stone circle (now gone) near present-day Kingussie, so that he could commune with evil spirits. In this stone circle and under the influence of Druidic forces, he was said to drink the blood of stillborn babies in the midst of unholy rituals. Of course, many of these tales (especially those about drinking the blood of infants) may well have been put about by his implacable enemy, Alexander Burr, Bishop of Moray, but they served to create the impression of a vampiric Highland warlord which still lingers to this day.

Tadhg O'Carroll

In Ireland, members of the ruling clans were sometimes portrayed as having a lust for blood. In the bloody years of unrest around the mid-16th and early 17th centuries, a number of tales circulated throughout the country concerning the vampiric tendencies of certain ferocious and cruel warlords. Many of these may well have been put about by their enemies, but they left an indelible impression on the general mind, that echoed down across the centuries. Tadhg (or Teige) O'Carroll, for example, one of the so-called "Dark Princes of Ely" was credited with drinking the blood of his prisoners. The ancient kingdom of Ely lay in the Irish Midlands and comprised most of Counties Offaly and North Tipperary. It served as a "buffer zone" between two great power blocs in the area—one headed by the Fitzgeralds, (the Earls of Desmond and Kildare), the other headed by the Butlers (the Dukes of Ormond and North Tipperary). The O'Carrolls were a particularly fierce and war-like clan who had probably been driven south from North Monaghan by an expansion of the more powerful O'Neills in neighbouring Tyrone. Politically skillful and devious, they were able to play the main regional power blocs off against each other whilst ruling their own lands with an iron fist. The most bloodthirsty of them all, however, was Tadhg Caoch (One-eyed Tadhg) who came to prominence in between 1540s and early 1550s. His stronghold of Leap Castle (between Birr and Kinnity in Offaly) had an extremely sinister reputation that it enjoys even today (it is believed to be the most haunted castle in Western Europe). An old legend says the mortar used to build the fortress had been mixed with the blood of the defeated O'Bannions, from whom the O'Carrolls had seized the land, leading to the ancient curse that is said to still hang over the place—"Raised in blood; blood be its portion." Tadhg encouraged this reputation and added to his own notoriety by cutting the throat of his elder brother Thaddeus, who was a priest, whilst he was at prayer in the chapel at Leap. This was an act of blasphemy, which condemned the chieftain to remain as a vampiric ghost within the gloomy corridors of Leap. Tadhg was killed by his own kinsmen during internecine disputes in 1553, but not before he had killed large numbers of the neighbouring O'Mahons and allegedly drank their blood, and before he had bricked up many prisoners in the extensive rock-hewn dungeons that extend for miles beneath the castle. Many of these remain sealed to this day, concealing the atrocities of Tadhg and many of the other O'Carroll chieftains. In 1617, following the chaos of the Rebellion of Hugh O'Neill and the Plantation of Ulster, the era of the O'Carroll chieftains eventually came to an end as Sir Charles O'Carroll accepted lands in the New World and his descendants went on to found the state of Maryland. One of them was a signatory to the Declaration of Independence. The sinister fortress of Leap Castle however, still stands, guarding a trail that runs through the Slieve Bloom Mountains, between the plain of Leix and the coast. It is said to be haunted by Tadhg's vampiric spirit and at midnight, an eerie light has been seen shining across the valley in which it is situated, from the window of the chapel where the evil warlord slew his brother. Few locals will venture there after dark.

Cormac Tadhg McCarthy

Another vampire warlord was reputedly Cormac Tadhg McCarthy of Carrickphouka Castle, west of Macroom in County Cork. In 1601, he was made High Sheriff of Cork by the English with the instructions to hunt down all Irish rebels. In this he was diligent, anxious to please his English masters. His main opponent was the chieftain James Fitzgerald, who was regarded as a traitor by the authorities in Dublin, and in order to capture him, Cormac invited him to a feast in Carrickphouka on the pretence of making peace. During the course of the banquet, he had Fitzgerald killed, but in order to assure the English of his loyalty and to impress them, he went slightly further. It is said that he lapped up the spilled blood and ate the raw flesh of the fallen chieftain, much to the horror and disgust of the English who were present. In defence of these horrific actions, the McCarthy clan claimed that Cormac had in fact been possessed by a spirit that had risen out of the rock upon which his castle was built. (Carrickphouka means "the rock of the phouka"—phouka or pooka being a malevolent and dark spirit or demon). Even so, this was not enough to prevent Cormac from going down in history as a "vampire Sheriff." Even today, tales still exist of alleged sightings of him in and around the castle, long after his death. Today Carrickphouka Castle is simply a ruin—it was destroyed during the Williamite Wars of 1690-91, but local people still stay away from it after dark and elderly people will cross the road when passing by it and will genuflect in protection, even in broad daylight.

Relish Cakes and Blood Pudding

The horrors of the Great Famine (1845–52) added another element to the vampire legends of Ireland. As the Irish potato crop, upon which much of the populace depended, began to fail, hunger and destitution began to set in all across the country. In desperation, people turned to other means of sustenance, one of which was blood. One of the most famous alternative dishes of the Famine period was "relish cakes" that in many ways resembled the English black pudding. These were made from dried blood, (usually that of pigs or cows), mixed with whatever greens were available—cabbage tops and so on—and heated in the fires of the cottages. In other localities, cattle were driven to certain areas, where a small incision was made in their necks and a small amount of blood drawn off. This was then used to make the relish cakes or, more than likely, drunk raw, similar to milk. Blood was believed to be a good source of iron and nutrients and was supposed to guard against the fevers and sicknesses that followed the Famine.

Epidemics of various diseases swept through a number of Irish counties independent of the Famine. Several years before the Great Hunger took hold there were outbreaks of typhoid and tuberculosis in places such as Counties Sligo and Clare. People began to sicken and waste away, coughing up flecks of blood that remained about their mouths. They sensed a weight on their chests and their skin became pallid to the point of looking similar to marble. These were all the classic symptoms of a vampire attack. It is interesting to note that Bram Stoker's mother came from County Sligo and that she had lived through a particularly vicious epidemic of tuberculosis there in the early 1800s.

England 18th Century

Although England did not suffer from such horrors, there were tales of vampiric corpses rising from the dead in English folklore as well. Instances of catalepsy and trances seem to have been common around the 1700s and into the early 1800s. Medicine as we understand it was, of course, simply finding its feet, and some of those who were pronounced dead were in fact not dead at all. Some of the horror that these unfortunates must have experienced is reflected in Edgar Allen Poe's macabre masterpiece *The Premature Burial.* Such burials were in all probability, much more common than might be imagined. There are tales from England, Wales, and Ireland of corpses suddenly "coming to" just as they were about to be coffined, or of corpses opening their eyes and sitting up when they were already in an open coffin.

Constance Whitney

In the chancel of the London church of St. Giles, Cripplegate, there is still a monument to the memory of Constance Whitney who died in the early 1800s. Her tomb is marked by a marble scroll, with a carving on it that depicts the lady rising from her coffin. Behind this representation is a rather frightening legend.

The unfortunate lady was buried whilst in a cataleptic trance and was only returned to consciousness when a greedy sexton opened her coffin with the intention of stealing a valuable ring from her finger. The lady rose up, putting the robber to flight, and lived for a number of years after her terrifying ordeal.

Ernest Wicks

In September 1895, a boy named Ernest Wicks was found lying on the grass in Regent's Park, London, seemingly quite dead. The body was removed to and laid out in Marylebone mortuary where it was examined by the mortuary keeper, Mr. Ellis, prior to the arrival of a doctor. During the course of this examination, Mr. Ellis noted that the chest was slightly rising and falling and he assumed that the subject might well be alive. He rubbed the boy's arms in an attempt to restore the circulation and it seems to have worked—the child sluggishly sat up as if he had been no more than sleeping. He then slumped back but continued to breathe regularly. When the doctor arrived, the child was taken to the Middlesex Hospital where the surgeon pronounced him to be "recovering from a fit." At an inquiry in 1902, it was revealed that the boy had "died" no less than four times and that his mother had obtained three certificates of death, all signed by reputable doctors. And Ernest Wicks was not the only person to be so afflicted.

Alice Holden

In 1905, a Mrs. Alice Holden, living near Accrington, suddenly "died," despite being only twenty-eight and in full health. Even though the circumstances looked more than a little suspicious, the doctor did not hesitate to issue a certificate of death and arrangements for her funeral were made. Luckily, an undertaker's assistant saw a flutter of her eyelids as he prepared to put the body in the coffin, and eventually the woman was revived and continued to live perfectly well for many years afterwards. Though this occurred at the beginning of the 20th century, a similar event took place in England in the 1990s. Here, once again, a woman was pronounced dead and, if not for an embalmer's eagle-eyed observation, she would have been buried. She is still living today, fit and well.

Resurrection Men

The horror of premature burial was coupled in the popular imagination with yet another terror—that of the Resurrection Men. As medical science made its faltering steps forward during the 18th century, a growing number of anatomists and surgeons began to look around for dead human bodies upon which they could experiment and with which they could teach their pupils. Initially executed felons provided a ready source for these—the English king, Henry VIII granted the Worshipful Company of Barber-Surgeons four cadavers each year to practice upon—but soon the demand was so great that the gallows struggled to keep up. In order to meet this demand, a new breed of criminal came to the fore—the Resurrectionist or "Sack-em-Ups." These were, in effect, bodysnatchers—those who would dig up freshly interred corpses and sell them on to the surgeons. It was a ghoulish practice and totally illegal. And indeed, some of the Resurrectionists augmented their supplies of cadavers with those whom they had themselves murdered. In many cases, those purchasing the corpses did not query the method of death too much. Gentlemen such as Dr. Robert Knox in Edinburgh (now notorious for his connection with the infamous bodysnatchers Burke and Hare) and Dr. Samuel Clossey in Dublin, were willing to "turn a blind eye" to irregularities that they found on the bodies, which today would suggest foul play. As early as the 1760s, the Edinburgh female Resurrectionists, Helen Torrence and Jean Waldie were dealing with dug-up bodies alongside a "Dr. Russell" and his associates who ran an "apothecary shop" in the old part of the city. In London, competing gangs led by Ben Crouch and Israel Chapman dealt with the United Borough Hospital and St. Bartholomew's between 1809 and 1813. Even as late as 1830, the Bethnal Green gang, led by John Bishop, was selling freshly dug-up bodies to St. Bartholomew's for eight guineas.

The idea of the body being buried before its time, and that of the cadaver raised from the grave by the attentions of the Resurrectionists, made an indelible impression on the popular mind. This fused with tales coming from Central and Eastern Europe to form the basis of the English vampire belief. It was but a small step from the "resurrected" corpse to the notion of the threatening vampire rising from its tomb to menace those around it.

An example of the English vampire theme is to be found in Augustus Hare's *Story of My Life* (1896) in which he recounted a tale told to him by a certain Captain Fisher whose family had lived at Coglin Grange in a remote area of Cumberland in the north of the country.

Coglin Grange

The Grange at Coglin was a long, low house, no more than one-story high. It was very old, and according to Fisher, the land sloped away at one side towards an equally ancient church, in a hollow below. Coglin Grange had been a home to the Fisher family for a number of years, but after a time, they began to find it too small and cramped, and they moved south to Thorncombe near Guildford. They rented out Coglin Grange and were extremely fortunate in their tenants—two brothers and a sister.

The new tenants of the Grange settled in extremely well and were well-liked by their neighbours. And because there was only three of them, Coglin suited their needs admirably. Their winter was spent settling in and establishing themselves, meeting new friends, and making themselves popular in the district. Spring changed to an extremely hot summer when the nights seemed long and clammy and it was difficult to get any sleep.

One evening during the hot spell, the family at Coglin dined on the veranda of the old house before separating for the night to their bedrooms, which were all on the ground floor. However, shortly after she got into bed, the sister found that she could not sleep and propped herself up on her pillows. Although she'd fastened the window of her room, she had not closed the shutters and so she was able to look out across the countryside, bathed in the silver light of what seemed to be an abnormally large moon. Her room looked out in the direction of the old church and a particularly thick and dark stand of trees. As she watched, she suddenly became aware of two lights, flickering along the edge of the tree line, along the edge of the churchyard. As she watched, she suddenly became aware of a shape that seemed to have coalesced out of the shadows and was drawing slowly nearer to the Grange. For a moment, she wasn't sure because the large, pale moon was scattering shadows everywhere across the intervening ground and from time to time, it seemed lost amongst these.

But as it drew closer, the woman felt an unimaginable terror rise in the back of her throat. Suddenly and without warning, the coalescing figure changed direction and seemed to be going around the house, moving towards a corner to her left. She leapt from her bed and ran to her door, ready to unlock it and see who this peculiar visitor to her home might be. As she did so, she heard a scratching sound at the window behind her and, turning, she saw a hideous brown face, the colour of withered leaves, looking in at her. The eyes of the Thing glowed like living coals with a terrible malevolence that scared her even more. She stood there, transfixed, but safe in the knowledge that the window was securely fastened. The face drew back and there was silence for a moment. Then she heard a sound from the window similar to a bird pecking and, to her horror, she realized that the creature outside was trying to unpick the lead around the window-frame. Unable to move through sheer terror, she stood where she was and at last one of the panes of glass fell into the room. The long, bony hand of the creature came through the aperture and seized the handle of the window opening it to admit the rest of its body. In an instant, it was across the room and had seized the terrified woman by the hair. Dragging her forward it bit her sharply on the neck. The bite seemed to free her voice and she screamed loudly, bringing her brothers running from their own bedrooms to find her door locked from the inside. A poker brought from the fireplace in the living room, soon smashed the lock. At their approach, the Thing had dropped its victim and darted back towards the window. When the brothers broke in, they found their sister kneeling by the side of her bed bleeding from a wound in her throat. One brother pursued the creature out into the night and over the ground towards the church, which the Thing covered in impossibly huge strides. On reaching the churchyard wall, it seemed to disappear into a group of shadows and did not reappear, so the pursuer returned to join his brother and sister in the bedroom at Coglin Grange. The girl was dreadfully hurt, but she was of a strong disposition and was not all that given to superstition. The three of them assumed that a lunatic had escaped from custody and had made his way to Coglin and attacked her. And that was the way it was left. The wound healed but the actual shock of her attack had unsettled the girl and had left her very shaken. Her brothers decided to take her to Switzerland in order to fully recover from her ordeal.

After some time travelling through the Alps, they returned to Coglin Grange at the girl's insistence. She was anxious to get back and resume their old way of life as quickly as possible. When they returned home, they began to secure the old place, barring all the doors and closing all the shutters at night, although one little place was left uncovered (as was the fashion in many old houses) in order to let some light in. The brothers themselves kept a brace of pistols in each of their rooms and close to their beds in case they should have any further unwelcome night visitors.

The winter passed peacefully and quietly. The following spring was warm and, although it was not quite summer, some of the nights were particularly muggy. One night, the sister was woken up by a sound that she remembered only too well—the scratching sound of long claws upon the windowpane. Looking up at the uncovered topmost pane, she saw the same horrid brown face staring down at her, the eyes burning red with a hellish fire. This time, her voice didn't desert her and she screamed as loudly as she could, bringing her brothers into the room. Grabbing their pistols, they rushed outside to confront the Thing but, by this time, it was already rushing down the slope across the open ground towards the church, darting in and out of the shadows as it went. One of the brothers got a shot off and seemingly hit it in the leg, but it kept on running, taking extremely large strides. Reaching the churchyard wall, it scrambled over and disappeared among the tombstones and into the vault of a long-extinct family.

The next day, the brothers summoned some of their neighbours from around Coglin Grange and in their presence, the vault was opened. It was full of coffins, many of which had been broken open with their contents scattered upon the ground. Only one coffin was intact and its lid was loose. Upon opening it, the searchers found themselves looking at the same hideous, withered face that had been peering through the window of the Grange. Trembling, they managed to cursorily examine the body and found the traces of a pistol shot in one of the legs. It was generally concluded that the creature in the coffin was a vampire, and the body was taken out into the daylight and burnt. From then on, there was no more trouble at Coglin Grange. Subsequent commentators on the above story have pointed out that there is no such place as Coglin

Grange, but have identified the house concerned as Coglin Low Hall in Cumbria. The vault, in which the vampire was found, also seems to have disappeared—there is nothing in Coglin Churchyard that might correspond to it, and no record of the family to whom it may have belonged to.

Whether strictly accurate or not, Hare's story was widely circulated and it fit in with the Gothic mood that had developed in England during the 19th century. The first vampire story is usually attributed to Dr. John Polidori who was born in London in 1795 as the son of an Italian émigré. In 1815, he completed his studies in medicine and entered the service of Lord Byron as the latter's personal physician, accompanying his master on a journey through Europe. Also accompanying them were the poet Percy Shelley and his wife Mary. On a stormy night in 1816, in the Villa Diodati above Lake Geneva in Switzerland, the group read through a Gothic ghost story book entitled *Tales of the Dead* and decided to write their own ghost or horror story. The most famous work to come out of that experiment was Mary Shelley's classic novel *Frankenstein*, but Polidori also penned a minor classic—*The Vampyre*. This moved away from the brutal lowborn vampiric creature of Slavic folklore and created Lord Ruthven, an aristocratic vampire who may well have been the template for Dracula himself. The novella was published in April 1819 in the *New Monthly Magazine* but was embarrassingly credited as a new piece by Lord Byron. Despite attempts to correct this mistake, it remained as Byron's work for many years afterward. Polodori died in 1821 under mysterious circumstances. He had been suffering from depression for some time and was thought to have committed suicide by drinking poison. Regardless, he had left behind the model for the vampire that we all recognize today.

Polodori's work was only one of a number of Gothic tales that began to appear during the early-to-mid 19th century. Many of these bore titles that suggested ancient and terrifying mysteries and the returning dead—*The Black Monk* or *The Secret of the Grey Turret; The Blighted Heart* or *The Old Priory Ruins; Blanche* or *The Mystery of the Doomed House; The Skeleton Clutch* or *The Goblet of Gore*. There were also other popular novels in circulation that had overtones of cannibalism and mass murder that had their roots in actual historical occurrences—works such as *Sawney Bean, the Man-Eater of Midlothian* and *Sweeney Todd, the Demon Barber of Fleet Street*, all of which raised a horror of, and a fascination with, the darker side of 19th century life. Every one of these ghastly titles probably sprang from the pen of one man who was making a veritable fortune in the genre. Foremost amongst these terrors was *Varney the Vampire* or *The Feast of Blood.*

Varney the Vampyre

The events as detailed in the story were alleged to have been based on fact and were supposed to have taken place in England, during the reign of Queen Anne (1702–1714), although no such record can be traced. These events may relate to some of the reports that were emerging from Central and Eastern Europe. *Varney* appeared as a lengthy volume in 1847 and is credited as being one of the early works of the writer Thomas Preskett Prest, the fabled author of Gothic stories that appeared in lurid horror magazines known as "dreadfuls." The volume boasted two hundred and twenty chapters, making it one of the longest books ever written in the genre. It was such a success, however, that it was reprinted in a number of serialized chapters by Messrs. E. Lloyd, who had printing premises in London's Salisbury Square and were purveyors of "shockers" and "dreadfuls" of the most gruesome kind, and with whom Prest had a close association. *Varney,* like all of Prest's stories, followed a formula, were filled with heaving bosoms, lustful roues, and gore.

Prest's work spawned a score of imitators, most of which are best forgotten but through their pages they built up a corpus of vampire lore that began to establish the vampire as one of the principal terrors of Victorian England. However, it was not only Britain that was falling under the thrall of the Undead. Across the ocean in America, a similar body of lore and tradition was beginning to establish itself.

The American Colonies

There had been whispers of vampiric activity in the New World since the early days of the European Colonists. As early as 1692, the Reverend Deodat Lawson, minister at Salem Village, Massachusetts, (scene of the infamous

Salem Witch Trials), complained of being attacked in the darkness on the doorstep of one of the afflicted girls, by an unseen creature who had attempted to bite him. This might be put down to something of the hysteria of the time, but for the Puritan colonists, America must have been a frightening and supernatural place. It was covered in deep and gloomy forests and the trackless bogs in which a man might be lost. And out in this wilderness were Native Americans who, as far as the colonists were concerned, practiced diabolical rites and might well be agents of the Devil himself. The forests and swamps were the homes of ungodly creatures.

Disease was also rampant in this new land. Following the War of Independence in 1775, epidemics of tuberculosis, cholera, and typhoid swept through the fledgling settlements scattered across the developing areas of early America. For many, the sicknesses were the work of Satan who was lurking in the wilderness. Normally healthy individuals suddenly began to inexplicably waste away, and eventually die. There was no warning—they simply turned pale and feeble, withering away before their demise. It could only be the result of some form of supernatural evil. Both English and German immigrants brought with them tales of ancient terrors from their own homelands and gradually these melded into the folklore of the New World. One element in this folklore was that of the vampire that had been brought to America mainly by immigrants from Central Europe. Even in an increasingly enlightened age, an explanation for such diseases was not sought in the fly-ridden bogs or in the scummy wells, which might have lain near to the early settlements; rather communities looked towards something uncanny which hovered around, just out of sight. The very primordialness of the landscape itself suggested that such things were possible. In such a place, the idea of the vampire that many Europeans had carried with them to America seemed all too real.

The vampire capital of the New World was not, as might be supposed, New York (Niew Amsterdam under the Dutch) or San Francisco (as it often appears in the movies). Instead it was the small state of Rhode Island. Amongst the isolated farms and communities, old ways lingered on and old tales were often repeated along the lanes that wound their ways amongst the apple orchards of the state. Rhode Island had experienced heavy fighting during the

War of Independence and remote, often overgrown cemeteries were filled with corpses from that time. There were also stories that some corpses lay unburied, hidden away in the woods where wounded British, German, and American soldiers had crawled away to die. There were legends of ghosts haunting lonely gravesites and of ancient beings from the time before the settlers that still dwelt in the deep woodlands. Memories of ancestral European terrors added a fresh edge to these fears and whispers.

Disease swept through Rhode Island towards the end of the 18th century. The arrival of tuberculosis was coupled with a fear that the British might try to reinvade the Colonies (this happened in 1812) and illness struck sporadically in communities that teetered on the edge of public panic and hysteria. The tiny state was to produce a tradition that was to become known throughout America (and further afield) as "the vampire ladies."

Sarah Tillinghast

The horror began in 1796 with Sarah Tillinghast, daughter of Stukely Tillinghast, an apple farmer from the South County area of the state. Nineteen-year-old Sarah was a quiet and demure girl, but exceptionally dreamy and given to wandering in old cemeteries where the buried Revolutionary War casualties lay. In the autumn of 1796, she suddenly fell ill, with what the local doctor diagnosed as consumption (tuberculosis) and died. Shortly afterward, other members of the Tillinghast family also became ill and died, wasting away in an inexplicable manner. Oddly enough, they had dreamed of Sarah a number of nights before their actual death. Fear spread through the community—not of tubercular contagion—but of vampire activity. Old stories were stirred up again and many became convinced that Sarah and some of her siblings had become vampiric creatures. These stories were perhaps fanned by the local minister, Benjamin Northup, who saw the Devil's hand in the deaths. As the hysteria mounted, Stukely Tillinghast became more and more unsure of what to do. He was losing members of his family on a regular basis to an unknown but relentless evil against which he and the church seemed powerless. In desperation, he travelled out to the lonely churchyard where his daughter lay and together with one of his farmhands unearthed her coffin. Opening it, he found

Sarah lying, just as fresh and beautiful as when she had been interred. Taking a large hunting knife, he cut out her heart and set fire to it. He'd heard about an old legend that said it was the only way to destroy a vampire. After that, the deaths in the Tillinghast household stopped, as did the dreams, but Stukely had lost half of his large family.

Nancy Young

Things were quiet in Rhode Island until 1827 when the "vampire epidemic" surfaced again. This time it was near the small town of Foster and it afflicted the household of Captain Levi Young and his wife, both natives of Sterling, Connecticut who had bought land in the area. Levi Young had been a captain of militia but had settled down to become a farmer in the Foster area. He had done rather well and was reasonably prosperous. He and his wife Anna Perkins had eight children and the Foster farmhouse rang with the sound of a happy and contented family.

In the spring of 1827, things changed. Levi and Anna's eldest daughter Nancy, began to sicken with what seemed, at first, to be a passing cold. It grew steadily worse—Levi thought she had taken a severe influenza—and she took to her bed, eventually becoming completely bedridden. She died shortly after.

As with Sarah Tillinghast, a few months after Nancy Young's death, other members of her family also began to sicken. Some of them complained that they too had dreamed of Nancy visiting them at night and had experienced an extraordinary weight upon them as they lay in bed. Stories of Sarah Tillinghast began to resurface in Rhode Island society and the chilling word "vampire" was on many lips. Again hysteria was bubbling just beneath the surface of the Foster community. Something had to be done. An elderly Foster resident known locally as "Doc" Lennox suggested that Nancy's body should be exhumed and burned. This was done by Levi Young himself, on a chilly autumn morning in the town's new churchyard and in full view of his neighbours. Doc Lennox had suggested that other members of the Young family should stand in the smoke from the pyre in order to protect themselves from former vampiric attentions. After Nancy was burned, the deaths stopped. Things would remain quiet in Rhode Island for almost fifty years.

Juliet Rose

The next of Rhode Island's "vampire ladies" is generally taken to be Juliet Rose, the daughter of William G. Rose, a businessman and civic leader in South County. Her story follows the now-established pattern of both Nancy Young and Sarah Tillinghast. A lively youngster, and the child of William's first wife Mary Taylor (who had died some years before), Juliet suddenly and inexplicably succumbed to what was described as a "harsh fever" and died in the early autumn of 1874. Shortly after her death, William's other daughter, Mary Griswold, began to show signs of an illness, wasting away. Almost immediately old stories of the earlier vampire ladies rose to the forefront of William Rose's mind. He was convinced that the vampire scourge had returned. Armed with his suspicions, he confronted his local minister, the Reverend Amos Cabot, but was told that he was still grieving for Juliet and was imagining things. Still convinced of the awful plague, William Rose went to the family cemetery deep in the Rhode Island woods. There, according to his own testimony, he beheld the form of his daughter standing over what was her grave. Although it extended its arms to him, begging for his warmth, the apparition vanished before his whispered prayers and William Rose commenced to dig up Juliet's coffin. Pulling back the lid, he saw to his horror that the winding sheet, in which the body lay, was badly stained with fresh blood. With a cry of despair, he drew his hunting knife and plunged in into the cadaver's heart. A scream rang through the graveyard. When he returned home, he found his young daughter recovering slowly from whatever it was that ailed her. This was taken to be indisputable evidence of vampire activity that was now laid to rest.

Mercy Brown

The area stayed quiet until 1892, when the last and most famous of Rhode Island's vampires made her appearance. This was Mercy Brown, daughter of George Brown, who owned a small farm between the settlements of Exeter and Wickford in the south of the state. The story had started, however, much earlier, with the death of George's wife Mary in 1883. Shortly after her death, his daughter Mary Olive began to complain of strange and terrifying dreams and of a crushing weight on her chest. She began to exhibit some of the signs of the strange sickness that had taken away her mother until June 1884 when she succumbed to the same death. Things remained quiet for about five years until George's only son Edwin also began to display the same ghastly symptoms that had carried away his mother and sister. He too experienced terrible dreams of suffocation and crushing, turning from a hearty young man into a pale and shambling wreck. His doctor suggested that perhaps the airs of Colorado might be good for him and so Edwin travelled there to recover his failing health. His health returned almost immediately, and he decided to stay there for a while. Whilst he was there, however, he received word that his younger sister, Mercy Lena, had been seized with a similar disease and was sinking fast. Edwin rushed home but was too late—Mercy was already dead. Notions of the vampires began to re-emerge from the shadows and a number of local people complained of feeling weak, adding that they had also dreamed of Mercy Brown on a number of consecutive nights. The people feared another outbreak of the "vampire plague" and decided that something had to be done.

On the morning of 18th March 1892, a group of town elders, headed by the local doctor, Harold Metcalfe, made their way to the tiny cemetery where Mercy Brown had been taken to rest. Because she had died in the winter when the ground was still hard with frost, Mercy had not actually been buried, but lay in a squat stone crypt on the edge of the burying ground. The coffin that contained Mercy Brown's body lay just inside the door, balanced on a cart. With due solemnity, the men opened the casket and threw back the lid. Mercy lay inside just as fresh and pretty as she'd ever been, with no sign of decay upon her. There were also traces of fresh blood on the inside of the coffin. Stepping forward, the doctor made a small incision in the cadaver and removed her heart and liver. These were ritually burned and water and vinegar were poured into the cavity from which they'd been removed. The men then left the cemetery and returned to their homes, praying that the scourge of vampirism which had afflicted Rhode Island was at last over. And indeed it appeared to be.

Edwin Brown himself died shortly after these macabre events. However, one of the local newspapers, *The Providence Journal*, seized upon the incident and carried a rather lurid account of the gathering in the churchyard in its issue of 19th March 1892. It followed the story in its 21st March issue, claiming that vampires were not a native Rhode Island superstition but "settled here," brought in by immigrants to the state. The article was lifted by some of the New York papers who used it to poke fun at the "superstitious" Rhode Islanders and the story became widespread all across America. The Mercy Brown case may have been yet another influence on Bram Stoker as he wrote his vampire novel. He had been touring part of the United States as secretary to the actor Sir Henry Irving and, it is thought, could not have failed to come into contact with some account of the incident. Indeed, after his death, his wife found cuttings from some of the American newspapers relating to the case amongst his possessions.

Nelly Vaughn

Mercy Brown more or less marked the end of the "vampire ladies," although there is one more that has not been mentioned. In a secluded graveyard, near Coventry, Rhode Island, stood a funeral marker bearing a curious inscription. The grave was that of Nelly Vaughn, who died in 1889, aged nineteen years and the inscription reads: *"I am waiting and watching for you."* The message may have been quite innocent—to a loving family or a secret lover but in the remote Rhode Island cemetery and with the alleged history of vampirism in the state, they took on a rather chilling aspect. In 1967, a teacher at Coventry High School informed his class that there was a vampire buried somewhere in the locality. After a degree of research, interest fastened on Nelly Vaughn's tombstone with its peculiar message. There was a myth in the area that no vegetation would grow on Nelly's grave though this may arguably have had more to do with the number of visitors at the site than with any supernatural agency. Besides the peculiar inscription, little is known about Nelly Vaughn's brief life and virtually nothing is known about how she died. However, the gravesite generated a massive amount of interest in vampires and ghosts in that remote corner of Rhode Island. In the 1980s, *Yankee* magazine ran an article entitled *The Words on Nelly's Tombstone,* which generated a fresh and more widespread interest in Rhode Island vampires. There were more visitors and Nelly's funeral marker became so desecrated and broken that it had to be removed in 1990. Perhaps poor Nelly can finally rest in peace.

Horace Ray

Rhode Island was not, of course, the only American state to experience an alleged vampire phenomenon. In neighbouring Connecticut, there were also suggested instances involving the Undead. In Jowett City, between the years 1847 and 1852, it was suspected that some sort of vampiric agency was at work in the locality. The vampire was supposed to be the unquiet revenant of Horace (sometimes given as Henry) Ray who had died early in 1847 and who was said to be preying on two of his sons who had survived him. When they too died, a number of people around the Jowett City area dreamed of them and awoke, experiencing exhaustion. Certain religious factions believed that vampires were at work and the bodies of Horace Ray and his sons were exhumed and burnt, whereupon the dreams and exhaustion stopped.

In the town of Griswold, historians investigated a local building site after some children had found a human skull there. The place was found to be a very old burying ground that included a stone vault. Here, the historians found a coffin containing some human remains that had obviously been treated for vampirism—dismembered in a very deliberate fashion. The skull had been placed amongst the bones of the chest and both arms and legs had been systematically broken. A closer examination of these bones revealed a tubercular-like condition. The coffin was marked "JB 55"—the "JB" being taken to refer to the occupant of the coffin and the "55" to his or her age. The skeleton was placed back in its coffin and no further examination was carried out, although anthropologists have suggested that this method of burial was not native to Connecticut but rather was common in Eastern Europe.

The Corwin Brothers

In Woodstock, Vermont, two brothers named Corwin were struck by an inexplicable illness towards the end of 1834. Before the year was ended, the eldest of the brothers had died and the other was starting to sicken. Stories concerning vampires who had been living in the forests which cloaked the Vermont mountains were suddenly remembered, and it was considered that the elder Corwen might be the victim of one of these, and that he had even become a vampire himself. His body was subsequently dug up and burned, the ashes placed in an iron pot and buried directly beneath the town square. A later account tells of how some youths attempted to dig them up late at night but were assailed by unearthly cries and screams, so they abandoned the idea.

Rachel Burton

An earlier and even more curious tale comes from Manchester, Vermont, concerning jealously and vengeance that reached out from beyond the grave. In the late 18th century, Isaac Burton, a naval officer, watched his young wife Rachel slip away with the ravages of a strange disease that resembled consumption. Distraught by her illness, he vowed that she was the love of his life and that if she died, he would never marry again. He laid her to rest in the Manchester cemetery. For a while, he mourned her loss, but then became attracted to pretty Hulda Powell who lived in the town. Soon the pair of them were married. Hulda made Isaac a good wife. A year or so after the wedding however, Hulda began to sicken with the same illness that had carried off Rachel. Significantly, she claimed to have dreamt of Isaac's first wife and a meeting of the town fathers including the local clergyman concluded that Rachel Burton was somehow drawing off Hulda's strength from the other side of the grave. Her body was exhumed and though she had been dead for over a year, her body was found to be remarkably fresh. The cadaver was ritually burned, but in 1793, Hulda Burton died, seemingly a victim of Isaac's former wife. The tale only added to the building corpus of Undead lore. Down through the years, the shadow of the vampire lingered on both sides of the Atlantic and all across Europe.

Dracula and other Vampire Fiction

In 1897, the Irish writer Bram Stoker published what was to become one of the seminal books of vampire fiction—the novel *Dracula*. Although he would produce other works, none would catch the public imagination as much as his tale of the vampire count, drawing as it did upon a number of social issues but also on a corpus of folklore. Indeed, the novel has supposedly never been out of print since the day that it was first published. Allegedly, the only book that can rival that record is the Bible. It established the idea of the Undead firmly in Eastern Europe, a part of the world to which Stoker had never been (although it's possible that he may have been aware of Dom Calmet's work in that region) and inextricably linked the vampire motif with a medieval Wallachian warlord. It also created the image of the Undead as the cloak-swathed aristocrat with which we are all familiar today.

The book and the ideas that it produced were so successful that it inevitably spawned a number of imitations, not least of all in the developing cinematic industry of the early 20th century.

Nosferatu

The most famous of all the early vampire films was produced by a small German film company, Prana Film. This had been set up around the end of 1919 to produce and promote films (then silent, black and white films) that had a supernatural theme. In the end, the studio produced only one film, but it was destined to become a classic. This was F.W. Marnau's *Nosfertu, ein symphonie des gruens (a symphony of horror)*. Although the title was "nosferatu" (a German word for vampire) the action of the film was set in the Carpathian Mountains of Eastern Europe. Marnau used a largely German cast, including the Berlin-born actor Maximillian Schreck, who had initially made his name on the German stage but was now increasingly seen in films. Schreck's own name is interesting—it is the German word for "terror" or "fight" and it led to the legend that it was not his name at all. In fact, he was at one time said to be an English actor named Alfred Abel, but this rumour was put to rest when the two men appeared together. Because he was a rather private man and not a great deal was known about his background, weird and unsubstantiated tales grew around him.

Schreck's portrayal of the vampire perhaps owed more to the tale of Coglin Grange than it did to the sleek and stately aristocrat of Stoker's novel. Count Graf Orlock is an emaciated and withered figure, slightly stooped and bald and with protruding fangs and long, claw-like fingernails. Even so, the film borrowed liberally from the *Dracula* novel and therein lay its downfall. The producers and writer (generally credited as Albin Grau) had not obtained the permission of the Stoker estate, and Florence Stoker, (Bram Stoker's widow), immediately instigated legal proceedings. A case of copyright infringement was found against Prana Film and Florence was awarded substantial damages. After making one film, the studio declared itself bankrupt. However, it had left behind what many consider to be an early masterpiece of cinematic horror.

Dracula: The Films

Universal

Universal Pictures in America was more circumspect when it released its own version of Dracula in 1931. Director Todd Browning had obtained all necessary permissions and had gone out of his way to choose an actor that he considered perfect for the job. That actor was Bela Lugosi. Lugosi had been born in Lugos, a town in Austria-Hungary (now Lugoj in Romania) and had a thick Hungarian accent, which Browning deemed ideal for the vampire count. During the 1930s, Lugosi became the quintessential vampire, full of East European menace and aristocratic evil. His version of the Count was probably closer to Stoker's ideal that Schreck's had been. He was less emaciated and more human, but there was still a sinister chill around his portrayal of Dracula. As Browning had imagined, his thick accent gave an air of eerie authenticity to the character. Who can forget his utterance as he listened to the howling of wolves outside his castle "*The children of the night—what music they make!*" or "*I never drink—wine.*" Despite all the authenticity of imagery, Browning took massive liberties with the script to suit American audiences. For example, it is Renfield, not Jonathan Harker, who visits Dracula in his castle. Whereas in the book, it is the other way around. However, largely due to the brooding presence of Lugosi, the film was an outstanding success. In fact, it spawned a string of what were called "Monster Movies" and Lugosi found himself heading a stable of other famous monster actors such as Boris Karloff *(Frankenstein* and *The Mummy)* and Lon Chaney Jr. (*The Wolfman)* who dominated much of the 1930s and early 1940s with their creepy films.

Hammer Films

Another actor, the London-born Christopher Lee, would also be forever associated with the vampire Count. By the late 1950s/early 1960s, Lugosi's leering elegance was starting to appear slightly jaded. A new and dynamic post-War era needed a more credible challenge. Christopher Lee, who was to firmly establish the ideal of the modern vampire, emerged out of a new English-based studio. Exclusive Films had been formed in London in 1935 by a Spaniard named Enrique Carreras and a former actor William Hinds (stage name William Hammer). In the late 1950s, they also formed a subsidiary with Hinds as Chairman, that was named Hammer Films. The new company was to distribute horror and supernaturally based films, mainly for the British market, but for wider distribution as well. Lee, who is a direct descendant of the Emperor Charlemagne on his mother's side, had already appeared in a number of horror movies and had worked for Hammer playing another demonic figure—the oriental fiend Dr. Fu Manchu in 1965. In 1966, he appeared in the film *Dracula, Prince of Darkness,* playing the vampire Count. His austere, aristocratic version was a triumph and set the tone for all subsequent films—many of which starred Lee himself as Count Dracula. A powerful and commanding presence on screen, Lee was perfect as the demonic nobleman and brought a sinister air of sophisticated menace to the role. In most films, just as in Stoker's novel, the Count faced Professor Abraham Van Helsing, played by another Englishman—Surrey-born Peter Cushing. Throughout the 1960s and early 1970s, the two of them pitted wits against each other in a series of films, becoming almost icons of good and evil in the public mind. Both continued, long after Hammer and its subsidiary Tyburn (named after a place of public execution in London) had folded. Cushing appeared as General Moff Tarkin in the *Star Wars* series (in which Lee also appeared) and Lee most recently as the wizard Saruman the White in *Lord of the Rings.* Their cinematic legacy, however, has lived on in countless vampire movies.

Vampires have continued to exercise a hold on the human imagination. Apart from the films, countless books, magazines, and television programs on the subject have been produced through the years, right up until the present day. In fact, one of the most popular television series of recent times has been *Buffy, the Vampire Slayer* that was based on a film. It portrayed the vampire myth in a teenage soap opera-style and was extremely popular with many young people. Things have moved a long way since Dom Augustine Calmet!

Two figures have dominated the vampire myth and in their own ways have shaped our perspective of it—Dracula and the Countess Elizabeth Bathory. It is interesting to look at both of these and to see how the legend of the vampire has grown up around them

Vlad Tepes: Dracula the Legend

In the 15th century, Eastern Europe was in turmoil. Christianity found itself under threat from a rapidly expanding sphere of influence controlled by the Muslim Ottoman Turks. Indeed, after the fall of Constantinople in 1453, Christendom found itself under almost constant threat from the forces of Mohammed the Conqueror, who sought to extend the Muslim faith throughout all of Eastern Europe. Desperately, Christianity sought some form of response to the steadily growing Ottoman expansion.

The Holy Roman Emperor Sigismund (elected in 1410) created a semi-secret organization known as the Order of the Dragon to defend the eastern lands from the advancing Turkish threat. Its emblem was a dragon, clinging to a cross, its wings outstretched. From around 1431, a certain warlord or Voivode (local ruler), Vlad II of Wallachia, was brought into the Order and had the dragon emblazoned on his coinage. The Wallachian name for dragon was "Drac" and he became known locally as Vlad Dracul. Interestingly enough, the word "drac" can also mean "devil" or "evil spirit."

Wallachia was a tiny territory, but it was important. It had been founded in 1292 by Radu Negru (Radu the Black) but for many years it was dominated by Hungary who laid claim to part of neighbouring Transylvania and Moldavia. It broke free of Hungarian influence in 1330, becoming virtually an independent kingdom. It still, however, maintained strong links with Transylvania, and in fact Vlad II's wife was a Transylvanian noblewoman. In fact, Sigismund was to make Vlad II military governor of Transylvania in 1431. Wallachia was also strategically important, forming a kind of "buffer" between the Christian states and the expanding Muslim powers. This was why Christendom considered Vlad II's support so important.

Vlad II, however, was a skilled politician and sought a kind of "middle way" between the two factions. He was in a dangerous position and had no wish to see his country either invaded by the Turks or used as a frontier for a Christian battleground. From time to time, he struck up alliances with both, however as Turkish influence increased, he began to side with them. When the Turks invaded Transylvania in 1442, he remained neutral, greatly angering the Hungarians under their leader John Hunyadi, the White Knight of Hungary. Hunyadi attacked the Turks and drove them out of Transylvania before turning his attention on Vlad II and forcing him to flee his throne. However, Vlad regained it in 1443 with Turkish support, but was forced to hand over two of his sons—Vlad and Radu—as hostages to the Turkish administration. An uneasy peace existed between Wallachia and Hungary with Hunyadi demanding that Vlad II fulfill his obligations as a member of the Order of the Dragon, but Vlad II resisting for fear of inflaming the Turks.

Eventually, Vlad II died in 1448. On hearing of his death, the Turks immediately released his second son Vlad and supported him as Voivode of Wallachia. Hunyadi, fearing Turkish domination of the region immediately placed his own candidate Vladislav II or Vladislav Dan, backed by the Hungarian Army, on the Wallachian throne. However, he angered his Hungarian overlords by adopting slightly pro-Turkish policies and the situation became even more tense.

In 1456, the Hungarians invaded Turkish Serbia. It was a disastrous campaign during which Hunyadi was killed and, in the resulting political confusion, Vlad was prompted to make his bid for the Wallachian monarchy. He ousted Vladislav and had him murdered before taking the throne as Vlad III or Vlad Dracula(Drac-ula—son of the dragon). His reign was a despotic one, during the course of which he stood up to the Turks and systematically began to destroy the old local landowner system that had existed in Wallachia. This may have been because the Hungarian-backed land owners of Tirgoviste had burned his elder brother Mircea to death—Vlad III was to exact a terrible revenge upon them, arresting, torturing, and eventually executing them. His cruelty became legendary.

In 1462, the Turks forced Vlad III to flee the throne by aiding a popular uprising against him, placing his younger brother Radu the Handsome (who had remained in Turkish custody after Vlad had been released) on the Wallachian throne. It is said that Vlad's wife leapt to her death into a foaming river near his castle at Arges to avoid being captured by Turkish soldiers. Vlad himself managed to escape and fled to the Hungarian court for safety. Here the Hungarian king, Matthias Corvenus (John Hundyadi's son), had him imprisoned as a traitor. It is not known how long he was held, but he was released perhaps around 1474 by marrying into one of the Hungarian noble families. He then formed an alliance with Count Stephen Barthory to reinvade Wallachia and get his throne back, which their combined forces did in 1476. By this time, Radu was dead and had been replaced by another Turkish puppet, Basarab the Old. Basarab's forces were easily defeated and Vlad took the throne once more. However, several months later, Count Bathory's armies departed for Transylvania leaving Vlad in a rather weak position. Taking advantage of this, a massive Turkish army entered the country and Vlad was forced to take up arms to defend his country with only a skeleton army. He was killed in battle near present-day Bucharest. His decapitated body was recovered from the Turks and was taken inland to be buried at the monastery at Snagov.

There is little doubt that Vlad III was a cruel man, but he may have been not so different from many other rulers around him. Some of his methods of torture and execution may seem extremely barbaric to us today, but we must remember that Vlad was forced to maintain a strict and authoritarian rule to protect his country from the forces that surged around it—namely Hungarian and Turk. Nevertheless, some of his methods appear to be quite unique as well as being incredibly draconian and brutal. For example, one of his favourite methods of torture and death was to place Turkish prisoners on the top of high stakes and let the forces of gravity pull them down as the point of the stake disembowelled them. This earned him the nickname "Vlad Tepes" (pronounced Tep-esh) or "Vlad the Impaler." A number of grizzly anecdotes are told about him as well. The most common tale is how he received three Turkish ambassadors at his court, each one of them wearing a fez. In accordance with their own custom, they did not remove their headgear when they entered his presence. Vlad took this as a sign of disrespect and instructed that the fezs be nailed to their foreheads. In a similar anecdote, a Saxon merchant was caught either cheating or stealing from a poor man. Vlad had him placed against a wooden door and had a bag of gold nailed to his hand. The merchant's eyes were then gauged out so that he could not see his wealth.

Aware of the vast armies of beggars and diseased persons that traversed his territory demanding alms, Vlad devised a novel way of alleviating the problem. He invited many of the beggars and invalids to a great banquet held in a barn and when they were inside, he had all the doors locked and the building set alight, burning those inside to death. In this way he solved the country's destitute problem "at a stroke." However, it should be noted that although he appears as an often cruel and barbaric man, there is no record of Vlad III actually drinking human blood. Nevertheless, from our own 21st century point of view, he seems to have been a horrific despot.

Vlad Tepes is celebrated and remembered in his native Wallachia as a good prince, a defender of his country (now part of Romania) against foreign invaders—the Turks and the Saxons. He is fondly remembered as a friend of the poor and a champion of the common man—a ruler who protected his subjects, (through the laws that he enacted), from scheming foreign merchants and vicious Turkish interlopers. In this respect, he is regarded as a national hero.

The legends surrounding this admittedly bloodthirsty Wallachian warlord must have attracted Bram Stoker when he came to write his novel. Although not familiar with the area itself, he had heard some of its legends through friends who had connections with that part of the world. In 19th century England, Romania was a remote and exotic land—perhaps something like Tibet appeared during the 1950s and 1960s. Transylvania—the land beyond the forest—had a mysterious ring to it, and where better to set a story of horror and mystery than in the mist-shrouded forests that swathed the lower slopes of the Carpathian Mountains? Stoker may also have been aware of the tales and legends concerning vampires that had emerged from Hungary during the 1700s and this may have influenced his decision to set his novel—its content perhaps influenced by Irish and American elements—in the Transylvania/ Moldavia areas. And although we have no evidence that he knew anything about her, another person from the same region may have coloured his perspective. This was the nightmarish Countess Elizabeth Bathory.

Countess Elizabeth Bathory

Elizabeth (Erzsebet) Bathory has often been described as "Countess Dracula." The Bathory family was an old and illustrious one—one of the oldest in Transylvania in fact. The family traced its descendency from Vid Bathory, a legendary and mighty warrior who had allegedly slain a dragon with a mace in what is now eastern Romania. This may have created the motif for the Romanian Christian knight Iorgi—also said to have killed a dragon—who later became St. George, patron saint of England. They were also related by what looks to have been incestuous marriages amongst various other members of similar clans. Her mother, Anna Bathory, was the sister of King Stephen of Poland, and her father Iorgi (George—her mother's third husband) was the ruler of several countries. However, instances of inbreeding had led to rumours of madness and monstrous births in former years.

Elizabeth Bathory was born into this troubled lineage in 1560. Her mother was a devout Calvinist and an exceptionally strong character, and her father, George, was a hard-working man who had held several administrative posts under the Hapsburgs. She had at least one elder brother, one of the many Stephens (a popular name among the male Bathorys) and two younger sisters, Klara and Sofia, who disappeared from history without trace.

In 1571 at age 11, Elizabeth was promised in marriage to the fifteen year-old Count Ferenc (Francis) Nadasdy, fabulously wealthy and reckoned to be one of the most eligible bachelors in Hungary at that time. Such young betrothals were not uncommon and were usually for political reasons rather than any sort of romantic notions. In order to acquire the notable family name, Francis changed his own to that of Bathory, giving him the tradition of that family, as well as its notoriety.

Francis and Elizabeth waited four years to marry, finally doing so on 8th May 1575. Elizabeth was sent from the Bathory castle and into the care of her mother-in-law, the formidable Lady Ursula Kasnizsai. Whilst she was at the court of Lady Nadasdy, plagues and epidemics raged through Eastern Europe, carrying away the poor and wretched in the villages of Hungary. The tides of illnesses and disease, however, simply lapped around the walls of the castle at

Savarin, keeping everyone there confined. Elizabeth found herself increasingly under the control of her severe and dominant mother-in-law. It was around this time that she was, according to legend, visited by a "black stranger," perhaps a forest demon to whom she is said to have given herself. What actually might have transpired is that she had an affair with one (or more) of the servants, leading to the supposition that she may very well have been sexually promiscuous.

When her mother-in-law died, Elizabeth joined her husband at the remote Csejthe Castle. By this time, the Muslim Turks were making advances and (as they had done in Vlad III's time) the Christian forces were trying to limit their expansion. Count Francis was now a solider in the Hungarian army and had distinguished himself in battle becoming known as "The Black Hero of Hungary." He was consequently away fighting against Turkish incursions for much of his time, leaving his wife alone in the gloomy fortress.

It was now that Elizabeth fell under various influences. The servants at Csejthe, for the most part, were local people, steeped in local lore and legend. The area seemed to have been superstitious and filled with old tales and practices, many of which stretched back across the centuries. Certain servants appear to have initiated Elizabeth into rather unsavoury practices. Elizabeth may well have been attracted to lesbianism (she had an aunt who was renowned throughout Hungary in this respect) and this may have played a prominent role in some of the occurrences at Csejthe. An old servant woman named Darvula—locally regarded as a witch—together with a maid named Dorottya Szentes, seem to have played a major part in the terrible acts that were to make Elizabeth Bathory's name a by-word for evil and depravation. To these may be added the name Janos (or Johannes) Ujvary, who is described as Elizabeth's majordomo. There seems little doubt that many of these "practices," whilst reeking of dark witchcraft, also contained sexual elements.

In 1600, Count Francis was killed in battle against the Turks and it was now that the real period of Elizabeth's atrocities began. She was now mistress of Csejthe and a formidable power in the locality. Since the death of her husband, she was also under the protection of her kinsman, King Matthias of

Hungary, which gave her added status. However, the depravity of her life was beginning to tell on her physically—she appeared to be growing old and haggard much more swiftly than she would have liked. It is here that legend takes over.

According to one popular tale, a young maidservant was brushing the Countess's hair when she accidentally pulled it. Angered, Elizabeth struck her across the face, so sharply that she drew blood. Later, looking at the area on which the girl's blood had fallen, the Countess imagined that the skin seemed younger and fresher than the skin around it. She consulted with the witch Darvula and learned that it was imagined in the countryside that the blood of a virgin, accompanied by certain abominable rites, had youth-giving properties. This set Elizabeth off on a bloody and murderous trail. Together with her accomplices, she began to recruit young local girls from the villages round about, ostensibly to work as servants at Csethje, but in reality to be murdered within the castle walls. Each day, the Countess would bathe in their blood in the belief that it returned at least some of her youthful looks. There were accounts of her actually drinking the blood as a restorative medicine.

Most of the girls whom Elizabeth and her cohorts murdered came from the Slovak population of Hungary—girls who were often considered of the "lower order" in society. For a while, the authorities did not overly worry about the disappearance of the girls. The official story was that they had contracted illness and died. For a number of years—roughly between 1601 and 1611—the Countess murdered innumerable servant girls with impunity and without any official enquiry. Many people, particularly in the locality, either knew or suspected what was going on within the castle but none dared voice it. Once a Lutheran pastor spoke out against her, claiming that there was a great and horrific evil going on in Csethje, including cannibal feasts and blood-drinking orgies, and although initially his words fell on largely deaf ears, some people started to pay attention. A legend says that one of the girls who the Countess was about to kill managed to escape and raised the alarm in the surrounding countryside, although this is not extremely likely. What is more likely is that the rumours surrounding the Countess continued to grow until they reached the ears of the Hungarian king, Matthias Corvenus, who had no other option but to investigate. Together with the provincial governor, Count Gryorgi Thurzo, the King invaded Csejthe early in 1611, and within the walls the two men discovered evidence of horrors almost beyond imagining.

In 1611, a series of trials conducted by the King himself were set up and the servants, Darvula and Dorottya Szentes, along with Janos Ujvary, were all found guilty of witchcraft and murder, and were executed. Elizabeth herself was not found guilty of any crime—indeed her noble rank saved her from criminal proceedings—but she was commanded to remain in Csejthe at the pleasure of the Hungarian king. To this end, stonemasons were brought in and Elizabeth was walled up in the apartments where she had committed the majority of her atrocities. Only a small aperture was left through which food could be passed into her. All the windows of that section of the castle were also bricked up, leaving her alone in the darkness. There she was to remain until she died.

On 31st July 1614, Elizabeth (then reputedly age fifty-four) dictated her last will and testament to two priests from the Estergom bishopric. What remained of her family holdings were to be divided between her children, with her son Paul and his descendants receiving the main portion. Shortly afterwards, two of her guards decided that they would try to look at her through the aperture through which she was fed—she was supposedly still the most beautiful woman in all of Hungary. When they looked through, however, they saw only the body of the Countess, lying face down on the floor. The bloody Countess was dead in her lonely, lightless world.

The records concerning Elizabeth Bathory were sealed for one hundred years and her name was forbidden to be mentioned throughout Hungary. The name "Csejthe" became a swear word in the Hungarian tongue and the Slovaks within the borders of the country referred to the Countess obliquely as "the Hungarian whore." The shadow of Elizabeth Bathory fell darkly across her lands for many centuries after her death.

Although there is no real evidence that Bram Stoker used the idea of the "Countess Dracula" in his vampire novel, there is no reason why he should not have known about her. In fact, she may well have served as the template for another Irish writer's vampiric tale. This was *Carmilla* written by Joseph

Sheridan Le Fanu, originally published in 1871 in the magazine *The Dark Blue*. In this tale, a vampiric older girl subtly and evilly influences the impressionable mind of her younger companion. There are, of course, undertones of lesbianism and bloodlust in the story that provide a tangible link with the "Blood Countess." In her own way, Elizabeth Bathory was as influential to the vampire myth as Vlad Tepes.

The dark and sinister figure of the vampire has proved to be one of the most enduring motifs of horror across the centuries. And this most enduring of monsters looks set to continue its haunting of the minds of men and women for many years to come. Look out into the dark! Is there a shape, shrouded in a black cloak lurking there? The vampire might be closer than you think!

Werewolves

'Tis like the howling of Irish wolves against the moon.

—William Shakespeare,
As You Like It

The wolf is perhaps Man's oldest enemy, with a history that goes back into the dim and distant past. Our earliest ancestors both feared and admired the creature with which they often competed for food. Man feared the wolf's ferocity but admired its cunning; they feared its predatory instinct but admired its stealth and swiftness; they feared its strength and tirelessness but admired its hunting prowess. In many respects, the wolf was the ultimate enemy they wished they could emulate. It is hardly surprising that perhaps some of these early hunters wished that they could take on some of its characteristics in order to aid them in their own hunting or to defend themselves from other predators. Almost as an extension of this wish, man and animal began to merge in the early mind as part of an overall longing to be similar to the creatures that so successfully shared their environment. But how could these desired characteristics be acquired? The answer seemed to be by supernatural means.

Ancient Stories of Transformation

Animus

By using powers from another world, humans could perhaps induce in themselves the strength, cunning, and aggressiveness that they themselves seemed to lack, but that creatures (such as the wolf) had in abundance. This type of transformation—from a squeamish human into a predatory animal—may well have been the preserve of Shamanism and ritual amongst our prehistoric ancestors. Perhaps the Shaman, in the course of such a ritual, may have adopted the *animus* of a wild animal, may have worn its skin, and may even have *appeared* animal-like.

Sorcerer of Trois Freres

These Shamanistic traits seem to be illustrated in the famous figure known as the "Sorcerer of Trois Freres," a cave drawing from the Palaeolithic period, discovered in a deep cave system beneath the Pyrenees. The wall painting depicts the "Sorcerer" as a curious creature—a hybrid of both human and animal. He appears to be in some sort of dancing posture, moving sideways and upright on human feet but slouched forward as if ready to drop into a four-legged stance, balancing himself on bear-like forepaws. Large antlers adorn his head, above a bearded, human-like face from which intelligent eyes stare owlishly out. But at his hindquarters, a bushy wolf's tail is clearly visible, swinging back to reveal a lion-like phallus. The cavern in which this peculiar painting has been created can only be approached by crawling almost horizontally through a connecting tunnel of about thirty or forty yards. Cultural historians such as Joseph Campbell have suggested that this awkward positioning of the painting is suggestive of a mystical and religious aspect. It is also suggestive of Palaeolithic suppositions of humans taking on the attributes of either animal hunters or of quarry. It is not hard to imagine the Shaman, pelted in animal skins, dancing in some remote cavern in order to call down the animalistic spirits that would ensure good hunting and plentiful communal larders.

Romulus and Remus

Arguably, it was the wolf that attracted much of early man's attention. Like humans, wolves were communal animals—they lived and hunted in packs, they obeyed strict laws of leadership, and they cared for their young. It was not surprising that, as societies developed, some ancient legends concentrated on linkages between men and wolves rather than on their aggression and adversity. Therefore, stories of children being raised by kindly wolves—children such as Romulus and Remus, the founding fathers of Rome—also became widespread in the ancient world. There seems little doubt that there *were* occurrences of children being raised by female wolves—who are, in many respects, maternal creatures—and indeed similar instances continue in remote parts of the world today. Tales of feral children, raised by wolves, living in the wild and exhibiting wolf-like behaviour must have strengthened the links between men and wolves, deep in the human mind.

Gilgamesh

So the wolf became both a predator and companion within Mankind's psyche. Elements of this confusion underpins old mythological tales emerging from the early civilizations. Interestingly, all of them involve men turning into (or being turned into) animals. From Greek legend comes the story of Actaeon, the youth who secretly glimpsed the huntress-god Artemis when she was bathing. In anger, she changed him into a stag and he was immediately torn to pieces by his own hounds. Perhaps even older is the Akkadian legend taken from the *Epic of Gilgamesh,* dated around the second millennium B.C., of a young shepherd who makes continual sacrifices to the goddess Ishtar. Even so, the capricious goddess transforms him into a wolf, and similar to Actaeon, he his torn to shreds by his own dogs. This tale is probably the oldest known tale of such a transformation, from man to wolf.

Artemis

The Greek goddess, Artemis, is also an interesting figure. To both the Greeks and the Romans (to whom she was known as Diana), she is a predatory hunting goddess, sometimes described as a "mistress of the animals."

But she also had another personification—that was as Phoebe or Selene (Luna in Latin), the goddess of the moon. She was considered to be a secretive and vicious entity, ruling the earth during the day and the sky at night. This creates a link between the predatory hunters (many of whom were nocturnal) and the moon, which provided them with light. Another of Artemis's incarnations was as the goddess Hecate, Mistress of the Underworld, and in this incarnation she is sometimes presented with three feral heads—usually those of wolves. This may have given rise to the legend of Cerebus, the monstrous triple-headed dog (or wolf) that guarded the Gates of Hell. This motif, however, gave the goddess sovereignty over the three main elements of the physical world—the air, the earth, and the Underworld. It is possible that in her original incarnation, Artemis may have been either a bear-goddess or a wolf-goddess, giving her a connection to the Palaeolithic period and the skin-swathed Shamans and animalistic rituals of that time.

Laignech Falead

As the civilizations of the world began to grow and develop, so their legends grew and developed with them—particularly the legend of the werewolf. Many of these legends, however, sought to connect with the warrior/hunter past. For example, there was a persistent belief in Ireland almost up until the 14th century that a tribe of wolf-men known as the Laignech Faelad dwelt somewhere in County Tipperary. Details of them appear in a very ancient manuscript, the *Coir Animann*, but are sceptically dismissed by the English historian William Camden in the 16th century. They were reputedly employed as mercenaries by the Celtic kings of Ireland when they made war on each other, and their ferocity and guile was seemingly unsurpassed. They were said to demand payment for their services in the form of flesh from young infants, which they divided and devoured amongst themselves.

Berserkers

The Vikings, too, had tales of *Berserkers,* ferocious warriors who devoured the flesh of their slain victims and smeared themselves in the blood of the slain. It is from these people that the word "berserk," meaning "uncontrollable," originates.

Certain of these berserkers wore animal skins, to add to their ferocious appearance and to terrify their enemies. An early description of these warriors comes from the Icelandic historian and mythologist Snorri Sturluson (1170–1241). In his *Ynglinga Saga*—a history of Sweden from extremely early time—she described the followers of the god Odin as those "who went without their mail coats and were mad as hounds or wolves, bit their shields, and were as strong as bears or bulls. They slew men but neither fire nor iron had effect upon them. This is called *berserkganger* (going berserk)." The word *berserk* itself comes from two root sources. The first part "*ber*" from the animal itself—the bear—and *serker*—shirt—implying that these men probably wore bearskin shirts to imbue themselves with frenzy. Similar groupings of warriors are to be found in Germanic traditions as well, where they were considered to be extremely fearless and vicious in battle. The idea of fierce warrior cults draped in bear or wolf skins probably strengthened the links between man and beast and added considerably to the idea that a man might transform himself into an animal.

Lykaon

One other aspect of ancient lore needs to be mentioned—the mysterious ritual on the top of Mount Lykaon, a remote spot in the highlands of Acadia in the Peloponnesus peninsula in ancient Greece. Mention of this place and the clandestine rituals that were held there comes from the Greek writer Pausanius. At the time of his writing, the lower slopes of this high country were enclosed by thick forests that were the natural abode of predatory wolves. The mountains, however, were bare and rocky and it was here that sacrifices were made to the sky god—the Lykaian Zeus. Pausanius refuses to divulge the ritual surrounding the sacrifice, but there is a suggestion that it may well have been human. In fact, the "Lykaian Zeus" may very possibly have been a much older, more feral god than the familiar deities of Classical Greece. Furthermore, it was believed that one of the participants in the ritual would be turned into a wolf for a specified period of nine years, provided he or she avoided eating human flesh during that period. If not, the unfortunate would remain in the wolf shape forever. This transformation was associated with a myth that a legendary king of Arcadia, King Lykaon, had sacrificed a baby to Zeus and was turned into the shape of a wolf for this crime. Another connected story tells of an Arcadian boxer named Damarchus who was a champion of the Olympic Games around 400 B.C., after having been changed into a wolf and then back to human form nine years later. Whilst not doubting Lykaon's original vile sacrifice, Pausanius doubts the notion of animal transformation. Whilst the Arcadian Olympic team may have had an unnaturally hirsute boxer in its ranks, the writer does not truly believe that he was once a wolf. However, many other Greeks were not so sceptical—Arcadia was an enclosed and mysterious world. The mountains that surrounded it had protected it from battles. Arcadia had retained its own dialect and superstitions—its inhabitants were believed to have a long pedigree and were immersed, or so the surrounding Greeks thought, in primal magic and witchcraft. To such people, the idea of a man becoming a wolf would not have seemed an impossibility.

Lunatics

As we have seen, from early times there has been a link between such transformations—particularly those into wolves—with the moon. The goddess Artemis, as the "Mistress of Animals" and sometimes portrayed as having a wolf's head, was also the goddess of the moon. In a sense, such a connection is understandable. Most of the more vicious predators were nocturnal, hunting by moonlight. Furthermore, animals such as wolves seemed particularly drawn to the moon, frequently howling at it in chorus. And even as late as the early 19th century, the forces of the moon were often associated with frenzied or irrational behaviour in humans. In fact, the description "lunatic" comes from the French *lune,* meaning the moon. Moonlight, it was held, had a certain influence on the human mind, robbing it of reason and allowing primordial passions and rages to come to the surface. What better connection, then, to ferocious behaviour than a full moon that could transform a seemingly cultured man into a ravening beast? The myth of the beast-man, influenced by the moon, was beginning to take shape.

Christianity and Lycanthropy

Christianity added a further complication. Important to this faith was the consumption of blood and flesh through the Mystery of the Sacrament. The Catholic doctrine of transubstantiation, which was widely accepted by the Church around the ninth century and fully adopted by the Council of Lateran in 1215, spelled out at length that the bread and wine consumed at the Mass actually became the literal blood and body of Christ at the moment of ingestion by the communicant. To emphasise this point, the priest muttered "*hoc est Corpus Christi*" as he placed the Holy Wafer on the tongue of those crouched by the altar rail. The idea of eating flesh and drinking blood was therefore not incompatible with strict church doctrine. What *was* incompatible was the thought of men supernaturally turning into the beasts of the field.

The Church's response to many of the old Pagan beliefs was rather piecemeal. To the dismay of many religious leaders, a number of major Pagan festivals and processions continued long into the Christian period.

Fertility Rituals

Writing in the 6th century, Cesarius of Arles noted with alarm, the fertility processions during the January calends (celebrating the beginning of the year—from which we get the word calendar), in which some of the participants dressed in the skins of stags, sheep, goats, and sometimes hounds and wolves. The purpose of these disguises was to ensure prosperity and plenty throughout the coming year, but Cesarius was appalled and disgusted at the apparent loss of humanity amongst the participants in Arles. Their behaviour was similar to the beasts that they represented; they howled, they roared, and they copulated in the open in a state of euphoria that approached ecstasy. The churchman lost no time criticizing them and urging them to turn to the more spiritual and serene ways. Even so, the sight of normally cultured people indulging in animalistic behaviour must have shaken both him and others.

The Wild Hunt

In some parts of Europe, the Church contended with other animalistic traditions—this was the notion of the Wild Hunt. Reference to this occurs in accounts from all over Europe—France, England, Spain, Germany and Scandinavia.

The Hunt was a nightly cavalcade—sometimes of the dead, sometimes of supernatural creatures—led by some mysterious and mythological figure. In some areas that figure was Odin, in others Berthold, Herne, or Frau Perchta. Female entities that led the Hunt evoked memories of Artemis or Diana and provided a distinct connection between Greek myth and the legends of the Celts and Germanic peoples. These nightly chases were usually carried out when the moon was full and were usually confined either to the deep forests or remote mountains, reinforcing Man's fear of the dark and the deep woods. Such traditions stretched back into the mists of antiquity and there was little that the church could do against them, except to condemn them as the works of the Devil. Those who were swept up in their passing became the property of the Enemy of All Mankind. They lost all vestiges of their holy humanity—Man had been created in the image of God—and became as animals, feral and ferocious.

The Black Death

Such diabolism was expanding with the spread of the forest. In the late 1340s and early 1350s, a terrible disease took the countries of Western Europe in its fetid grasp. This was the Black Death—a deadly mixture of bubonic, pneumonic, and septicaemic plagues—and it is estimated that it killed somewhere between 25 and 45 percent of Europe's population. Whole villages were decimated at a single stroke; towns became tombs for the victims of the disease. Many of the 25 million who died were of the labouring poor and those who worked on the land, so as a result, one of the Death's first victims was the rural economy. Crops rotted in the fields, livestock died for want of care and, more importantly, the forests that had been cut back, began to expand again. And with the growth of cover, the wolf population began to increase. As they competed for food, wolf packs became more and more aggressive, particularly during the cold winter months when game was scarce. From time to time, starving wolf packs would attack human settlements, adding to the general notion that they were vicious killers with a taste for human flesh. In some cases, the Church taught that such attacks were a direct chastisement from God on a sinful world. If men behaved like animals, then they would be judged like animals.

British/Celtic Wolflore

Wehrwulf/Wodfreca

The first usage of the word "werewolf" occurs in English and in a Biblical context. It is referenced in the Ecclesiastical Ordinances of Cnut, a Danish king who ruled a great part of England between 1017 and 1035. The term "wehrwulf" is used in a passage that has little connection with a human transforming into a wolf. The text involved is Matthew 7:15. "Beware of false prophets, which come to you in sheep's clothing, but inwardly they are ravening wolves." The author of the Ordnance—intriguingly named Wulfstan—urges both priests and bishops to be vigilant in protecting their flocks (congregation) "in order that the ravening werewolf should not too widely devastate their spiritual flocks. In his exposition, the holy man uses the rare Saxon term "wodfreca" (*wod* meaning "bold" and *freca* meaning "grasping" or "greedy" alongside the term "wehrwulf." This has been translated by some scholars as the Saxon equivalent of berserker—a wild, vicious man who lived in the woods. By using the adjective *wodfreca,* Wulfstan drew a clear connection between the unchristian person and the wild ravening animal. Later in Saxon England, the term was used to describe any form of outlaw or outcast. These people were associated with viciousness and bloody slaughter; a butcher who gave no mercy. The notion of the wild, wolfish man was becoming deeply entrenched in Christian as well as Pagan mythology.

Irish Wolfhounds

It was in Ireland that a written werewolf legend made its appearance. With its deep woodlands and open boggy stretches, Ireland was especially plagued by wolves. So bad was the problem that in 1652, Oliver Cromwell issued an edict at Kilkenny forbidding the export of Irish Wolfhounds, that had been specially bred to deal with the predator. Wolf hunts were common throughout the country—an old ballad "MacDermott" described one of them in Munster. This may have been a reference to the "Black and Tan" hunt that rode through Ireland in medieval times, killing wolves as it met them. Around the 1650s, there were stories of travellers around Lough Neagh in the North being attacked by packs of wild wolves as they walked towards Belfast. An old travel book entitled, *The Travels of Cosmo* written in 1669, describes Ireland as Wolfland because of the number of the animals that were to be found there. It is not surprising that early tales of werewolves come from Ireland.

Giraldus de Barri

The writer of the story is Giraldus de Barri (called Giraldus Cambrenisis or Gerald of Wales), a churchman and a member of the ruling Norman aristocracy in England. His book, *A History and Topography of Ireland* (sometimes referred to as *Irish Wonders and Miracles*), was written around 1187. For many 12th century Englishmen, travelling to Ireland was similar to travelling to another planet—it was a mysterious and apparently hostile place. Yet Giraldus had journeyed there in the retinue of Prince John (then Lord of Ireland and to whom he acted as Confessor) and during the course of his stay he visited his distant relatives, the Fitzgeralds of Wicklow.

If Giraldus had a failing it was that he was far too credulous and believed everything that he was told. For instance, he believed that washing one's hair in a certain well in Meath would restore greying hair to its natural colour; or that somewhere in the country was a lake in which the fish had teeth of gold. Two other tales, however, interested him greatly—one concerning a man-ox that had been brought to his relative's castle and the other an old werewolf tale that was widely told. The incident, he specifically asserts, occurred three years before Prince John's expedition to Ireland, around 1182 or 1183.

Clan Altan

A certain priest, travelling from Ulster to Meath on church business, had set up camp for the night in a forest on the borders of Meath. He and his only companion, a small boy, were resting beside the fire when they were greatly shocked and alarmed at the appearance of a large wolf in the forest. More shockingly, the animal spoke to them, telling them that they really should have no fear of it. Despite this reassurance, the priest still had a fear of the creature. However, he questioned the animal and heard a strange tale.

The wolf was in fact a man. He and his wife were members of Clan Altan, a group of people who inhabited a village in the Diocese of Ossory and who had run from a certain irascible saint—the Abbot Natalis who had cursed them all. The terms of the curse were this: every seven years two of the Clan (a man and a woman) were exiled from their community and forced to take the shape of wolves for seven years. They might be hunted down or attacked by other wolves, but if they survived that period, they would be allowed to return to their village and resume their human form. Two others, however, would then take their place.

The wolf told the priest that his companion was ill and likely to die and the creature wished the holy man to come and minister to her in her final hours. Although still terrified, the priest followed the werewolf to a hollow tree deep in the forest, where his mate lay. She too behaved in an almost human way although the cleric was still wary. Was he correct in administering the Offices of the Church to such an inhuman creature? He completed most of the Rites of the Church without offering the final communion. Then, using the male werewolf's paw like a hand, he cut through the skin, peeling it back and revealing the face of an elderly woman underneath. The cleric, now convinced of the creatures' humanity, offered her the Blessed Sacrament, which she received with due penance and devotion. The werewolf then escorted him back to his camp and after uttering several prophesies concerning the English who were living in Ireland, disappeared back into the forest promising to meet the priest upon his return from Meath. The holy man, however, was delayed, and never saw him again.

Although Giraldus insisted that the story was uniquely Irish, there are several familiar elements from other cultures. For example, the period of the seven years of Natalis's curse reflects the nine years of werewolfery in the Lykaian myth from ancient Greece. Two similar stories turn up in other sources—one from an Irish/ Scandinavian tradition where the 13th century *Kongs Skuggsjo (Speculum Regale)* states that St. Patrick turned members of a certain Clan who opposed his teachings, into wolves, their condition lasting for seven years. The second is a fragmentary tale from the Harz Mountain region in present-day Germany, in which a number of "Godless people" are turned into wolves for seven years by an irate St. Willibrod because they worshipped Pagan deities in the form of standing stones.

One current theme runs through Giraldus's account and the other stories as well as the Lykaian legend—that the transformation of a person into a wolf is the result of a curse, placed upon the unfortunates either by primal gods or by Christian holy men. It is doubtful that many early clerics used the notion of the "beast lurking within" to symbolize the more ferocious aspects of human nature as opposed to Christian charity and culture.

Marie de France

Another contemporary besides Giraldus was Marie de France, a Norman writer who produced a series of *lais* (epic poems) concerning various aspects of early medieval French life. Much of her work contains a stern moral theme and, although little is known about her, it is quite possible that Marie herself may have been a nun who mixed with the troubadours at the Gascon court.

The Lai of Bisclavret

One of these poems, *The Lai of Bisclavret*, is centred around a garwaf, that Marie describes as a werewolf-like creature known to the Normans. The name "Bisclaveret" itself is something of a linguistic puzzle. Marie insists that it is Breton and indeed it seems to derive from two Breton words *bisc* meaning "short" and *laveret* "wearing breeches." This may refer to other stories of fierce little men, dwelling in the woods, who wore breeches of animal skins and attacked travellers as they passed through the French forests. Such a motif is an adaptation of the Wild Men of the Woods that appears in the myths of many lands, including England. Other linguists have intriguingly linked the name to the ancient Breton *bleiz lavaret* (speaking wolf) or *bleiz laveret* (thinking wolf).

Garwaf

The protagonist of *The Lai of Bisclavret* is a Breton knight, considered to be extremely brave, and also married to a beautiful lady. He is, however, surrounded by a mystery. For three whole days each week, he disappears without explanation from his castle, apparently departing into the deep woodlands. These continued disappearances both alarmed and upset his wife who begged

him to tell her where he went. Seeing her obvious distress, he finally relented and explained to her that he was a garwaf and must go into the forest for three days each week in order to take the shape of a wolf. As soon as he laid aside his clothes, the transformation occurred. His disclosure only further alarmed his wife who was determined to be rid of him. In order to do this, she planned to steal his clothes (without which he could not return to human form but must remain a wolf forever) and got the nobleman to divulge where he left them—in a hollow stone, concealed by a bush near an ancient chapel deep in the forest. The lady then contacted a former paramour who became her lover and persuaded him to steal the clothes, thus condemning the knight to the permanent wolf-form.

A year passed and Bisclavret had not returned from the forest. The woodlands were searched but nothing was found. It was assumed that he was dead. His former wife married her lover and gradually his name began to fade from memory. The king, however, was hunting through the forest when his huntsmen found a wolf and his hounds seized upon it. The king, however, showed mercy and spareed the creature, taking it back to the palace as a pet. There it became a favourite of the court, earning many friends by its good nature and gentleness. One day, the monarch gave a great feast, and amongst those invited was the new husband of Bisclavret's former wife. As soon as it saw the nobleman, the wolf's mood suddenly changed. Far from being kind and gentle, it turned ferociously on the visitor, leaping upon him and sinking its fangs into him to the astonishment of everyone present. The king himself managed to drive the animal back with a stick, allowing the treacherous knight to escape further injury. Because the creature was so amiable and the attack so unexpected, many began to suspect that there was more to the matter and the king decreed that the incident was to be fully investigated.

First, however, there was to be a hunt, and once more they passed through the woods near Bisclavret's former castle. As they camped there, many of the local nobility came to pay their respects to the monarch, including Bisclavret's former wife. As she entered the king's presence, the placid wolf at his side changed once more and sprang forward to attack her, biting off her nose in its ferocity (a common torture in the medieval world). The courtiers managed to beat the creature off. Then one of the king's counsellors, noted for his wisdom, pointed out that the wolf had never attacked anyone save that woman, and her second husband. He also reminded the monarch that this was the wife of a brave knight who had disappeared in mysterious circumstances. The king enforced his decree and investigated further.

Under torture, the hapless pair revealed what happened. The lady admitted that she had been responsible for the theft of her first husband's clothes from the hollow stone near the abandoned abbey. The king ordered the return of the garments and when they were brought, he placed them in front of the wolf, which at first shied away from them. The wise counsellor told the king that, because it was a shameful thing, the transformation from wolf back to man must be done in secret with no-one watching. So the king took the wolf back to the royal bedroom and left it alone with the clothes. Shortly afterwards the brave and handsome knight emerged from the room and the king rushed forward and celebrated his return to humanity with great joy. Bisclavert was confirmed in his lands and his treacherous former wife and her husband were banished from the kingdom. They went to live in a distant land where they raised many noseless children.

Although Marie de France treated Bisclavret sympathetically, she was at pains to point out that the garwaf was a terrifying creature. She described it as a "beste salvage." Bisclavret revealed that he hunted in the woods by night, similar to a beast of prey, killing and devouring, doing great harm, and that he had a desire to attack and kill humans. She also told of the king's terror when, during the hunt that captured Bisclavret, he was confronted by the cornered wolf. She described the ferocity of the creature as it attacked its former wife, ripping away her nose.

Gorlagon

This lai dates from the 12th century, but it is probably based on an older Breton folktale. Indeed, several ancient Celtic stories contain roughly the same themes concerning the werewolf, one of which is the Welsh Arthurian legend of Gorlagon. This story has many variations, but in a generally-accepted Latin version, Arthus is challenged by his queen to discover the ways of womankind.

In order to do this, he sets out for the castle of neighbouring King Gargol. Although this king cannot help him, he directs him to the fortress of another local monarch, King Torleil. This king cannot help him any more than the first but directs him even further, to the castle of King Gorlagon. This king agrees to tell him a story that will aid him in his quest, although he will only be slightly wiser at the end of it.

His tale concerns a king with a garden or courtyard in which grew a magic sapling. If this sapling were to be cut and the person who cut it tapped himself upon the head with it whilst reciting a certain spell, he would be transformed into the shape of a wolf. His treacherous wife, who had availed herself of a handsome young lover, managed to discover the secret of this sapling, had it cut, and used it to transform her husband. The werewolf-king fled into the forest where he met with a she-wolf and raised a family of wolf cubs whilst his wife married her paramour. When his cubs were almost fully grown, the werewolf-king entered the town and attacked two princes who were the sons of his former wife and her lover. However, the creatures were pursued back into the forest by the lady's cousins, and the cubs were killed, although the werewolf-king himself escaped.

Maddened by the slaughter of his offspring, the werewolf-king began to attack the settlements of local shepherds, decimating their flocks. He was hunted and chased out to another land where he was no more welcome. Travelling to a third country, he found a refuge for himself in a deep wood where he thought he might be safe. However, one night he overheard two locals saying that the king was coming that way to hunt the werewolf-king. It is here that the legend begins to closely follow the tale of Bisclavret, in that the wolf managed to stop the king en route to the hunt and convince the monarch not to kill him. He further persuaded the king and his retinue that he was a friendly wolf, and he became much loved by them—almost a pet. Nevertheless, the king's wife does not approve of the animal, and whilst her husband was away, she mistreated it. At the same time, she was conducting an affair with one of the servants, thus cuckolding the king himself. One night whilst they were engaged in their lovemaking, the wolf attacked them, inflicting deep wounds upon the servant. In order to retaliate, the queen locked her own son in the deepest dungeon and swore that the wolf had eaten him and had even attacked the servant who had tried to defend him. The wolf, however, managed to get the king to follow him to the deep dungeon where the prince was discovered unharmed and the queen's treachery was exposed. When the boy revealed what had happened, the servant, who was also involved in the plot, was hanged whilst the queen was pulled apart after being tied between wild horses, and her remains burnt.

It was now becoming apparent that the wolf was more than simply a dumb animal, and that it possessed an almost human intelligence. The king came to the conclusion that it might be a man in a bewitched state and he asked the creature to lead him to its own country. The wolf led him to his native land where it was discovered that the evil queen and her new husband had become fearful despots. The king invaded with a mighty army and forced the queen and her husband to surrender. Threatened with torture, the queen confessed what she had done to her former husband and was made to fetch the magic sapling and turn the wolf back into her husband.

Impressed by the tale, Arthur was determined to know if it was true. "Who is the mad-looking woman who sits opposite you?" he asked Garlagon, "Who weeps over a bloody head set on a platter before her and which she kisses whenever you kiss your wife?" "That," explained the king, "is the treacherous queen. For I was the werewolf in the tale that I've just recounted. The two foreign countries in the story are those ruled over by my two brothers Gargol and Torleil. My former wife was not killed but is condemned to carry the severed head of the lover with whom she betrayed me everywhere she goes. I remarried and decreed that every time I kissed my new wife, she should kiss the dead lips of the man who seized my throne. In this way, the country would be reminded both of her great wickedness and of my absolute rule."

This tale contains a number of interesting elements. The names of the three kings are significant. Each one of them is a name for a werewolf. Gorlagon is a variant of the Old Welsh word *Garlion,* signifying a creature that is half man, half wolf, similar to the Norman *garwaf.* It is probable that in the original tale (for the story is much older than the Arthurian legend) the three kings were one man. And the original tale, some scholars have suggested, may be the one (or a similar one) to that which Marie de France used for her Bisclavret lai.

Eastern Creatures

During the medieval period, travel to places on the very edge of, or beyond Europe, began to increase with those who brought back fantastic tales of places and creatures that they had found. They also encountered Crusaders, returning from what is today the Middle East, and recounted stories of fabulous and exotic realms inhabited by strange breeds of people who often defied conventional physiology. Those who journeyed further East returned with descriptions of races that almost defied imagination. There were tales of giants and pygmies; of Troglodytes—squat little men who dwelt in caverns far beneath the deserts of Ethiopia; of the Anthropophagi and Laestrygonians—wild and ferocious men who dwelt on remote islands in the Aegean and who ate human flesh (descriptions of these had existed since Greek times); of Amazons—a fierce tribe of women who lived around the headwaters of a mighty river away to the West; of Sciopods—one-legged creatures who lay around protecting themselves from the sun's rays by shading their bodies with a gigantic single foot; of the Astomi, who did not eat as they had no mouths, but lived on the smell of rotting apples; of the Cylcops—one eyed giants who killed and devoured all those who came near; and of the Panotii, men with exceptionally long ears in which they could wrap themselves as they slept. The whole bizarre panoply sounded similar to science fiction. Amongst these monstrous races, perhaps the best known, were the Cynocephali—the Dog Heads—creatures with the bodies of men but with the heads of dogs. Accounts of them had existed since the days of the writer Pliny, who located them somewhere in India. They had no understandable speech but barked like hounds in order to communicate with each other. They were extremely primitive, little more than prehistoric hunters, dressed in animal skins and dwelling in caves. Their crude weapons consisted of bows, spears, and javelins, but they were regarded as ferocious fighters. Many legends of their viciousness had been circulating for a long time, probably since the days of Alexander the Great and certainly well before the Middle Ages. As time went on, however, many of their attributes became exaggerated—their feral nature, their guile and cunning, their enormous and rending teeth. Their cries, echoing through the mountains and canyons where they lived may have sounded similar to "bar-bar," and this may have been one of the sources from which the Greeks devised the word "barbarian" describing what they considered to be the uncouth and uncultured peoples whom they encountered. The notion of a Dog-Headed race of men may have evolved from baboons with their hairy bodies and long dog-like muzzles, glimpsed by those travelling East—creatures that displayed at least some characteristics but also showed immense ferocity. The idea of bestial races or of men somehow transforming themselves into wild animals—particularly the wolf—was drawing more closely together.

The Church's Position on Evil

How did the church react to such alleged discoveries? It has often been said that if life were to be found on other planets, then the modern church would have to re-evaluate its perspectives, and so it was with its medieval counterpart. The Dog-Heads in particular (a widespread and popular tale), caused ancient clerics some concern. Although the 11th century "Theodore" Psalter (now held in the British Library) contains an illustration of Christ preaching to a group of dog-headed figures, this was uncommon in the medieval world.

Dogs

For Christian thinkers, the dog or wolf represented the feral, uncontrollable element in Man as opposed to the cultured, compassionate Christian that their teachings sought to encourage. Of special significance to them was a verse of Scripture, taken from the Psalms and said to depict the Passion of Christ. Psalm 22 v. 16 states, "For dogs have encompassed me; the assembly of the wicked have enclosed me." Now this passage lends itself to a number of interpretations, but for some of the early Fathers, these words were to be taken literally, and as an oblique reference to the Dog-Heads of foreign shores. They were evil and were opposed to God and his servants, almost beyond the Word of God. Even though there were suggestions that some of the Dog-Heads might have been Christianised through the interventions of the Apostles (there was even a suggestion that St. Christopher had originally been a Pagan Dog-Head named Reprobus before becoming converted), this was not generally accepted. The Dog-Heads were too far off base to understand the sacred precepts of the Christian message. But although they were considered to be well "beyond the Pale" of the Christianised world, the popularity of the Dog-Head legends showed no signs of diminishing. Indeed, in 1430, a map of the world was drawn up by medieval cartographers that showed a people known as the Beni Chelib, living in Ethiopia under a Saracen king called Ebinichebel, all of whom were dog-headed. This seems to be a deliberate attempt to equate the vicious and war-like Dog-Heads with the developing religion of Islam, considered to be Christianity's main competitor in the Eastern lands. The notion of the sinful, hostile werewolf, associated with dark, foreign, customs and practices was now gaining ground.

At the end of the 15th century, Europe stumbled uncertainly towards the first glimmerings of the Enlightenment. In such a period, the Church tried desperately to exercise its former power over the hearts and minds of its people whilst they in turn and, in the face of mounting social change, tried to cling to the certainties that had sustained them through the last thousand years. This was the period of the great European witch hunts, as old superstitions made one final assault on the popular mind. It was believed that the end of the world was approaching and the Devil was loose, working through his agents to ensure the downfall of the Godly. The first stirrings of Protestantism vied with Catholicism for the hearts and minds of men and women before it fractured and splintered into various sects, only adding to the spiritual confusion of the time. In an attempt to promote Catholic unity, the Church turned on the enemy in its midst—witches and evil-workers. Pope Innocent VIII (1484–1492), seeking to divert attention from the apathy and worldliness of the Papacy, turned his attention to the Mainz and Treves regions of Germany where ancient practices were still said to flourish. It was Pope Innocent who commissioned the churchmen Heinrich Kramer and Jacobus Sprenger to draw up what was to become the infamous witchcraft manual of the Holy Inquisition—the *Malleus Maleificarum* (the Hammer of the Witch). Kramer, who had been Chief Inquisitor in the Tyrol, was well versed in ideas about witchcraft and used them to embellish the sinister volume. The book was used as a means of detecting, judging and despatching witches and was widely used by witch-finders everywhere. Even today, long after the witch persecutions have ceased, it is still a best-seller. In conjunction with *Malleus,* Innocent issued a Papal Bull against witchcraft and in doing so started a hysteria which would rumble on for almost two hundred years.

Witches/Shapeshifters

Throughout the latter half of the 16th century and most of the 17th, witches were everywhere. They had magical powers—one of which was to transform themselves into other forms, usually those of animals. Back in the 12th century, Giraldus deBarri had confidently asserted that it was within the power of all Irish woman to change themselves into hares and stoats in order to drink milk from the udders of cows (a belief that was still held in many Irish rural areas at the beginning of the 20th century), and soon animal transformations had become part and parcel of the witch belief. Witches, it was widely believed, went about the countryside in animal disguises, seeking to do harm against their neighbours. Potions and unguents were used in order to transform them into the guise of stoats, weasels, cats, ravens, and other creatures. Witches galloped around the countryside in the guise of horses, trampling crops and breaking down fences or gnawing through grain sacks in the guise of mice. The forms that they could take were endless, and it was not very long before the wolf was added to this list.

Peter Stubb

Perhaps one of the most celebrated werewolf cases of the late 16th century was that of Peter Stubb (alternately spelt Stubbe, Stumpf, or Stube), the werewolf of Cologne, Germany, whose trial took place in 1589. The widespread knowledge of the case can be attributed to the pamphlets, detailing many of his horrendous crimes, that circulated throughout Europe, and were translated into a number of languages. A number of learned writers of the time, such as Martin Del Rio, subsequently made comments on the case, adding to its notoriety.

Witchcraft was involved in the transformation—the dark powers centering around a magic belt with which, by buckling it around his waist, Stubb could transform himself into a ravening wolf. He was described in *A True Discourse Declaring the Damnable Life and Death of One Stubbe Peter,"* an anonymous pamphlet published in 1590, as "strong and mighty, with eyes great and large, that in the night sparkled like brands of fire; a mouth great and wide, with the most sharp and cruel teeth; a huge body and mighty paws. And no sooner would he put off the same girdle, but presently he should appear in his former shape, according to the proportion of a man as if he had never been changed." Whilst in his wolf shape, Stubb was incredibly ferocious, viciously attacking a number of people who crossed his path and then escaping into the surrounding countryside, easily outdistancing the hounds that were sent after him. It was alleged that his first choice of prey, whilst in the wolf shape, was human but if he could not find any, he would attack the sheep and cattle of his neighbours. He had, it was stated, murdered no less than thirteen young children and savaged at least two pregnant women, ripping the unborn babies from their wombs in order to devour them. The horror of his attacks could not be overemphasized. In addition to these bestial crimes, he was accused of incest with both his sister and daughter, and of actually murdering his own son whilst in human form and of eating the boy's brains in order to staunch "his greedy appetite."

Whilst in his wolf-form, Stubb was cornered in some fields near the town of Bedbur by a pack of hounds that had been sent against him. In order to elude them, he removed the magic belt and appeared simply as an ordinary traveller, walking towards the town and leaning on his staff. But those who were following the hounds claimed that they had never taken their eyes from the wolf and had seen the miraculous transformation. Stubb was arrested and, under strict torture, gave a full account of his abominable life. The magic belt, however, was not found and (under torture) Stubb admitted to having abandoned it "in a certain valley," just before he had been captured. The valley was searched but nothing was discovered and it was assumed that the Devil (whose servant Stubb was supposed to be) had reclaimed it.

Stubb's case had now become so celebrated that he could not escape the full rigor of the law. Every horrid detail of the affair had shocked the populace of Germany and beyond. He was sentenced to be strapped to a wheel and large sections of his flesh were ripped from the bone using red-hot pliers. His arms and legs were then smashed with a wooden axe, after which he was finally decapitated and his corpse was burnt on the same pyre as those of his daughter and mistress, who had also been executed for their crimes. After the execution, a memorial was set up in Bedbur consisting of a long pole pushed through the broken execution wheel and with the likeness of a wolf, framed in wood near its summit. On the very top, however, Stubb's head was impaled as a warning to all who might be tempted to follow him and take on the guise of a wolf. Around this grisly reminder were hung sixteen pieces of wood, representing the sixteen victims whom Stubb was alleged to have murdered as a werewolf.

Although this German werewolf was perhaps the best known, it was in France that many of the trials for lycanthropy occurred. Indeed, contemporary with and even before Stubb was brought to trial in Bedbur, there were several notable French trials, including that of the famous Gilles Garnier.

Gilles Garner

Gilles Garnier, the "hermit of St. Bonnot," ranks as one of the earliest and most famous French werewolves. During the early 1570s, he was dwelling in great poverty, along with his wife in the rough and wooded countryside of Armanges, near the town of Dole. He was not a native of the area, having initially come from Lyon, and he was considered odd and rather belligerent in his ways. About the time he came to live at Armanges, a large wolf began to prey on the flocks of local shepherds, spreading fear and alarm. Additionally, several children were carried off to be devoured in the forest—witnesses claimed that a werewolf was responsible. As time passed, such attacks became more and more frequent, to the alarm of many of the parents in the area. Naturally, suspicion fell upon the surly anti-social hermit dwelling in the woods, but there was not enough concrete evidence to confront him. However, the local parlement (governing body) did take some action. It issued a proclamation that the populace should assemble with pikes, arquebuses, sticks, and halberds to hunt, seize, and kill the werewolf. The vigilante assembly soon hunted down its prey in November 1573. It was reported that a little girl was rescued from the jaws of a wolf in La Poupee meadow, between Authune and Chastenoy. She had been badly mauled by the creature and her shocked rescuers thought that they recognized human features on the wolf as they drove it off. For many, the animal bore an uncanny resemblance to the misanthropic hermit of St. Bonnot. The parlement at Dole ordered that he be arrested and questioned. Garnier's confession (perhaps elicited under torture) gave a graphic and horrifying account of his activities as a werewolf. Much of the gruesome details concerned the murder and devouring of two children in particular—two boys, ages ten and twelve years of age, one of whom he had killed in the locality of Dole and the other (in August 1570) in a pear-orchard near the village of Perrouze. In this latter case, he had been driven off (still in his wolf form) by the approach of some labourers. In that same October, he had also killed a ten-year-old girl in a wood known as La Serre about a mile or so from Dole. He claimed that he found her flesh "especially sweet" and took some of it home for his wife to eat.

Unlike Stubb, however, Garnier was slightly vague about how he actually transformed himself into an animal. There was no magic belt given to him by the Devil. Rather he seems to have become a wolf through "sorcery" and in most of his evidence, he speaks of "strangling" his victims whilst in his werewolf-guise. Could it be possible that the weak-minded and confused Garnier simply imagined that he became a wolf in order to commit several murders? It is also possible that cannibalism may have been common in some of the more remote parts of Europe than is perhaps commonly supposed, and that the wretched Garnier and his wife might have given in to such abnormal urges in order to survive. Such mental niceties, however, were not taken into account by the officials in Dole, who eventually found the hermit guilty of the most ghastly of werewolf crimes. Ironically, he was not offered the mercy of strangulation before his body was completely burned—an unusually harsh punishment that was said to reflect the awfulness of his offences. It probably also reflected a wide-spread fear of a beast lurking within the midst of a civilized community.

Michael Verdung

Gilles Garnier was not the first werewolf to terrify the French people. Around 1520, three of the creatures had been discovered in the village of

Poligny in the Jura region close to the Swiss Alps. This was a remote and mountainous area and well-suited to tales of the loup-garou, a wolf-like creature that was, in actuality, an evil spirit going about in the form of a massive hound. The first of these wolf-men to be discovered was Michel Verdung (also known as Michael Udon) who had allegedly been wounded whilst in his wolf form by a traveller whom he had attacked. Following the trail of blood, some local men found their way to Verdung's hut, where they found a woman with whom he lived, bathing his fresh wounds. The matter was put in front of the Inquisitor-General at Besancon who commenced a rigorous investigation. Under torture, Verdung implicated another man whom he knew—one Pierre Bourgot, known locally as Big Peter. This man was known for his surly attitude, irascible temper, and strange ways, and it came as no surprise that he should be involved in something so dark and sinister as werewolfery. Under torture himself, Peter confessed to how he had first become a werewolf. Whilst hunting for some sheep that had been scattered by a storm, he was approached by three dark horsemen to whom he told his troubles. One of them promised Bourgot help and contentment if he would agree to serve these three masters and do whatever they asked. Bourgot promptly accepted and found his lost sheep soon afterward. A few days later, the three horsemen arrived at his house to seal the bargain they had made and the one who had spoken revealed himself to be an instrument of the Devil. He made Big Peter deny his Christian birthright and to take an oath to serve Satan by kissing his left hand. Later, Bourgot began to doubt the wisdom of his agreement and as he was considering going to the priest to confess what he had done, Michel Verdung appeared at his door. Verdung informed him that he had been sent by the Devil and promised him gold and great wealth if he would renew his oath of allegiance to the Evil One. He then made Peter disrobe and applied an ointment to him that changed him into the form of a wolf. In this guise, Verdung told him, he could attend the Devil's Sabbat. Verdung was able to restore him to human form by means of another ointment that he (Verdung) kept. When in the wolf form, Peter experienced awful lusts and desires, including the desire to eat human flesh. He had, for example, eaten the flesh of a four-year-old child and had found it sweet and delicious. He had also broken the neck of a nine-year-old girl and had devoured her as well. Not only this, but Verdung had assumed a wolf-shape as well. Not only had he assisted him in his foul crimes, but together they had also copulated with wild female wolves. Faced with such a catalogue of horrors, there could be no other option save execution and burning. The imprint of the werewolf had, however, been set in the popular mind.

Jacques Roulet

Stories of Gilles Garnier and the lycanthropes of Poligny began to circulate around Europe, adding fuel to the fire of the werewolf panic. However, he was not the only French werewolf to arouse both fear and hatred. In the summer of 1598, a soldier walking through the fields near Angers, in the French northwest, together with some local peasants, came across a wild beggar, cowering half-naked in the bushes. Upon pulling him out, they found blood smeared across his hands and face, and pieces of what looked similar to human flesh embedded under his long and filthy finger nails. On searching further, they also found, the body of a murdered fifteen-year-old boy.

The beggar's name was Jacques Roulet and he was both mentally retarded and an epileptic. This did not prevent him from being taken back to Angers to be interrogated. Although there is no record as to whether the interrogation was actually carried out, it probably involved torture and resulted in a full confession of werewolfery to the court of Judge Pierre Herault. Roulet admitted that he had a magic ointment that, when rubbed into his skin, changed him into the form of a wolf. The judge asked him if that meant he was *dressed* as a wolf, but Roulet denied this. He said that he was an actual animal and that his hands had become rending paws. He could not, however describe his head but thought that whilst his body was that of a wolf, his head remained human. He also confessed to have taken part in the Devil's Sabbat at which others of his kind had participated.

There is no real record of what actually befell Jacques Roulet, following his confession, but it is likely that he was burned—not as a werewolf—but as a witch and a heretic. The court records, containing the details of his abominable crimes, were ordered to be burnt and so only fragments of them survive.

However, the year 1598 seems to have been a particularly troublesome year in France with regard to werewolves, for the weak-minded, flesh-eating beggar was not the only such case in the country. Indeed, this year was to produce a veritable epidemic of werewolf accusations. One of the most notable occurred in Chalons, where a tailor, living within the town boundary, was found to have committed a number of cannibalistic crimes. He attacked children who ventured into or near his place of work. In nearby woods and fields just outside the town, he ate their flesh, which he found particularly succulent. He stored their bones among some chests and barrels at the back of his shop. When these were accidentally discovered, the tailor's game was up. Like Jacques Roulet, the lycanthrope tailor of Chalons was probably sentenced to death and once more the directives of the court were destroyed.

Devil's Sabbat

The notion of the Sabbat tied werewolfery inextricably to witchcraft and to the enemies of the Church. Sabbats were believed to be great gatherings, attended by the vilest of witches and presided over by the Devil himself. Their primary purpose was to do evil, but there was also an element of revelry to them in which the participants often adopted the characteristics of animals—baying, howling, and copulating at random. The whole idea of such gatherings was to strip away all that was good and ordered by God, and to give in to one's primal desires in order to affect great harm on Christian communities. The ravening beast was now seen as an agent of the Evil One and an enemy of all Mankind, to be hunted down and destroyed.

Pierre Gandillion

In the area of Franche-Comte, near the Swiss Alps, not far from Poligny where Michel Verdung and his companion had terrified the populace, a whole family of werewolves had been discovered as well. The region was very remote and was thickly forested with the mountains rising majestically behind it. Two children were picking fruit near the village of St. Claude in Burgundy in the spring of 1598 when one of them, sixteen-year-old Benoit Bidel, momentarily left his younger sister at the foot of a great tree whilst he climbed into its branches. Whilst he was still climbing disaster struck. A "tailless wolf" suddenly sprang from the surrounding forest and attacked the defenseless girl. Benoit, who was armed with a knife that he'd been using for cutting down fruit, jumped to the ground and prepared to defend his sister. The wolf, however, which seemed to have a human face and fur-covered hands, struck the knife away and delivered the boy a fatal blow on the neck. The girl screamed and her cries alerted some peasants who were working in the fields nearby. They found Benoit close to death, but he was able to pass on crucial information concerning the "wolf" before he did so. The workmen now began to search the area and in some woodlands close by, they found a girl, Perrenette Gandillion, wandering among the trees. There were traces of blood on her dress and, both outraged and frightened, the mob tore her to pieces.

The Gandillions lived close by, and now the people of St. Claude turned their attentions upon the family. They had been under suspicion for some time as being witches and Devil-worshipers, and this incident gave the local authorities the excuse they needed to investigate further. Other members were now arrested and brought to trial. Perrenette's sister, Antoinette, was accused of being a werewolf and of being able to create hailstorms that had flattened the crops of her neighbours. She was also accused of having attended a witch's Sabbat where she copulated with the Devil, who had come to her in the guise of a goat. Her brother, Pierre Gandillion, was similarly accused. Subject to swoons and epilepsy, he was said to lie at home in a cataleptic state whilst his spirit roamed through the woods in the guise of a werewolf, doing harm. He was also accused of attending a Sabbat, convened by the Devil and comprised entirely of werewolves. Under torture, he revealed how Satan had given both him and others clothes of wolf's skin that covered their human shape, and had made them run throughout the country on all fours, attacking both humans and animals to satisfy their unholy lusts. Pierre's son, Georges, also confessed to having a salve or ointment that could turn him into a wolf and, together with Perrenette and Antoinette, killing two goats belonging to a neighbour.

Henri Boguet

In the St. Claude cases, a new and slightly sinister figure emerged—Henri Boguet. A Grand Justice for the Franche-Comte region, Boguet was a University-educated lawyer who had made a special study of witchcraft cases. His book *Discours des sorciers* was an exhaustive (if biased) work that would become the staple text for French witch hunters and magistrates for years after his death in 1619. His record of finding witches in the Franche-Comte and Jura Mountain regions was exemplary. At one stage he boasted that he was responsible for over 600 executions for witchcraft between the years 1598 and 1616. He was especially adept at fining instances of witchcraft amongst the Jews of his area. At the time of the St. Claude cases, his witchcraft book was already in print, and he was widely regarded as France's leading demonologist, but as he investigated the evidence, Boguet decided to release a second edition of the work that would include a lengthy chapter on lycanthropy. He used the Gandillion family as an example of how the Devil could corrupt God's people and turn them into beasts. He said that he had observed members of the family walking on all fours around their cells, just as they had done in the fields, and he observed that Pierre Gandillion was so disfigured that he actually resembled a beast. All of them had shown an appetite for human flesh.

Sawney Bean

Although it is questionable as to whether the Gandillions were indeed werewolves, it may be possible that they were actually cannibals. Indeed, some scholars have argued parallels between those who have been convicted of werewolfery and cases such as that of Sawney Bean and his family in 14th century Scotland. During the reign of the Scottish king James I (1406–1437), Alexander Bean (also known as Sandy or Sawney Bean), a surly and uneducated man, the son of a hedger and ditcher, absconded from his East Lothian home with a woman as brutish and unlettered as himself. Bean is described as insolent and overbearing, and his new partner displayed similar characteristics. They went to live in a deep cave at Bennane Head near Ballintrae, which was then part of Galloway (today it is part of Ayrshire). They would live there for more than 25 years, making little contact with the local villages, so that few knew of their existence. During that time, they sustained themselves and their family by capturing and killing travellers on a nearby moor, taking their bodies back to the cave, and cooking and eating them. It is said that when discovered, the cave resembled "a butcher's kitchen." Sawney and his partner raised a brood of children around them—some of whom were very badly deformed—all of whom had a taste for human flesh. As travellers in the area began to disappear with increasing frequency, the authorities in Ballantrae became alarmed. Word reached the ears of King James and he decided that the matter should be investigated. By now bits and pieces of human remains had washed up along the coast as the Bean's discarded some of their food. To the horror of some of those who found them, they appeared to have been gnawed by human teeth. The King himself now took personal charge of the investigation and ordered a hunt with hounds all along the coastline near Ballintrae. He had heard vague stories of a hermit and his wife who lived somewhere around the area. The hounds and men soon found the concealed entrance to Sawney Bean's cave and recoiled from the horrors that it held. It is said that the King himself was violently sick at the stores of human remains, some of them half-eaten, that were laid out deep in the cavern. Here, too, were piles of clothes, wallets, money, and valuables that the cannibals had stored away without actually realizing the value of what they held. Bean and his family were so used to their cannibalistic lifestyle that they could not understand that they had committed any crime. But in the eyes of the law, they had committed the most abominable of crimes and they were all arrested and taken back to the Tollbooth in Edinburgh. From there, they were taken to Leith where they were formally tried and sentenced to death. So gruesome was the effect of their crimes on the Scottish people that the method of their execution in many ways reflected the horror of their lives. The men were sentenced to have all their limbs amputated and to be allowed to bleed to death whilst the women were to be killed as slowly as possible. Some of Sawney Bean's children died wondering what they had done wrong. The name of Sawney Bean, however, passed into folklore as "the Maneater of Midlothian" and actually spawned a number of stories and plays as well as a Shockfest underground film in the style of "Cannibal Holocaust."

Although he was not classed as a werewolf—rather as a cannibal and a mass murderer—Sawney Bean's case may reflect some of the aspects of the French lycanthropy trials. Lonely men and women such as Gilles Garnier, Sawney Bean, and the Gandillion family, dwelling in the utmost poverty in remote rural areas, may have preyed upon their vulnerable neighbours in order to sustain themselves without having to work. They may have looked on those around them as a ready source of food during desperate times, and therefore cannibalism may well have been much more widespread than we commonly suppose. However, it was men like Henri Boguet who made the connections between the rapacious beast and the agents of evil, and it was they who stoked up the notion of werewolves.

Nicholas Remy

Having burnt the Gandillions, Boguet turned his attention to seeking out other werewolves in the Jura region. It is unclear whether he found any, but his efforts against witches seems to have increased. Numbers of those people brought before the courts for practicing witchcraft grew dramatically. However, although Boguet insisted that werewolves were lurking everywhere in society (he continually cited the instances of Poligny and of the tailor of Chalons), the number of actual citations of werewolfery are extremely scant. Indeed, although instances of witchcraft trials went up, their total number was remarkably less than the likes of Boguet were to later claim. Boguet's counterpart in Lorraine, the judge Nicholas Remy, himself a writer of a major book on witchcraft entitled *Demonoltary*, was to grandly claim that he had tried and executed no less than 900 persons for sorcery, including werewolfery. The actual records however, suggest that the number was far, far lower. And yet, the notion of witches and werewolves were potent figures that lurked deep in the French mind. The werewolf was still seen as the agent of the Devil.

France, Religion, and Terror

Part of the reason for much of the terror during early times may lie in the changing of the times that plagued France throughout the mid-to-late 16th century. The difficulties, (social, religious, and economic), were, of course, reflected all over Europe. But in France they seemed to take on a special resonance. The nub of these problems seemed to be the steady emergence of a Protestant tradition, that promised freedom and independence from a perceived Catholic tyranny. This was not only a purely doctrinal standpoint but, as with most religious teachings, it had political ramifications.

Huguenots

The austere Protestant Huguenots looked upon the French monarchy with something akin to disdain and sought to administer their own affairs in a "Godly way"—that is, separate from the laws laid down by the king. Many of the Huguenot towns operated almost as independent republics, and Huguenot leaders and ministers encouraged the nonpayment of ecclesiastical tithes—usually 10 percent of overall income—to the Church authorities. In doing so, they placed themselves on a collision course with the state. Violent protests against tithes flared in areas such as Languedoc and Aquitaine, placing strains on the levying of secular taxation and disturbing the government immensely. Such a situation could not be allowed to continue. As the civil disobedience and riots continued all through the 1560s, the authorities realized they had to take action.

St. Bartholomew's Day Massacre

On 24th August 1572, large numbers of French Protestants streamed into Paris to witness the marriage of Henry of Navarre to Margaret of Valois. The occasion, St. Bartholomew's Day, was supposed to be a holy and joyous one. It was also the day that the Catholic machinery of state chose to act. The army was unleashed and hundreds of Huguenots were massacred, souring the air between Catholics and Protestants for years to come. The event ushered in a period known as the Wars of Religion, a series of civil wars in which Protestants and Catholics vied for control of their respective regions. In 1598, the formerly Protestant French king, Henry IV, tried to ameliorate the situation by enacting the Edict of Nantes that promised religious tolerance to all French citizens. Less than a hundred years later in 1685, however, Henry's grandson, Louis XIV, revoked this Edict, outlawing Protestantism, making France a Catholic country, and expelling the Huguenots. Mixed in amongst this religious and civil unrest were other factors such as plague and personal and economic hardship that often touched daily lives. Religious hatred, disease, poverty, and civil war all had a corrosive effect on the social structure, particularly in relatively isolated areas. In times of uncertainty and pestilence, people looked around for scapegoats, and communally religious certainties sought to reassert themselves. God was in His Heaven but the Devil was in the world, and he was determined to attack and destroy the righteous. Nor could the populace look to the central authorities for any sort of stability, because they too were in a dangerous state of flux. The uniformity of state that had characterized the reign of Henry II now gave way to a period of vacillating and weak administration under those of his sons. Francis II had ruled for little more than a year, guided as the Scottish Protestant Reformer John Knox (Francis was married to the young Mary, Queen of Scots), by "the vile whispers of Popish priests." He was only fifteen when he ascended the throne in 1559 and realizing that the new monarch was young and impressionable, the various great French houses—such as the formidable Catholic house of Guise—strove to advance their own fortunes. By 1560, after a year of ineffectual and indifferent rule, however, Francis was dead from a cancer of the ear (vindication, said Knox, that the whisperings of the Catholics were poisonous) and was succeeded by his younger brother Charles IX. Charles was only a weak-minded child and so the country was in effect ruled by his powerful mother, Catherine de Medici. A skilled politician, Catherine was able to play off one side against the other, but was set on France remaining a Catholic nation. All the same, she did not want a powerful Catholic family such as the Guises to have involvement in affairs of state and take powers from her easily influenced son, and she even courted some of the leading Protestants to counterbalance their influence. She was also acutely aware of the rise of the powerful Huguenot factions within the country and it was she who authorized the St. Bartholomew's Day Massacre, although her weak-willed son, the king, ordered it.

The massacre proved to be a turning point for the country, deepening divisions and turning French Protestants firmly against the monarchy. The years that followed were troubled with the Catholic Church trying to gain a hold on the minds of the people and the Protestants striving just as hard towards the same goal. In such a heated atmosphere, it is not surprising that demonologies began to emerge, gripping the public imagination, even at village level.

By the time Charles IX died in 1574, his reign had divided France as never before and his younger brother Henry III inherited a poisonous mess. The Guises had formed the violent Catholic League that was being aided by the great Catholic king, Philip II of Spain, whilst the Huguenots were already arming themselves for conflict. In a desperate bid to prevent a full-scale civil war (there had been many minor clashes and local "wars" between the two factions), Henry proposed a middle way that seemed to be acceptable to the politiques (moderates on both sides). He also struck up an alliance with his cousin, the Huguenot Henry of Navarre, in order to attack the Catholic stronghold of Paris, where the Guises had been stirring trouble. Before such an invasion could take place, however, Henry III was assassinated by a Dominican friar and, as he had no children, he was succeeded by his cousin from Navarre who became Henry IV, the first of the Bourbon kings. Having to retake large areas of his kingdom by force from the grip of the Catholic League, and in order to placate the Parisian mob and many of the important Catholic nobles, Henry changed his religion from Protestantism to Catholicism, declaring that "Paris was well worth a Mass." This helped him, as a tolerant Catholic king, to enact the Edict of Nantes that went some of the way to resolve the yawning differences between the religions. The Huguenots continued to remain a problem from the monarchy for almost a century to come. Henry himself would be assassinated in 1610, leaving the throne of France to a nine-year-old boy—his son Louis XIII.

The instability of the monarchy, the turbulence of the times, and the uncertainty of human life stalked the country as local wars raged. They all contributed to an overall feeling of doom. For many, the end of the world must surely be at hand and the forces of evil were abroad. Furthermore, localized fighting and wide-spread plague had left many bodies unburied, especially in the countryside attracting wolves from the surrounding woodlands in search of easy prey. Stories of wolf attacks may have become mixed with local stories of demonic forces, as exemplified in the writings of Henri Boguet and Nicholas Remy, stirring up popular fears and causing terrors to be seen everywhere.

Inarticulate and bizarre-looking strangers such as Jacques Roulet or sullen hermits such as Gilles Garnier were the reasons for the general social unease of the time. The wolf attacks were often linked in the common consciousness with demons lurking in the woodlands, and the evils that beset a local community might be exorcised by executing them. And of course, the shadow of the wolf, watching from the woodland tree line was enough to frighten everyone. The idea of the diabolic man-wolf, the enemy of Mankind, was inching ever closer.

Jean Grenier

This case, which is generally perceived to be the end of the 16th century werewolf terror in France, occurred in 1603. This ended in the trial of Jean Grenier, known as the last French loup-garou. Most of what we know about the case comes from the account of a French witch hunter named Pierre de Lancre. De Lancre was a famous magistrate who sought out and tried witches not only within French territory, but also those who had crossed the border into Spain and, similar to Burguot, was considered something of an authority on the diabolical arts. The Grenier case had come to his attention when he was acting as a lawyer for the parlement in Bordeaux and had been referred from a lower court at St. Sever.

Jean Grenier was a strange, fourteen-year-old boy, possibly suffering from mental abnormalities, who liked to frighten small children and young girls with the claim that he was a werewolf. As time went on, his assertions grew wilder and wilder. He had been approached by a mysterious stranger (possibly the Devil or one of his agents) who had given him a wolfskin cape that, together with a magic salve, could transform him into a wolf for the space of one hour on certain nights of the week. He also claimed to be the illegitimate son of a priest—his accepted father was not his real father—and, he claimed that the sons of priests grew up to become werewolves and serve the Devil. In his werewolf shape, he had attacked several dogs but had found their blood disgusting.

Far sweeter was the blood and flesh of young girls and small children. Whilst these were clearly the fantasies of a rather disturbed mind, they were taken extremely seriously by those in the surrounding neighbourhood. One girl to whom he had told these stories, a thirteen-year-old named Marguerite Porier, with whom he'd been attending some sheep, accused him of attacking her whilst in his werewolf guise. Whilst Jean had gone off somewhere, she was approached by some kind of wolf-like animal. She managed to beat it off with her staff, but it had only retreated a little way, and then slumped back on its haunches to glower at her savagely, upon which she had turned and fled. The beast, she said, was much smaller than an actual forest wolf and its tail was a mere stump. It was, she thought, some way between a wolf and a human. It could only, she averred, be Jean Grenier.

Given the severity of the accusation, the boy might have been expected to deny it. But surprisingly, he seemed eager to admit it and indeed confessed to a number of other similar crimes. Over the past months, a number of children had gone missing, and this added an immediate importance to his somewhat rambling confession. Indeed, the courts took a great deal of time in checking some of the detail, but found nothing of consequence. In the meantime, Jean's stories grew wilder and wilder, symptomatic of a disordered mind. He now implicated others whom he said had hunted with him. One of these was his father and a neighbour, both of whom were arrested and imprisoned. There were more searches of the Grenier house, particularly to find the magic salve of which Jean had spoken, but nothing was discovered. Jean's father was ordered to be tortured and he confessed that he had indeed been a werewolf and had sought out little girls but he had not eaten them, just "played with them". It might be inferred that the older man was a pedophile who interfered with small children and that his son shared some of his predatory sexual abnormalities. However, this was well beyond the 17th century French court. Emboldened by the ongoing trial, several young children who had seen their friends carried off by wolves now came forward and added to the accusations against the Greniers. Under further torture, Jean's father laid the blame squarely on his son and recanted of his own actions. He was spared for the time being. Based on the admittedly circumstantial evidence and on his own crazed

confession, Jean Grenier was brought before the judge at Coutras in June of 1603 and the court swiftly convicted him. He was sentenced to be hanged and burnt. However, the courts were not yet finished with him.

Le Maitre de la Foret

Jean Grenier's case was reviewed by the parlement of Bordeaux in September of that year. Again, he told his story of becoming a wolf, adding embellishments as he did so, seeking to implicate others whom he felt had turned against him. He told the court that, at the age of eleven or twelve, he had been taken deep into the woods by his neighbour to meet with a "black man" whom he called Le Maitre de la Foret (the Master of the Forest). This man, assumed to be the Devil, had scratched him with his nail, leaving a mark, and had given him the magic salve and wolf-pelt cloak that he needed in order to change shape. He also confessed that whilst in a wolf shape, he had entered an empty house in a village whose name he could not remember and had dragged a baby from its cradle and had eaten it. When he encountered a true wolf, he gave him what was left of the child. Later, in the parish of St. Antoinne-de-Pizon, he had attacked a small girl in a black dress who was looking after some sheep. He had partially devoured her as well. In fact, St. Antoinee-de-Pizon had become a favourite hunting ground of his, and two months earlier he had attacked and eaten a small boy playing in a yard, whilst six weeks before that he had devoured another child walking on a stone bridge. He had also fought with several dogs, killing most of them except one in Eparon, where the owner had appeared and had driven him off with a rapier. Once again, he repeated the allegation that his father was not his true parent and that he was in fact, the illegitimate son of a priest. He claimed that this fact gave him "special powers." This was found to be a fabrication—the fantasy of a confused mind—and that his father was indeed the labourer who had been arrested and tortured. There was some animosity between father and son—Jean's mother had died and his father had remarried. Jean and his stepmother didn't get along well—she found him strange in his ways—and so his father had put him out of the house, reduced him to beggary, and forced him to wander the countryside seeking food. He did try to get work but was notoriously unreliable. He was reduced to terrorizing small girls with tales of werewolfery and Devil-worship.

Relations had soured between Jean and his father and it was no surprise that he tried to implicate him in both his real or imagined crimes. When he had to face his father in court, however, his testimony began to fail; he crossed himself in his evidence and withdrew some of the allegations. He told the court that his stepmother had thrown him out because she had seen him behaving like a dog and further had witnessed him vomit up the fingers of a small child. He had made her afraid and she had driven him from the house. The father was dismissed without charge.

Despite all his crazy allegations, Jean Grenier was taken seriously by the courts. And yet, the sentence that was passed down to him shows the changing attitude of the time. He should have been burnt, indeed he was already sentenced to be so. However, the court took a more lenient view than the lower judiciary. It took into account the boy's "stupidity," the fact that he was a beggar and was malnourished, that he was bereft of a real mother and had been raised by a cruel stepmother, and that he'd been left to fend for himself without anyone to take an interest in him. Such a miserable specimen, in the court's view, was easy prey for the Devil and his agents but he was not beyond salvation. So, instead of condemning him to death, the court sentenced Grenier to live out his days as a prisoner in a Christian monastery. Here, it was hoped, he would renounce his formerly evil ways and turn to the path of Christ.

Bete de Gevaudan

It is generally accepted that Jean Grenier was the last instance of werewolfery in France and, with his trial, the whole French episode drew to a close. However, the beast, lurking at the back of the French mind, refused to go away. It resurfaced in 1764 with the infamous Bete de Gevaudan high in the Massif Central region. In the village of Langogne, in the Gevaudan, a ferocious wolf-like beast began killing people who strayed too near the edge of the forest. The death toll rose rapidly to eleven, including two labouring men. Although the deaths were probably the work of packs of wolves rather than any single animal, it did not take long for the ancient lycanthropic fears of earlier centuries to resurface. Although the probability of attacks by genuine wolf packs was acknowledged, folklore and folk-wisdom also hinted at the possibility of a werewolf. Old folktales and rumours began to circulate, accompanied by a wealth of broadsheets and printed material. Many of these included diabolical-looking woodcuts, showing monstrous and threatening figures, half-man, half-wolf. There were accounts, too, fuelled by the ongoing hysteria, of strange partially-human creatures seen slinking through the woods at Mazel-de-Grezes. (One account even said that although one of these figures was in the shape of a wolf, it wore brass buttons on its front as if the wolfskin were on an overcoat which some human had put on.) A women going to Mass had been accompanied for part of the way, by an especially hairy man who had vanished as soon as she had screamed the name of Christ. This was a sure sign that her companion had been a werewolf and in the service of the Devil. The Bete was never caught and soon the killings stopped. The terror, however, lingered on.

Many of the alleged sightings of the beast were no more than rural folktales and imaginings, but they serve to illustrate that, although there was a formal acknowledgement that, werewolves did not exist, there was still an element of uncertainty about this, particularly in the rural mind. Folktales concerning people who could transform themselves into animals or of wolves who could speak with a human voice (in order to tempt God's people) still circulated widely, especially in France.

Le Grande Mal Garou

The French collector of such supernatural tales or contes, Charles Perrault, recognized the importance of such stories. In 1697 he published a collection of folktales that contained one werewolf-themed story in particular—the notion of a speaking wolf that would create mayhem. It dealt with a petite fille, a pretty child, who has to journey through a dark wood in order to take some groceries to her grandmother who is ill. She is dressed in her favourite cape, made from a red material. On her way through the wood, she meets with a wolf, who engages her in conversation. The animal questions her and obtains the exact directions to her grandmother's house, also learning that the old lady is both ill and housebound. It does not attack her, however, due to the presence of some woodcutters nearby. The wolf then expresses concern about the old woman and says that it will visit her as well, but suggests that they take different paths to see who will get to the grandmother's hut first. The girl takes the longer path, but is distracted on her way by picking wild flowers and chasing butterflies. The wolf, meanwhile, has already reached the door of the hut and, by mimicking the little girl's voice, encourages the grandmother to allow it in, whereupon it leaps on the old woman in the bed and devours her. It then puts on the corpse's nightgown and climbs into the bed to wait for the little girl to arrive. This she does and the wolf pretends to be the bedridden old lady. There is some conversation between the two concerning the largeness of eyes, mouth, and teeth. At the very end, the wolf reveals itself, pounces upon the little girl and eats her. There is no happy ending to this tale. The story is, of course, the original narrative of the well-known children's fable *Little Red Riding Hood*; the version which Perrault collected at the end of the 17th century seems to have its source in the stories of Gilles Garnier and of Jean Grenier and of the Werewolves of Poligny, over a century earlier. Here, the wolves attacked feeble and defenceless victims—small children such as Red Riding Hood and the bedridden grandmother—harking back to some of the allegations during the French werewolf trials. Indeed, it is perfectly possible that Little Red Riding Hood started out as a gruesome werewolf tale. It is strange that Perrault's heroine is not afraid of speaking to a wolf or that she does not sense that something is wrong when the creature speaks to her. It has been suggested that initially, Little Red Riding Hood meets the werewolf in its human guise (Perrault is careful to display the werewolf as a wolf and not as a hybrid half-human creature), which doesn't frighten her, but later encounters it in its animal shape when it eats her.

The original French tale ends with the death of Red Riding Hood in the jaws of the wolf, but a German variant collected by the Brothers Jacob and Wilhelm Grimm, has a much happier and satisfactory ending. This story was published in 1812 in their famous *Kinder-und Hausmarchen* tales. This German story is known as *Rotkappchen* or Red Cap, which gives us the familiar title *Red Riding Hood*. In this version, which to a point closely parallels Perrault's narrative, the little girl's cries draw the attention of a passing huntsman. Suspecting what has happened, he attacks the wolf, slicing its belly open with his hunting knife, allowing Red Cap and her grandmother to escape. Throughout this entire procedure, the wolf appears to be asleep, gorged after its meal, and so Red Cap fetches a large stone that they sew into the creature's belly. The wolf wakes up and tries to run off but the weight of the stones weight it down and it dies.

The story of Red Riding Hood undoubtedly reflected a number of ancient legends and tales, stretching back long before Perrault. The colour of the heroine's hood or cap is the colour of blood; the girl is either extremely naïve or else deliberately misled by talking to the wolf (thus putting the creature in the role of Tempter); the notion that a demonic force (the wolf) masquerades as a human: all have traditions that stretch back almost as far as prehistoric times. And there are all sorts of political connotations—it has been suggested that the original Red Riding Hood legend is an old Huguenot tale. Allegedly it was circulated following the St. Bartholomew's Day Massacre, designed to symbolize the savagery of the French Monarchy—red being the colour of freedom (red caps were sometimes worn by the Huguenots as a symbol of their independence). Whatever the tradition, there is little doubt that the legend of Red Riding Hood and other tales like it kept the figures of the wolf and of the werewolf at the forefront of the popular rural mind.

Dr. Johann Wier

This is not to say, however, that such beliefs—the notion of men and women who could transform into animals and who were guided by demons—were completely and uncritically accepted. Even from the mid-16th century, when witch and werewolf trials were getting underway, some voices questioned the entire underlying principle of such notions. One of these early sceptics was a German physician. Doctor Johann Weyer (or Wier, 1515–1588) sought some sort of medical explanation to the eerie and supernatural powers to which some of these unfortunates confessed. In fact, Weyer is thought to have been the first man to use the term "mentally ill" to describe the conditions that some of these people had claimed for themselves. A logical and humane man, he argued that some of the unfortunates had deluded themselves into thinking that they had consorted with devils, had become animals, or had supernatural powers and that, rather than condemning them, the authorities should treat them with compassion In his book *De praestigiis daemonum* (The Illusion of Demons), first published in 1563, Weyer attacked the *Malleus Malificarum,* the witch hunter's guide-book, together with the Church's persecution of confused and mentally vulnerable people. Weyer was a follower of the Cologne sage. Heinrich Cornelius Agrippa von Nettesheim (1486–1535), who acknowledging the dark arts, had also argued that everything, including occultism, philosophy, and medicine, formed part of a cohesive whole. Weyer's work is counted as one of the earliest books displaying a much more enlightened view of the alleged imminence of the supernatural and indeed extends many of the underlying facets of modern psychiatry towards the whole credulous theory of witchcraft and shapeshifting.

Amongst the manifestations of alleged witchcraft that he considered, Weyer made specific references to werewolves. Those who had been accused of such crimes, he argued, had been suffering from a "disorder of their melancholic humour." He detailed a list of medical symptoms that might encourage them to rise from their beds at night to prowl the country thinking that they were wolves or other beasts. And, he argued, they might be "cured" by a number of means: by the letting of blood to restore the balance of the humours, or by eating juicy fruits and a strict variation in diet. (Weyer was first and foremost a physician, after all.) He further considered the case of the Werewolves of Poligny, who had confessed to eating small children and attending the diabolic Sabbat. His conclusion was that these men were not mentally ill, but were simply deluded. Acknowledging that they might well have met with the Devil or his agent (although what "the Devil" might be taken to be in his terminology is open to question), Weyer continues that the Master of Lies had so muddled their minds that they believed many things about themselves that were not true. According to Weyer, this may have been compounded by the salves and unguents with which the men smeared themselves before the transformation—the elements of such ointments may have held hallucinogenic properties, which confused their minds even further. The explanation that Weyer gave was a logical and medical one combining many strands of early psychoanalysis and references to psychotropic drugs. In these inferences, the German doctor seems to have been far ahead of his time.

Reginald Scot

Weyer's work was soon followed by one or two other individuals who questioned the reliability of witchcraft (and by implication, werewolf) cases. One of these was an Englishman, the Kentish Squire Reginald Scot (1538–1599). Scot was a Justice of the Peace for Kent and, as such, had seen many confused individuals come before him, accused of fantastic crimes. It also has to be remembered that Scot was a Protestant and took every opportunity to criticize what he perceived as the superstition and credulity of the Catholic Church. His most famous work, *Discoverie of Witchcraft,* first published in 1584, (nineteen years after Weyer) mocked the gullibility of those who believed in the tenets of witchcraft and accused poor and often mentally deficient people of it. He quoted Weyer, and much of his work seemed to mirror the German physician's argument, suggesting mental problems in those who were accused.

Sigmund Freud

Despite the enlightened works of people such as Weyer and Scot, the hysteria concerning werewolves remained in the deepest recesses of the communal mind, resurfacing from time to time with passing hysterias. Indeed the word "hysteria" was to come to the fore in the work of a much later medical figure—the father of psychoanalysis, Sigmund Freud. In 1897, Freud developed the theory that a "hysteria" such as was now suggested in a number of werewolf cases might be a delayed emotional reaction to an earlier sexual abuse or to repressed infantile sexual fantasies. Certain aspects of this theory may agree with the Grenier case in 1603 and perhaps also in the earlier Gandillion trial. Freud may well have been influenced by some of Weyer's theories—there is no doubt that he had reader Weyer, in a French translation, as he cited the work as one of his ten most influential books during an interview in 1906. According to his own account in 1914, Freud found himself face to face with a patient who expressed a connection to the werewolf motif. In fact, Freud named him the Wolf Man both in his notes and in his account. The patient is described as a twenty-seven-year-old man from a rather well-to-do Russian family, who, during the course of his analysis, described a dream that he'd had in infancy concerning wolves. He dreamt that he'd been lying in bed in his own bedroom when suddenly the bedroom window had slowly opened and, looking out, he'd seen about six or seven white wolves sitting around the foot of a big walnut tree outside. They were all watching him intently. None of the wolves made a move or seemed threatening in any way—nevertheless, the boy screamed, woke himself up, and had to be comforted by his nurse. There is also a curious folk element to the case, of which Freud and the patient were both well aware. The patient's birthday was 25th December (in many legends anyone daring to be born on the birthday of Christ was destined to become a monster and an agent of the Devil) and also he'd been born with a caul (a translucent membrane across the face which usually comes off at birth) that was considered an ill omen in parts of Russia. Freud also records that the nurse who had attended him as a child was deeply religious and extremely superstitious and took the caul as the sign that her charge would grow up to be a werewolf. With this in mind, the dream of wolves took on an added significance. Freud completed analysis on the Wolf Man by revealing that the child was most probably a wish to return to the womb and completely dismissed the old folk-wisdom that the nurse had passed on concerning the caul. It is interesting to note, of course, that Freud himself was born with a caul.

Werewolves in Film

Although both psychiatry and science were seeking to find alternative explanations for the supposed lycanthrope condition of a man who could turn himself into a wolf, whether willingly or unwillingly, still held a dark fascination for many people. And, as an idea, it was ripe for commercial exploitation. By the early 1930s, the werewolf's counterpart, the vampire, was making big money at the cinema box office. Cinema was now a popular form of entertainment; popular films were big earners and horror was an up-and-coming genre. A film adaptation of *Dracula* starring the sinister Bela Lugosi, together with a similar offering of *Frankenstein* starring Englishman William Henry Pratt (who had changed his name to the more East European-sounding Boris Karloff) had proved great successes. The film industry searched around for a comparable horror to unleash on the cinema-going public. They found it in the werewolf.

Lon Chaney, Jr.

Throughout the 1930s and into the 1940s, Universal Studios was the leaders in the field of Gothic horror. It was Universal who had released both *Dracula* and *Frankenstein* to popular and critical acclaim in 1931, and the company was now looking for another box-office smash. In 1935, they had released the *Werewolf of London* to moderate success but, by 1941, they were determined to release what today might be described as a werewolf blockbuster. It was to be called *Wolf Man* and was to bring the werewolf motif into cinematic legend. The man whom they had chosen for the central role was not a huge and menacing figure—he had nowhere near the sinister screen presence of either Lugosi or Karloff—but he was an actor of moderate talent. His name was Creighton Chaney and he was the son of the legendary silent movie actor Lon Chaney. Although his father had advised him not to take up film work, Creighton was determined to make it in the movies and, never one to discard a family connection, took the name Lon Chaney Jr. after his father's death in 1931. His mixture of rather brutish looks and child-like innocence, however, made him an ideal candidate for the cursed man.

From the beginning the movie had a disadvantage. Universal's other two big money-makers—*Dracula* and *Frankenstein*—had been based on recognized works of literature by Bram Stoker and Mary Shelley. Cinema-goers would have been familiar with the story or could go home and read the book. There was no comparatively famous literary work associated with the werewolf, and so, the film had to stand on both the plot and on Chaney's performance.

The Wolf Man

As with the vampire and, to some extent, Frankenstein, Universal introduced some folklore-like elements of its own into the story. The screenplay, written by Curt Siodmak, passed off certain inventions of his own as gypsy tradition. For example, although many of the werewolf trails and panics occurred in France, the werewolf becomes a creature mainly confined to Germany and Eastern Europe. This was to fit in with Universal's other two major horror creations that had an Eastern European location. The protagonist did not use a magic salve or a wolf-skin cloak or a belt, but was actually transformed unwillingly into the beast by the rays of the moon. This led to the famous quatrain that was widely attributed to ancient Romany gypsies but in fact had been created specially for the film by Siodmak and his team of writers:

> "Even a man, who's pure in heart,
> And says his prayers at night,
> Can become a wolf when the wolfsbane blooms,
> And the autumn moon is bright."

Coupled with this was the notion that a man could become a werewolf if he was bitten by another such creature. The change would then occur at the first full moon after the bite. This again had no basis in myth and legend, but it added to the suspense and horror of the situation. As well as this, Siodmak introduced another invention—an apotropaic that could repel and destroy a werewolf. This was once more to blend the werewolf legend in with that of the vampire (that could be repelled and destroyed by the crucifix). This was the use of silver, which Siodmak was to claim was Romanian gypsy lore. It was nothing of the sort. Although the werewolf featured in gypsy tradition, it was not a significant terror. Indeed, the people of rural France were much more terrified of the creature than the gypsies. As well as this, Universal introduced the notion of a pentagram, an ancient Romany talisman for warding away werewolves. Once again, this has no basis in tradition, it simply brought it into line with a number of "devil films" that were starting to appear, mainly from Universal.

Most importantly, the film created the impression that the change from man to beast did not involve a man transforming himself into a real-looking wolf but into some form of hybrid figure—not wholly human, not wholly wolf. This, according to the film, was a man-like being with added feral traits. In fact, in some of the earlier films, the werewolf looked more similar to a shaggy ape than a member of the canine species.

Wolf Man was a reasonable commercial success for Universal—enough to ensure several follow-ups and a team-up with Frankenstein. It would serve to keep the figure of the werewolf in the popular mind through the succeeding years.

Although never as big or as menacing a creature as the vampire or even *The Mummy* (which again featured Boris Karloff) the werewolf exuded a certain primal horror.

Later filmmakers were to take a tongue-in-cheek approach to the werewolf theme with such movies as *I Was A Teenage Werewolf* (1957, starring Michael Landon, who would go on to make his name as Little Joe Cartwright in *Bonanza*) and the classic *American Werewolf in London* (1979). Some films such as the UK production *Company of Wolves* (1984, and based on a book by Angela Cartwright) and *The Howling* (1981) did try to add some depth to the figure, but they still contained the pseudo-folkloric additions of previous movies. For instance, it was now claimed (using an allegedly Romany tradition) that only a silver bullet could kill or injure a werewolf. No such tradition ever existed—the only means of disposing of the beast, said conventional wisdom, was to burn it, the same as with each of Satan's minions. The picture that was starting to emerge in the latter half of the 20th century was an extremely confused one. Nevertheless, interest in the werewolf never died.

And even in today's relatively sophisticated society, a fear of the beast still lingers. It is not a great distance in many instances, from the thronging streets of a busy city to the cool of the remote and shadowy forest. And who knows what lurks in the dappled shade under the low boughs—a crouching beast, waiting to strike and to tear us limb from limb. Werewolves may be far closer to us than we would prefer.

Voodoo and Zombies

Cockroach, he don't wear no crockin' shoes when he creep into the fowl house.

—Creole proverb

The image of the zombie—the walking dead of Afro-Caribbean lore—with its shambling gait, dead eyes, and slack jaw, is perhaps one of the most frightening in all of terror iconography. The idea of a corpse, raised from the dead and somehow animated by magic is enough to send shivers down the spine of even the hardiest of individuals. Maybe this is why the zombie has maintained a constant appearance in many horror films through the years. There are other elements that have been added to the basic motif—that the zombie has inhuman strength; that it has supernatural powers (for instance, it can enter a room through a keyhole in the form of smoke); that the zombie did not die naturally but was magically murdered and turned into the monster through hideous sorcery; and that zombies eat human flesh similar to cannibals. Through the years, the notion of the zombie has assumed a menace that cannot easily be rivalled by more "sophisticated" monsters.

Zombies are, of course, inextricably linked in the popular mind with Voodoo, a religion found in West Africa, the Caribbean, and some parts of America.

Therefore, no examination of zombies can be carried out without first examining the belief system. However, because of its complexity, Voodoo is incredibly difficult to study. In its purest state, the religion that we refer to as Voodoo is only one of a myriad of beliefs that reflect either the ideologies of their practitioners or the area from which they have come. Some are even fragments of what may have once been broader and more wide-ranging beliefs; others have been adapted to suit the area in which they flourished.

Thus, Santeria, Umbanda, Quimbanda, Mami Wata, Shango, Moyambe, and Candomble are all considered as variants and aspects of the Voodoo religion. Even the name creates problems because "Voodoo" is something of an Anglicised construction, and other variations are given as voudon, voodun, vudoun, and voodoux. An even further Anglicised word, Hoodoo, is also sometimes used. The original terminology comes from the language of the Ewe/Yaroba peoples of the Arada area of Dahomey (now Benin) in West Africa and literally means, "to draw water." Eventually, it became modified to mean "to draw down spirits." This was done by means of a weave or coloured pattern that was spread upon the ground.

Loa

Although they were extremely powerful, the forces and powers (loa) in which the various tribes believed were also very child-like—they were curious and easily offended, but they could also be easily placated. They sulked, threw tantrums, and misbehaved similar to human children. They were also attracted by many things—bright colours, unusual patterns, and loud noise. Any of these might be used to placate and control them. Any person who could both read and control their moods was, through them, assured of great powers. They were the witch doctors, sorceresses, and Shamans who were treated with awe and reverence by their fellow tribesmen and followers.

Houngans and Mambos

The mediation of the relations between humans and spirits became the centre of the voudon faith of the Yaroba people, and those who controlled or interposed in that relationship were known in Voodoo terms as houngans (male) or mambo (female). The places to which the spirits were called—the Voodoo temple—was known as the hounfor, all of which gave Voodoo the recognizable trappings of a loosely organized faith.

It has been argued that Voodoo is a slave religion that adapted to the servile conditions amongst the peoples that were carried from the West Africa coast by European slavers. They brought indigenous religions, often centered on natural forces that became moulded into their servile situation in the plantations into which they were subsequently sold—estates in the Caribbean: the West Indies, South America, and parts of Northern America. Mixed in with the native faiths were some elements of Christianity. Dahomey had been largely colonized by the French, and French Franciscans had sought to establish their creed and culture there since the 1660s. Consequently, there was a certain "Frenchness" to the religions that the Africans practiced and this conveyed itself to the slavers to other parts of the world. This "Frenchness" often appeared in the language that was used; in some of the rituals and in the outlook of the slaves themselves. French Catholicism also influenced some of the belief systems that the slaves held—indeed some elements of Voodoo were simply a mixture of African Pagan observances and a form of Christian theology. Thus, ancient native gods became fused with Christian Saints; certain aspects of Christian ceremonies were moulded into the fabric of what was essentially "Pagan" belief, and Saint's days became the focus of Voodoo ritual and were celebrated as "special times."

Voodoo, and variants of it, flourished on the plantations, in the Caribbean, in South America, and on the North American continent. It also flourished around American slave ports, primarily in Louisiana (New Orleans) and in the realm of the Rice Kings in South Carolina (Charleston)—anywhere where slaves concentrated in large numbers. And the Voodoo sects spread quickly wherever they took root. As early as 1782, Governor Galvez of Louisiana specifically forbade the importation of slaves from Martinique, because he believed them to be "steeped in Voodoo" and that they would make the lives of the citizens of New Orleans and of the state in general "very unsafe." A decade later, several slaves from Santo Domingo were publicly burned in New Orleans for practicing "the heathen rites of the Voodoo."

Christian-seeming Worship

In the early 1700s, many Christian plantation owners forbade their slaves to practice Christian or "Christian-seeming" worship and many of the Voodoo rituals (which were loosely based on Christianity) slid away into the jungles, swamps, and forests, becoming secretive and mysterious. Legends grew up around it, as Christians speculated about what went on at these clandestine gatherings. Clearly there was some sort of spirit possession as the loa, drawn by the veve, took over the bodies of their followers in order to prophesy and heal, and this alarmed the Western Christian minds. Such a concept, for Western Christians, held echoes of medieval demon possession in Christian lands and they quickly equated possession by the loa with possession by the Devil himself. The copying of portions of Christian ritual was suggestive of the Black Mass, that was said to have been practiced by European witches and heretics. There were tales, too of cannibalism amongst the slaves.

Le Cochon Gris

In parts of the island of Martinique, where the Voodoo religion was supposed to be extremely widespread, certain cults were said to devour "le cochon gris" (the grey pig) which was a coded reference to human flesh. Whilst there may have been instances of the eating of human flesh, there is little evidence that it was in any way widespread. However, some of the white planters and settlers may have had good reason to be alarmed.

Bokor

Similar to many other religions, Voodoo had its darker side. If the loa were like children, then they could be unpredictable and capricious. They knew neither good nor evil, they could just as easily commit a sinister act as a righteous one. They could be duped into committing diabolical and anti-social acts by unscrupulous magicians known as "bokor." Once the bokor had the spirit under his or her control, it could be turned against humankind and had the potential to unleash great evil. As well as that, the bokor might summon up dark and vicious sprits that had no love for Mankind. Although in most cases, the spirits and forces were drawn down for benign reasons—to heal, to give aid for specific tasks, and to bring good luck. An alteration in the pattern of the veve could encourage less welcome forces, the substance of African nightmares.

Bori, Tikoloshi, and Dodo

These were beings similar to the Bori—a shapeshifting, often invisible, entity that engaged in acts of extreme violence. Then there was the Tikoloshi, a Xosha water demon that could either appear as a bird with an abnormal head, as a baboon, or the Dodo of Ghanian folklore, often assumed to be the blank-eyed ghost of a dead man who prowled the forests, ready to tear travellers asunder with claw-like hands.

Gegbo

Many of these terrors reflected the regions from which the slaves themselves came or from where their people had originated—mainly from West Africa or the Congo basin. The art of calling them down was known as *gegbo*, the evil side of Voodoo. Practitioners often chose to live well away from the main settlements or plantations and were often considered to be witches or sorcerers.

Gods of Voodoo

If the Voodoo religion was a complex affair, then so was its pantheon of gods and forces. Many of these reflected the native gods and powers, that characterized regional beliefs. But as Voodoo spread into other countries, there were some variations relating to the country in which the slaves found themselves.

Olorun and Obatala

In the Yoruba/Ewe pantheon, the supreme deity was Olorun, who was remote and unknowable. This did not, however, prevent him from interfering in the world, and he might have spoken to his followers through an intermediary or demi-god known as Obatala. Similar to children, the two deities often fought and were in conflict, which might be mediated for the benefit of Mankind, by an experienced houngan.

Minor Gods

Beneath these two entities was a pantheon of minor gods who in many ways resembled Catholic Saints. They might be approached in order to intercede with Olorun or they might have supernatural powers that they could use themselves. Amongst such entities were Ogou Balanaji, a god with healing powers, and Zaka, who presided over agriculture. There were, too, rather dangerous deities who had to be approached extremely carefully. Amongst these were Shango (or Shago) who controlled storms—especially lightning,—and maybe the most dangerous of all, Dambala-wedo, the great serpent. This pantheon was an ancient one which had arrived with the slaves from Arada in Dahomey and is refereed to as the Rada (or Arada) pantheon.

Le Danse de Don Pedro

However, just to confuse matters, a later Spanish variant of the original voudun threw up a wider pantheon that incorporated deities not found in the former. The story is that this strand of Voodoo belief started amongst slaves in the Spanish colonies in the Caribbean and the Americas and was much more flamboyant than the traditional African one. The traditional story concerning the origin of this particular form of the religion is that a Spanish-African slave named Don Pedro combined a mixture of rum and gunpowder and drank it. As he did so, he became inspired by a much more lively form of loa that made him behave in outlandish and bizarre ways. The central ritual of his followers was known as Le Danse de Don Pedro which gave rise to a form of Voodoo called Petro. In this form, the drumming was wilder than it had been before, the movements of the dancers were greatly exaggerated, and the colours used were more striking. Blood played an even greater part in the rituals than it had done in Rada. Animal sacrifice (usually a cockerel or a goat) had played a significant part in the ceremonies of both forms, but in the Petro ritual, the dancers, often inflamed with rum, smeared themselves with the animal's blood liberally as a symbol of devotion.

Papa Legba

Petros Voodoo also introduced an entirely new set of loa or minor deities to the pantheon, including Papa Legba, who acted as a kind of "gateway"

between the spirit and human worlds. He was the first of the loa that the houngan called up in the ritual and through him, other spirits might be contacted and brought forth. Within this Voodoo form, the forces of the Otherworld took on some human semblance—Papa Legba, for instance, often appeared as an old man, leaning on a crutch, a wholly recognizable figure amongst the slave communities. His mistress or wife was Erzule Frieda, the deity that controlled both love and lust—a huge, grinning, buxom figure, sometimes carrying a fruit basket. Again this was a recognizable figure on many of the plantation and served to "humanize" the loa.

Baron Samadi

The most famous of all the Petro Voodoo pantheon was Baron Cemetiere (graveyard), also known as Baron Samadi (Saturday) or Baron La Croix (the Cross), the Lord of the Graveyard. Often depicted as a skeleton dressed in grand style (sometimes in a gentleman's tuxedo and top hat), he was the Master of the Unquiet Dead and certainly not to be trifled with. He was placated with both rum and tobacco and could take awful vengeance if these items were not regularly offered. The Baron was an entity of the slave plantations of the New World and had no African equivalent.

Ghede

There was another added element to the Petro version of Voodoo as well—that was the Ghede, or ancestral ghosts. Whilst ghosts and ancestral spirits had been acknowledged in Rada Voodoo, they had been slightly less important than the primeval deities and loa. Now, these spirits assumed a vengeful role, turning against humans and had to be supernaturally restrained. They were under the command of Baron Cemetiere who often used them against the living unless he was given gifts and offerings.

The Elements of Voodoo

Both Rada and Petro Voodoo often placed a reliance on either wambi or gris-gris (charms). These concentrated the forces of the loa through tangible elements—for example, rooster's feet, black crows, and other such items. Much has been made of the concept of "Voodoo dolls," tiny effigies of a living person in which pins and sharp objects were stuck in order to cause that person pain or death. In fact, although many of these are actually sold as Voodoo items, they have very little to do with the religion itself. Indeed, they are not specifically African in origin. In early English tales concerning witchcraft, mention is made of the mommet, a clay image into which sharp objects and pins were placed by English witches in order to cause injury or illness. The same was also true of alleged European witchcraft. Besides the gris-gris, Petro sorcery also placed great emphasis on poudre—herbal preparations and powders. Many of these were natural remedies used to cure illness and resist infections, but others were said to be used for more sinister purposes, such as poisons and hallucinogenics.

Haiti

Zombies played a role in many Voodoo-related ideas. For example, it was considered illegal under Haitian law to use zombies (men without wills rather than actual dead men) in the cane fields or to exploit them as cheap labour. Those who did might have found themselves liable for a fine under the employment legislation.

Papa Doc

Also in Haiti, there was an added political dimension. During the brutal regime of Francois "Papa Doc" Duvalier who came to power in 1957, Voodoo was used to keep the dictator in power. Born in Haiti in 1907, Duvalier had started out as a simple country doctor who had been involved in the treatment of yaws (a common bacterial skin infection that had crippled large parts of Haiti). His treatments of the disease were highly effective, leading him to make the claim that he was healing through the power of Voodoo.

Code Noir

The Voodoo cult had flourished in Haiti since roughly the mid-18th century, with whispers of the infamous "Code Noir"—a blasphemous tome written in French, that outlined a number of ghastly ceremonies for calling down loa. It is possible that Duvalier was a member of a local cult and that he used this suspicion to gain control over those around him. Gradually he began to rise in power and influence through the ranks of Haitian society, moving into the fluctuating power vacuum left after the withdrawal of American troops at the end of World War II. He began to model himself after Baron Cemetiere who was then a feared figure in Haitian folklore.

Ton Ton Macoute

In 1957, Duvalier seized power, emasculating the already weak Haitian army and appointing a number of thugs to protect him, led by his friend and ally, Clement Barbot. These were the Ton Ton Macoute, who took their name from a bogeyman in Haitian folktales. This vicious group acted as a form of secret police and were known to use Voodoo ceremonies to create fear and unease in the populace. In their stronghold at Fort Dimanche, they tortured Duvalier's unfortunate opponents and allegedly committed acts of cannibalism and sorcery. "Papa Doc" himself began to use the trappings of Voodoo to intimidate those who spoke out against him—placing skulls and dark candles on his official desk and claiming that he was a powerful bokor. He was rumoured to drink human blood and devour human flesh in the privacy of his own quarters—rumours that he personally encouraged to intimidate his enemies. It was widely reported that he could not be killed and he also spread the suggestion that he had a veritable army of zombies, ready to do his bidding. During his oppressive regime, Haiti became, in the public mind, the Voodoo capital of the world.

Baby Doc

Despite all his alleged Voodoo powers, Duvalier died in 1971 and was succeeded by his equally brutal but less politically adept son, Jean Claude, known as "Baby Doc." Unable to maintain his hold over the minds of the people, or to continue the "Voodoo mystique" in the way that his father had done, Jean Claude's grip on power failed, bringing an end to the Duvalier regime. Even so, it had proved a powerful political tool for almost twenty years and had turned Haiti into the "land of zombies." Since then, Haiti, its economy almost decimated by the reign of the Duvaliers, has traded on its sinister reputation in the hope of attracting tourists and the curious.

American Voodoo: New Orleans

Perhaps it is the practitioners—the houngans, mambo, and bokors—who have added to the Voodoo and zombie mythology, especially amongst the slaves of America. Two American slave ports with their surrounding areas are recognized as centres for the religion. These are Charleston, South Carolina, and New Orleans, Louisiana. The latter of these two seems especially soaked in Voodoo culture with its largely French ethos, shadowy alleyways, and its hinterland of dark and mysterious swamplands and bayous where runaway slaves tended to gather.

There were always whispers of blood sacrifice (usually animals or cockerels) in some areas of the city, and, there were sometimes tales of strange practices imported from ancient Africa. In October 1863, a riot threatened when a dismembered human torso was discovered in the home of a suspected Voodoo practitioner. There was talk of the "goat without horns" (human sacrifice) which made its way into the city newspapers.

ElizabethSunderland

New Orleans was already on edge. Tales of "darkie worship" had been circulating for some time. Over eight years previously in 1855, the home of a known Voodoo practitioner named Elizabeth Sutherland had been mobbed by her neighbours who believed that she'd put a spell on them. The police rescued her and held her in protective custody in the Third District Station. A crowd then gathered outside the station, demanding that the witch be released. Fearing widespread civil unrest and of being seen as accessories to Voodoo, the police allowed Elizabeth to escape out the back door of the station and then told the crowd that she'd turned herself into a black cat in order to elude them. In this guise, she had squeezed through the bars of her cell.

Bessie Tolendano

Voodoo queens who could allegedly command fantastic powers, such as controlling the walking dead, were now rife in New Orleans. One of these, Bessie (or Betsy) Tolendano, "a stout and intelligent free woman of colour" according to one newspaper report, was brought to trial on a variety of charges, including trying to raise a corpse and of kidnapping children for use in blasphemous Voodoo rituals. She expressed surprise at some of the allegations, but claimed her position as a Voodoo queen through rights of inheritance. She displayed some of her gris-gris to the court and boasted of her great powers. She seemed quite sincere and declared it her right to convene Voodoo gatherings in any part of the city that she chose. She was, she claimed, the descendant of ancient Congo Queens and for her, Voodoo was a religion.

Hoodoo Mag

Another of the great New Orleans Voodoo queens, Hoodoo Mag, was also brought to court following the death of a prostitute named Julia Henderson in which she was said to have been implicated. She was accused of murdering Henderson by supernatural means—probably involving zombies or some form of fatal gris-gris. Hoodoo Mag was not a free woman but a slave in the service, (according to the *Daily Crescent)*, of one, Mr. Marpolis, a leading slave-holder in the city. The paper referred to her as "a black hellcat named Margaret...known throughout New Orleans as Hoodoo Mag." She was charged with stirring up the coloured people in the city against both their white and coloured masters. What became of her is unknown, but the trial left the municipal authorities extremely jittery.

Since 1817, a Municipal Ordinance in the city had forbidden slaves to gather in large numbers for any purpose, whether it be talking, drinking, or dancing. Fears of a slave uprising were everywhere and such gatherings were considered as the birthplaces of sedition and unrest. Nevertheless, by the mid-19th century, the enactment was largely ignored. Groups of slaves and "free people of colour" would often gather in the city's Congo Square, especially on St. John's Eve (23rd June—a sacred day in the Voodoo calendar) to drink and dance. Often, several Voodoo queens or mambos, and a number of hougans were also in attendance. What was beginning to worry the authorities was a number of curious white people who were also making their way to such gatherings and taking part in them.

Helen Thomas

Around 1853, a Voodoo queen named Helen Thomas conducted a massive gathering in the square where two white women were present and took part in the dancing and the rituals that went on. The *Dictionnaire Universale du XIX Siecle* described a raid by New Orleans police on a Voodoo gathering in which fifty nude women were found taking part—several of them white and prominent socialites. Inflamed with pambai (a form of rum punch) infused with a concoction which contained High John Conqueror Root (St. John's wort) the revellers danced all night in many parts of the city. However, many held that it wasn't the real thing—the real Voodoo dances were held in private, not in public.

Joe Goodness

It was not only the Voodoo queens who commanded such gatherings—many of the secret dances were conducted by male houngans or the babalawo (fathers of secrets).

One of the earliest "father of secrets" in the Algiers area of New Orleans was Joe Goodness, a houngan who had inherited powers and charms from his grandfather, also named Joe Goodness. This babalawo conducted a number of secretive rites throughout the city in the 1850s in which chickens were allegedly torn to pieces, dolls made from human skin and bone were reputedly studded with pins, and large amounts of liquor was consumed. There was even some talk that zombies were raised from the dead, but perhaps part of this is only legend. There are also stories of white people dancing and consuming gumbo in the city, which had been made there. An altar, decorated with goat's horns, was said to have been the centrepiece of the ritual.

Dr. John

One of the most important of all the early Voodoo practitioners in New Orleans was Dr. John; also known as Dr. John Croix, Voodoo John, and Bayou John, who dwelt in the city during the mid-to-late 1800s. A towering and imposing free man of colour and the owner of several slaves himself, Dr. John's ancestry was said to lie in Senegal. In fact, he was said to be a Senegalese prince. His face was covered in scars that he claimed were the ritual markings of his royal house and which gave him a particularly ferocious aspect. Captured by Spanish slavers, he had been sold to a gentleman of some rank who had been travelling to Cuba. In return for good service and for his excellent cooking, his master had eventually granted him freedom. He returned to Senegal to find that his father had died and that life there was not to his liking. He became a sailor, visiting many ports all over the world and finally quitting the sea when his ship reached New Orleans. There he took on work as a common miller in the docks area, working alongside other coloured employees over whom he seemed to exert a considerable power. Noticing that the other slaves seemed to fear him, his former master made John an overseer.

As his reputation increased, John began to realize that people were willing to pay for his services. Soon he had set himself up as a babalawo and zombie master and had increased both his notoriety and his wealth. He bought a plot of land out on Bayou Road and built a grand house there. Indeed, he began purchasing slaves himself, many of them female. Some of these he married, assembling a personal harem, and performing the marriage ceremonies in the Voodoo style. He would later boast of having fifteen wives and fifty children, all scattered across Louisiana. His wealth and influence increased throughout New Orleans and he soon travelled in an open carriage through the streets, dressed in the style of a refined gentleman.

Whilst he was a babalawo, Dr. John took little part in the dances and ceremonies of the Voodoo followers; these he left to the Voodoo queens and, if he did attend any, it was merely as an onlooker. He conducted most of his own business from a dark room in his house on Bayou Road. The place was full of animal and human skulls, the latter stolen from local graveyards, along with snakeskin, stuffed lizards, and embalmed scorpions. There were unmentionable poudres and potions in stoppered bottles and in bowls. From the middle of this supernatural clutter, Dr. John sold his charms, curses, and spells for a fee.

It is said that the last of his wives was white and that in his later years, she administered his affairs for him. Dr. John also conducted séances, issued prognostications, and prepared astrological charts, sometimes using pebbles to assist him "in the old African way." It is said that he also prepared gris-gris and love potions that were often bought by heavily veiled white ladies. He also sold protections to parents in order to keep their children safe. But there was a dark side to him, too. It was said that he commanded a legion of zombies (which he created through his magic) to do the work around his house and run nefarious errands for him (such as digging up corpses for parts) as soon as it was dark.

In spite of all his alleged supernatural powers, however, Dr. John was finally caught with a simple trick. Although he was a babalawo and a master of dark magic, the doctor could not read nor write and depended on some of his wives to manage his affairs for him. As he grew older, he desired to take his business into his own hands and decided to become educated. He hired a young black man to help him to read and write. The young man made him practice his signature on blank pieces of paper and therein lay the Doctor's undoing. Within several months, he had "signed away" most of his fortune and the house on Bayou Road. Within a year, he was practically a pauper.

He could never rightly understand what had happened to him and made several attempts to regain his lost fortune through the lottery, but his supernatural powers of prediction seemed to have deserted him. Once again, he tried to re-establish his position as foremost babalawo in New Orleans, but youngsters had taken over his clientele. Many of his wives deserted him and he was forced to take shelter with one of his children that his wife had borne him. It seemed that the great Doctor himself was the victim of a wambi or curse. Death came soon after.

The writer Lafcadio Hearn noted the passing of "John Montenant," also known as Dr. John, John Bayou, or Voodoo John. Hearn lavishly claimed that he was over one hundred years old (later accounts were to claim that he was almost two hundred). In reality, he was probably around eighty-two. Voodoo men were always fond of exaggerating their ages to give themselves supernatural credence. However, he had left a legacy behind him. Dr. John was one of the first houngans to mix Roman Catholicism with the snake worship of ancient Voodoo. On his desk in his darkened consulting room, amongst the fantastic and grotesque impedimenta of African witchcraft, stood a statue of the Virgin Mary. This he considered just as important for his powers as the dried toads and snakeskin that he often used. He was also the first of the houngans to devote much of his powers to foretelling the future and to healing, and he certainly was the first to establish his agencies throughout the city of New Orleans. He had truly established Voodoo as a reality all across the city. After his death, there was not another babalawo similar to him.

Even in death, Dr. John would not lie still. His restless loa was said to possess some of his devotees. It is thought that one of the most famous New Orleans R&B singers and piano players, Malcolm Rebennack, who played in the early 1970s with Professor Longhair and His Shuffling Hungarians, was possessed by his loa, causing him to adopt the name by which he is known today: Dr. John. This connection was established by the title of his first solo album, *Gris-Gris.*

Doctor Yah-Yah

Although Dr. John was one of the most important of the New Orleans Voodoo men, he was not the only one. Doctor Yah-Yah, a Voodoo practitioner and zombie-master, operated in the Lake Pontchartrain area around the same time as Dr. John. He broke all the traditions that claimed all babalawo were free men of colour. Doctor Yah-Yah was a slave whose real name was George Washington. He imitated Dr. John and seems to have practiced divination and astrology. However, he did not include healing in his supernatural repertoire. He was also known to issue gris-gris and curses for a price and, similar to Dr. John, was believed to have a number of zombies at his disposal. His career finally came to an end when he was arrested for selling poison to an Italian fruit-trader as a cure for rheumatism. Wary of the Voodoo man, the Italian wisely had the potion analysed and when it was found to contain poisonous substances, he lodged a formal complaint against Doctor Yah-Yah. The Doctor was briefly held by the authorities, but his master paid his fine and shipped him off to end his days as a field hand on a plantation, an undignified fate for a babalawo.

Doctor Beauregard

Another significant Voodoo man, Doctor Beauregard, flourished in New Orleans around 1870. He was one of the more exotic "foreign" practitioners, having come to the city from Kentucky. He was a man of awe-inspiring appearance, mainly due to the fact that he had never cut his hair and tied it up in a number of strange knots. In these, he carried some of his gris-gris in little packets and small bottles. He carried a monkey-skull rattle wherever he went, shaking it in order to let loose a wambi at an unfortunate enemy. Some of his techniques may have been later copied by the American R&B singer and songwriter, Screamin' Jay Hawkins, during the late 1950s and 60s. (Hawkins was one of the performers to explicitly use Voodoo imagery in his stage act. His most famous composition, *I Put a Spell on You*, recorded in 1956, hinted at the cult religion and was banned by several U.S. radio stations whilst his later *Feast of the Mau-Mau* was suggestive of cannibalistic ritual.) One of his most famous and financially successful "Voodoo recipes" was salted beef heart that was considered to ensure virility in men. From time to time, this fantastic figure would go around, brandishing a hoot-owl's head at his enemies and cursing them. Besides being a figure of curiosity, he was also a figure of fear and after badly scaring some ladies, he was arrested. He tried to terrify the police by throwing the hoot-owl's head at them and issuing curses, all of which proved ineffective. He was briefly held in custody and on his release, he apparently vanished and was assumed to have returned to Kentucky.

Don Pedro

The successor to Dr. John was as a Spanish slave named Don Pedro. Not much is known about him except that he was frequently in trouble with the police. He was said to have conducted a number of sexual orgies in his home and at Raquette Green in which white as well as coloured women took part. Raquette Green has long since disappeared, but it was once the site for a number of Voodoo gatherings. Don Pedro, however, seems to have disappeared without a trace.

Joseph Mellon

The other main Voodoo practitioner in New Orleans around this time was Joseph Mellon, who was said to issue some of the most ferocious curses in the city. However, he took a fancy to an engaged woman and tried unsuccessfully to entice her away from her fiancé by supernatural means. Before they could be married, the woman's fiancé suddenly and inexplicably died. Although it was suspected that Mellon had poisoned him, nothing could be proved. However, the death did him no good, for the object of his desire treated him with disdain and died an old, unmarried woman. Mellon himself seems to have died not long after. Other Voodoo men were to follow him: Delton Boussard, Papa Gris-Gris, and Doctor Cheveneux, but none could match the menacing legacy of Dr. John.

Mama Calliba and Dr. Maurice

And of course, there were the Voodoo queens. One of the earliest of these women was Mama Calliba, a mambo who held a number of Voodoo revels near an old brickworks on Dumaine Street. Most of these seemed to have been little more than orgies with naked men and women dancing wildly and, in many respects, Mama Calliba seems to have been little more than a brothel keeper, but her name as a "voodooiene" (female Voodoo priest) seems to have been widely circulated in the city. Together with her partner, known as Doctor Maurice, she presided over some of the wildest excesses of 19th century New Orleans. There are also suggestions that the mambo may also have been an abortionist—helping white women get rid of unwanted pregnancies by various means, sometimes by poudres and potions, at other times by more physical devices. Although she was considered to be a woman of some power, she disappeared without a trace. Doctor Maurice seems to have continued for a time, allegedly raising zombies and casting curses, but he, too, eventually seems to have faded into obscurity.

Mother Dede

A number of Voodoo queens followed, such as the notorious Madame Roux in Charleston, who flourished briefly but left little mark on the societies in which they lived. Most of their names exist merely in legend or folklore. The first queen of any importance seems to have been a black woman from Santo Domingo who had the name of Samitie (or Semetee) Dede, also known as Mother Dede in New Orleans. Brought to the city as a slave, she is said to have used her sorcerous influences on her master in order to procure her freedom. Although she boasted great Voodoo powers, she worked as a stall-holder, selling either sweets or trinkets. She is said to have taken over from Mama Calliba as the premier Voodoo queen in the city and to have continued the revels by the old brickworks on Dumaine Street. Under continuous surveillance by the police, she moved these revels to the banks of Lake Pontchartrain. By 1825, her power in the city was at its height and her revels were attracting participants from both white and black communities. What eventually became of her is unknown but it is possible that she may have fled the city following a number of police raids on her gatherings. By the early 1830s, she seems to have disappeared from Creole society.

ZozoLaBrique

Mother Dede was briefly succeeded by a former slave woman known as Zozo LaBrique (though she may also have had several other names) who appears to have been half-demented and who sold buckets of brick-dust from her stall. This came from an old tradition that some of the Creole housewives had claiming that steps of houses had to be scrubbed with brick-dust to keep away evil spirits or to wash away a curse placed on the house by an enemy. Just how this crazy creature became a principal Voodoo queen is unknown, but at one time she was the most consulted voodooiene in New Orleans. However, her reign as premier Voodoo queen was very brief as she had to make way for the most powerful of all the New Orleans voodooienes, Marie Laveau.

The Three Marie Laveaus

The legacy of Marie Laveau has lived on until the present time. In 1971, the Los Angeles-based rock band Redbone, led by Native American brothers

Pat and Lolly Vegas, scored a massive hit with *Witch Queen of New Orleans*, reputedly penned in her honour. However, any study of her long career as Voodoo queen is fraught with difficulty and contradictions because she may not have been one person at all, but *three* (there were at least two), all of whom took the name Marie Laveau. In 1830, her name echoed around the city whilst in 1895, she is recorded as presiding over a Voodoo gathering at Bayou St. John. Some people believe that Marie Laveau was still living in 1918 at the end of World War I and for a period after. A report in a newspaper stated that she had died in 1881 and that she had been a Voodoo queen for well over eighty years. The pirate Jean Lafeyette was said to have kissed her when he entered New Orleans with the American troops following the Battle there in 1815. A century later it was said that she was the mistress of Lafcadio Hearn. There is no official gravesite for her and she is said to lie buried in a number of places, including St. Louis No. 1 Cemetery, although others strongly declare that she is not buried there at all.

Marie Laveau: Marie 1

The first Marie Laveau appears in the marriage records of the old Cabildo district of New Orleans in 1819. Her wedding was performed by Pere Antoinne, a much-loved priest in the area, who for over fifty years was one of the best known religious figures in the city. At the time, New Orleans was a melting pot of cultures with a more European (French and Spanish) presence than American. It had also a large Creole population; Creole was in fact one of the major languages used in many districts. Grand dances for people of colour, known as Quadroon Balls, were the height of popularity amongst city society. Large sections were Roman Catholic and the French influence was especially strong, while white Anglo-Saxon Americans were looked upon as barbarians and dullards.

Jacques Paris

Marie's husband's name is given as Jacques Paris, a quadroon, and a free man of colour, reputedly from Santo Domingo. Marie was also dark skinned, with a reddish cast. She was also said to be exceptionally beautiful. She seems to have been a mixture of black, Native American, and white and, it is said, boasted a regal ancestry in each.

About a year after her marriage, something strange seems to have happened—Jacques seems to have vanished completely and Marie started calling herself "The Widow Paris" indicating that he was dead. However, there is no record of his death until *six* years after the marriage, which means that five years of his life are unaccounted for. Was he still married to Marie? Or was he indeed dead and his death had not been registered? The latter seems unlikely because Marie herself was a staunch Catholic and attended the St. Louis Cathedral on a daily basis. She had also gone with Pere Antoinne to attend victims of an epidemic of yellow fever that was sweeping the city. She was living in a house on what is now North Rampart Street and which had formerly belonged to her father, who was believed to have been called Charles Laveau. However, after the first year of her marriage, she seems to have been living there alone.

About a year and a half after her marriage, Marie began to advertise herself as a "hairdresser," entering the homes of prosperous white people in the well-to-do areas of New Orleans. These were pre-beauty parlour times when wealthy women called in their own "professional beauticians" to arrange and coiffeur their hair prior to important social engagements. Many of these "beauticians" were free women of colour. It was not clear as to whether Marie was a "hairdresser" or not—some said that, besides styling hair, she sold gris-gris. Others still say that she was a prostitute, visiting the husbands of those whose hair she styled. It has to be remembered that New Orleans was not an American city; it was a mixture of French, Spanish, and Creole, and standards, moral and otherwise, were quite different. When the Americans did settle in the city, they were shocked by the lax and flagrant ways of those around them. All accounts agree however, that this period was the start of Marie Laveau's career as a principal Voodoo queen in New Orleans.

During the mid-to-late 1850s, Voodoo fever was at its height in New Orleans with Marie presiding over what were rapidly coming to be known as "shows" in various parts of the city. These drew large crowds, a good number of them from the white districts, and were always fuelled by strong liquor and sexuality. No matter how many times the law tried to close them down and arrest Marie, she always seemed to elude punishment and the gatherings continued unabated. The horror and thrill of witchcraft coupled with unbridled sexuality provided a heady mix for all kinds of people inhabiting the city. Marie was becoming incredibly rich. So rich in fact, that she was able to build another house, near Milneburg.

Christophe Dunimy de Glapion

Marie seems to have been enjoying herself and familiarizing herself with the developing culture of the city. A few years after the "death" of Jacques Paris, she took up with another quadroon man named Christophe Dunimy de Glapion. Like Jacques Paris, he was originally from Santo Domingo and a free man of colour. He was also something of a war hero and had fought in the Battle of New Orleans. Soon he had moved in with Marie and lived with her until he died in 1835. Little is known about their relationship except that Marie bore him fifteen children in rapid succession and that they remained together until his death.

Shortly after she took up with Glapion, Marie began to advance herself as a Voodoo practitioner and soon she was a Voodoo queen. The New Orleans Voodoo cult was at that time in disarray and she was competing with a number of other queens, such as Samitie Dede and Marie Saloppe. Taking some of the methods that had been espoused by Dr. John (or John Bayou as she called him), she began to turn the Voodoo gatherings into spectacles, to which she often invited white people on a paying basis. Marie built her ceremonies on the trappings of Le Grand Zombi—the snake, the black cat, and the roosters. She also added a sexual content as most of her gatherings usually ended in a kind of mass fornication. She also added some of her stock Roman Catholic items: the statues, the incense, the holy water together with prayers, and invocations. She took issue with those who said that the followers of Voodoo had originally been Devil-worshippers and branded it as one of the world's most ancient religions, far older than Christianity. From Voodoo, Marie argued, the Christian faith had taken many of its ideas, and she was only an instrument, letting those old powers free again. Many considered what she had done to be incredibly blasphemous and she was denounced by some as "a servant of Satan."

The rival queens were quickly deposed and driven away and soon Marie Laveau reigned supreme in all areas of New Orleans. Some of her rivals actually died, and it was thought that Marie had used some extremely powerful gris-gris against them. Others swore loyalty to her and became a kind of sub-queen in certain areas of the city. The Widow Paris now thrived. She took charge of the revels in Congo Square and presided over gatherings on the shores of Lake Pontchartrain; all in defiance of bans that had been enacted. She remained untouched by the law, and though a number of charges were laid against her, none of them ever reached the courts. This was put down to her great "magic" although it had probably more to do with her contacts in high places. And seemingly, she became incredibly wealthy. Using the contacts that she had made while carrying out her "hairdressing," she began to draw affluent whites into the Voodoo culture. She attracted great publicity, which added to the uniqueness of her gatherings. Rumours spread that she was blackmailing several prominent city politicians, but nothing could be proved.

She was able to buy several new houses all across the city from which she conducted much of her Voodoo work. Her main base of operations was a small cottage on St. Anne Street, between North Rampart and Burgundy Streets, close to Congo Square, which she had allegedly obtained through her gris-gris. Around 1830, a young man of quality, from an extremely wealthy and prosperous family had been arrested in connection with a crime where the evidence against him was supposedly very strong. He protested his innocence, but it looked as though he was going to be found guilty and sentenced. In desperation, his father consulted Marie and offered to reward her handsomely for her aid. On the very day of the trial, Marie entered the St. Louis Cathedral very early in the morning and knelt for several hours at the altar rail. She had three Guinea peppers in her mouth. Then she secretly crept into the courtroom and places these peppers under a cushion of the judge's chair. The trial went ahead but, surprisingly, the judge dismissed the case and the young man was freed. Overjoyed, the father presented Marie with the small cottage that he owned on St. Anne Street where she was to live until her reported death. There was no doubt that her magic had somehow influenced the judge's decision and the gris-gris that she used were typical of her magic—a combination of older, African elements (the Guinea peppers) with her prayers in a

Catholic Cathedral. The mixture was both a potent and effective one, appealing to the innate desire for Christian miracles as well as the native African belief in magic.

In 1835, Christophe Glapion died at the house on St. Anne Street and his death seems to have occurred in June. His age was given as sixty-six. His funeral attracted large numbers, at which Marie sold her gris-gris, told fortunes, and removed curses. She was never one to ignore a business opportunity. After his death, the "Widow Paris" (Marie had never renounced that title, even when she was living with Glapion, perhaps in deference to the Catholic Church) became even more powerful across the city. Similar to Doctor John, she had agents stationed in every part of New Orleans (she ran almost what amounted to a secret service that kept her supplied with information) and she knew many of the secrets of local society, probably culled from her "hairdressing" days. She was also not averse to employing certain techniques that she had observed in some other cultures into Voodoo ritual—one of which was the famous Voodoo doll.

Mommet

Clay images, stuck with pins in order to do harm, were common in some West African cultures, but not all. The purpose of such magic was to fashion an image of a proposed victim and magically link it with its human counterpart. Thus, whatever befell the image would also befall the victim. This harmful aspect was a feature in many English and Continental witch trials. In England it was referred to as a "mommet," appearing in a number of both Scottish and West Country allegations. In Africa, witchcraft dolls were sometimes used to excite passion in the heart of a desired partner or to make individuals do things that they would not ordinarily have done. Occasionally, the image was harmed with the intent of harming the individual, but this was not widespread amongst the West African slaves. Marie introduced some of the European belief into Voodoo with the notion of the dolls that gave her power over her enemies.

Papa Limba

Marie also had a number of enemies in the Voodoo world. From time to time other Voodoo practitioners would try to usurp her position in New Orleans but she was able to see them all off. The most famous of these was a man who called himself Papa Limba (Papa Limba was a Creole name for St. Peter that held great and magical connotations amongst the slaves) and who operated out of a house on Frenchman Street around the late 1840s. Little is known about him except that he seems to have been a rather refined elderly gentleman, a free man of colour, who affected the stylish European dress of a black frock coat when he went out in public. Papa Limba was said to control shadows that he sent out to do “dark business” and harm people. This idea may have been the origin of some of the zombie stories around New Orleans at the time. The Papa used to boast that his magic was stronger than that of Marie Laveau and that his gris-gris could “do away with her” if he so chose. He also claimed to be the direct and true descendant of Doctor John and that Marie was only an impostor. For a while he flourished and may actually have been something of a threat to the empire that Marie was building, but his sudden and inexplicable death put an end to any challenge that he might have offered and only increased Marie’s standing. It was widely believed that her own superior powers killed him.

Mama Eunice

Another competitor was Mama (or Maman) Eunice who sold gris-gris and poudres around Bayou St. John. She does not seem to have been much of a threat to Marie, but she did conduct a number of gatherings at which a mixture of rum and gunpowder was consumed and frenzied, sexual dancing took place—a mirror of Marie’s own gatherings. Outraged at this, Marie warned her to stop. For a while, Mama Eunice took no notice and continued to hawk her charms around the city and engage in sexual antics at her gatherings. In the end, Marie openly threatened her with death and this seems to have focused the Mama’s mind. Marie instructed her to leave New Orleans and not to return and Mama seems to have readily complied.

Maison Blanche

Marie eventually bought another house near Milneburg called "Maison Blanche" and, though she used it herself for various activities, it became the centre of operations for her daughter, who was to become the second Marie Laveau. The house was described as having six rooms, one of which was a large common room where special ceremonies and dancing took place. All non-members of Marie's' "cult" were excluded. Many of the Voodoo rituals that were carried out there are thought to have been Petro Voodoo, performed largely by slaves from Santo Domingo, who always seemed to be around the house.

Marie now moved around the city in the style of a film star today. Everywhere the Widow Paris went, she was accompanied by bodyguards and attendants who kept the public (and the law) at bay. They were led by one of her sons—a burly man who bore the name Christophe Paris and who acted as a kind of "head of security" during her appearances.

The gatherings became wilder and less inhibited. Marie usually wore a full-length blue dress and mostly she was the only one wearing any clothes at all. The display of public nudity, coupled with the sexual dancing, outraged the moral guardians of New Orleans society.

In the mid-1850s, Marie Laveau began to take an interest in the welfare of prisoners. Previously, during a yellow fever epidemic, she had nursed the sick, which had given her the reputation of being a thoroughly kind woman in reality. She began visiting Parish Prison and became a well-known figure there, particularly amongst the men awaiting execution. It is said that she sometimes prayed with them or else prayed for them in the prison chapel. She brought food and even sat and talked earnestly with some of the more violent inmates. Gradually her visits came to be noticed by the Press.

John Adam and Anthony Deslisle

The first report of her visits was in 1852 (although they had been going on long before that), when she visited the cells of two murderers—John Adam and Anthony Deslisle—who had both been convicted of the brutal murder of a young girl. They had bludgeoned the child to death as they attempted to rob the house of her mistress, Madam Chevillon, but had been subsequently caught, brought to trial, found guilty, and sentenced to death. Their trial excited great interest all across New Orleans, possibly because of the viciousness of the crime. Marie visited frequently and talked seriously with them, especially with Deslisle.

On the day of the execution, a gallows had been erected on Orleans Street and a large crowd assembled. It was a beautiful day, warm and cloudless, with the sun shining brightly. Many of the people had brought their children to see the execution. Upon his appearance on the scaffold, Deslisle began a long, rambling, and almost hysterical oration, proclaiming his innocence and castigating the "barbarous Americans." As a Frenchman, he declared and desired a grand funeral that only Frenchmen should attend. In the middle of his harangue, he suddenly gave a terrified scream and pointed upwards. Overhead, a black cloud had suddenly appeared, whirling and swirling like a living thing. What had been a beautiful morning suddenly became a dull, gray twilight. A moment later, the sky turned almost black and people murmured that it was "like the Crucifixion." Rain began to fall in a flood. Despite the increasingly jittery mob of onlookers, the execution went ahead as scheduled. As both bodies dropped, lightning suddenly split the sky followed by a clap of thunder, signalling the impending doom. The crowd screamed and panicked but held firm. The bodies hung on the end of their ropes, which were now cut, allowing the corpses to fall to the ground. Suddenly, Deslisle moved and appeared to be trying to crawl, even though his right arm was bloody and broken. Adam, too seemed to be still breathing. The crowd surged forward and the police had to use their clubs in order to hold them back. Carrying the victims into the prison, they attempted to revive them with only partial success. Ten minutes later, the prisoners were carried out and hanged once more, this time quite successfully. All at once the storm clouds passed and the sun shone through again. On the edge of the crowd, a tall woman, her face covered by a veil but her hands showing her to be a woman of colour, turned away and disappeared into the maze of side streets and the whisper went about that it was Marie Laveau. The Adam-Deslisle case was a major talking point for many years after, but it was not the only such case in which Marie was involved.

Antoine Cambre

Antoine Cambre, a Creole from an old and well-established family, had shot and killed an old city lamplighter during a drunken argument. Cambre had led a wild and dissolute life—a fact that would count against him when on trial; it was likely that he would be hanged for the murder. This was indeed the result of the trial. Marie visited him in his cell and said, "Before you die, what would you like to eat?" The young man had other things on his mind besides a meal; however, Marie promised him that she would cook him a gumbo like no other that he had ever tasted. She brought it to him on the day of his execution and when the guards came to take him to the scaffold, they found him writhing in agony on the floor of the cell. He died soon after and although poison was suspected, no trace of it could be found. There was no doubt, however, that Cambre had eaten some of Marie Laveau's gumbo.

James Mullin

This was not the only high profile gift that she was to bring a condemned man. In 1859, she achieved notoriety all over New Orleans by bringing the murderer James Mullin his coffin. This coffin was both interesting and unique as it was decorated both inside and out with religious pictures. Marie and some others had worked on it for a long time beforehand. There was also the rather gruesome feature of a pillow made from the dress of Mullin's three-year-old daughter. Marie visited him and prayed with him every day until he was hanged.

Marie's Other Good Deeds

She further visited a number of other notorious murderers, all of whom added to her reputation as a "witchy" woman and a Voodoo queen. Among those she worked with were Heinrich Haas, Peter Smith, and Joseph Linsay, all of whom were sentenced to hang. Haas in particular received a great deal of her attention and she is said to have helped him decorate his condemned cell with many religious pictures. Her attentions toward Joseph Bazar in 1868 proved to have a positive result. Bazar had been convicted of killing his wife's lover, by battering him to death with a large stone whilst in a fit of drunken rage. As he stood on the gallows with a rope around his neck, a messenger suddenly galloped up, carrying a Commutation of Sentence, signed by the

State Governor Warmouth. This was put down to the supernatural intervention of Marie Laveau who had been exceptionally sympathetic towards Bazar.

Despite her seemingly good works, both the Church and many upright New Orleans citizens still remained hostile towards the Widow Paris, declaring that her visits to the prisons were no more than publicity-seeking exercises. This hostility was exacerbated by newspaper reports that Marie had imported a "heathen idol" from Africa and had used it in her rites, sacrificing goats and cockerels to it whilst naked followers danced all around it. "Voodoo Virgin" trumpeted the headlines together with the claim that Marie was replacing the holy statues with pagan idols. The rift between Marie and the Church widened and though she still attended Mass from time to time, her reception was distinctly cool. Many believed that she had taken Voodoo down a diabolical path and into the realms of darkest sorcery.

Marie Laveau was now an old woman and folktales speak of a withered crone with yellow skin and tufts of white hair peeking from under a dark skullcap. She was now arthritic and a little infirm, but her eyes, say the accounts, were still bright and full of hellfire. However, not even a witch can live forever and it is thought that the first Marie, the Widow Paris, died somewhere around 1880/81, though nobody is actually sure. By that time, she was succeeded by another Marie Laveau, who was in all probability her own daughter.

Marie Glapion: Marie II

Marie Glapion, who was to become Marie II, was born on 2nd February 1827, the daughter of Marie Laveau and Christophe Glapion. She was only one of Marie's many children, but she was intensely beautiful and bore a remarkable resemblance to her mother. Indeed, the legend said that somehow the first Marie had magically "rejuvenated" herself, a notion that her successor did not dismiss. Similar to her mother, she had begun work as a "hairdresser" and using some of her mother's money had opened an establishment on Royal Street. Later, she would open another premise on Bourbon Street, between St. Peter Street and Toulouse Street. In both establishments, she established a "Voodoo altar" that were said to hold statues of both St. Peter and the

Virgin, both covered with a sheet. From time to time there would be gatherings at the back of these shops at which, according to local folklore, rum would be consumed and queer rituals observed.

Whilst the first Marie Laveau had exhibited many endearing and humanitarian traits, such as her helping of those in distress and her nursing of the victims of yellow fever, few of these were evident in her daughter. The second Marie inspired and ruled by fear. Gradually, she took on a greater role as a Voodoo queen, driving her aged mother more and more into the background. At the house in St. Anne's Street, Marie II added a narrow back room and it was here that the first Marie Laveau was kept, practically under house arrest, whilst her daughter reigned supreme in New Orleans.

Mama Antoine

Every Monday night, Marie II would go to the house of a Voodoo practitioner called Mama Antoine on Dumaine Street, where gatherings were often held. These gatherings were known as parterres and were designed to encourage the spirits to come amongst them. A grand feast was reputedly laid out for the loa on a white table that included congris, apples, red peppers, chillies, and oranges. These feasts were overseen by a woman named Georgina Laveau, who was thought to have been a sister of Marie II and another who styled herself "Josephine Bayou."

There was dancing, too. A popular mystical dance called Fe Chauffe was described as being "really wild" and that was performed with the dancers often balancing lighted candles on their heads. A number of white ladies were also said to be in attendance, each paying Marie a substantial amount of money for being there—many of whom copulated with quadroons and other black men who were there. Many of these Monday night gatherings had the reputation of being little more than orgies disguised in quasi-religious trappings.

This brought in another side of Marie II's activities—her acting as a procuress. The Maison Blanche was already recognized, even in her mother's time, as a "place of ill repute" where white men could often meet young coloured girls, but at least the elder Marie had the sense to keep such activities relatively secret. Her daughter had no such inhibitions and let it be known far and wide that she offered such services for those who wanted them.

Doctor Jim

The major male figure in Marie II's life was a certain man of colour—part Native American, part black—named James Alexander, the self-styled Doctor Jim. He proved her first real challenge. Doctor Jim had come from Mississippi, with his wife, who was by no means a Voodoo practitioner herself. There were a number who said that James Alexander wasn't his real name at all—that it was Laurensky Avery—and that he was part Native American. Many people simply referred to him as "Indian Jim." Unlike Marie II, he was more sympathetic to his clients in the way that the original Marie Laveau had been—it is said that his gris-gris were more about healing than doing harm. Gradually, a kind of feud began to grow between the two Voodoo practitioners, and Marie II clearly saw him as a palpable threat to her carefully constructed empire. The feud was reported in the *Daily Picayune* as a "Voodoo war" in New Orleans and stated that supporters of both factions had threatened to clash, leading to the call-out for police support who dispersed the crowds and arrested several individuals for disorderly conduct.

Doctor Jim seems to have done quite well and soon was able to buy a house near Johnston Street, which he used as a base of operations. His influence now extended across the Mississippi River to Algiers, where he is said to have driven out several evil spirits, including demons, which had been sent by Marie II to torment her enemies. He was quite willing to work with some of the babalawo there, including a well-respected leader named Papa Sol. In many of his treatments and "exorcisms" in the Algiers district, Doctor Jim frequently used beer, which he would sprinkle over furniture in "diseased houses" or over people who were possessed by unfriendly loa. He began to preside over a number of Voodoo gatherings and was reckoned to be one of the "best Hoodoo dancers in New Orleans." He mixed traditional Voodoo dances with more recognized formats such as the Calinda and also added an element of Indian war dance that made the whole performance seem frenzied and bizarre. Unlike Marie II, he was also extremely careful to keep his followers out of "police trouble" and although his dances attracted the interest of the authorities, nobody was ever arrested. He ran several large gatherings out at Lake Pontchartrain, some of which were conducted on boats, adding to their novelty. There is no doubt that Doctor Jim was a great showman, often appearing clad only in a long blue sash and white frieze drawers.

Marie II's response to this was to surround herself with more and more gruesome and "mystical" trappings and to adopt a more haughty and mysterious image. Her rooms now contained elements of the dead, such as skulls and human rib cages; she is said to have kept complete skeletons in her armoire. Poisonous snakes were said to crawl across the carpets and deadly spiders hung in cobwebs from the ceiling. Simply to visit her must have taken a great deal of courage. She concentrated even more or curses and love potions. Her speciality was said to be a special file (seasoning) which, if added to food (such as gumbo) would induce both love and lust in those who consumed it. But despite the now-fantastic stories about her, she seemed powerless to limit the growing influence of Doctor Jim, especially in the Algiers districts. Then she had a stroke of luck.

One Yoy Lisvaudais

Doctor Jim met a sudden and violent death, which many people attributed to the supernatural influence of Marie Laveau. Whilst treating a simple-minded boy named One Yoy Lisvaudais, his patient suddenly and inexplicably became irritated and struck him on the temple with a rock. Doctor Jim was dazed, but recovered temporarily. However, the wound became infected and developed into an abscess that eventually killed him after several days. Many in New Orleans said that this was the work of his great rival in her house at the Maison Blanche.

Clementine Alexander

His estate now descended into chaos as his widow, Clementine, tried to claim her inheritance. All that he seemed to have left her was his house on Johnston Street, but there was also a great deal of money hidden somewhere. There were legal complications about claiming the house because it was revealed that his name had been neither James Alexander or Laurinsky Avery as had been commonly supposed, but rather Charles LeFontaine. It also emerged that he had owned other properties—mainly between Gentilly and Spanish Fort—under a variety of names, but that all the paperwork had been done in

the names of James Alexander, or Charles LeFontaine. It was years before the case was finally finished, although it was thought that there was a vast amount of money—perhaps lodged under yet another name—that has never been recovered, even today. Doctor Jim's death, however, left Marie II pretty much as the undisputed leading Voodoo practitioner in New Orleans. A few figures, such as Papa Sol and Madame Roux raised their heads, trying to claim Doctor Jim's legacy in Algiers, but she was able to see them off and her reign was absolute across the city.

On 16th June 1881, many newspapers in New Orleans carried the story that Marie Laveau, the famous Voodoo queen, had died. This was, of course, the Widow Paris, the first Marie Laveau, who had been languishing in the back room of the Maison Blanche whilst her daughter conducted her Voodoo gatherings. She was now said to be an old and withered woman whom very few people saw and who, when she was released from her room, shuffled vacantly about the house in a vaguely bewildered state. Of course, as soon as her death was announced, legends began to form around this event. One said that there had been a thunderstorm over the house at the very moment of her death; another said that there had been shrieks and howls and clanking of chains from the room itself and that a strong smell of sulphur had pervaded the general area around the Maison Blanche and St. Anne Street. However, the most astonishing thing about the death was that before Marie died, she had been attended to by a priest only hours before. She had renounced the Zombi and all her "old African wickedness" and had accepted the Sacraments. In other words, she had died a good Catholic. Indeed, some members of her family seethed with indignation at the mere suggestion that she had ever practiced Voodoo. As part of her will, she urged those who loved her to administer to the fever-ridden hospitals of the city. She was now treated as a virtual saint, both by those who had followed her and by the Church—something of an achievement! At the time of her death, her daughter, Marie Glapion (Marie II) was fifty-four years old and immediately formally assumed the name "Marie Laveau," although she'd been using it for years.

Following the death of the Widow Paris, cracks and schisms began to appear in the Glapion family. Marie II was unmarried, although she had several lovers and reputedly a good number of children, some of whom had changed their names in order to marry. Given their newfound "decent" status, they began to look disapprovingly on their mother as what was effectively the mistress of a brothel. Some of them also disapproved of her "Voodoo ways" and wanted little to do with her.

Madame LeGrande

Marie II also banished her sister, "Madame Legrande," from the Maison Blanche over some trifling matter and sent her to live in the St. Ann Street house. Madam Legrande threatened to have her new home torn down. Marie was also in dispute with the children from her mother's first marriage to Jacques Paris who now styled themselves as "Laveaus." She had seized as much money as she could from her mother's fortune, denying her first children any portion. She evicted John Laveau from a house that she owned and turned both him and his family out onto the streets. She was now pretty much an outcast from the majority of her family—both for the treatment of her mother and her indifference towards the family. This was exacerbated by her relationship with a "Doctor Theophile," an old and much loved babalawo who operated in the Algiers district and who claimed to be a direct descendant of Doctor John. He had gathered many of Doctor Jim's followers who were incredibly hostile towards Marie II, whom they blamed for the death of James Alexander. Either she or her agents seem to have been responsible for the death of Doctor Theophile as well, for he appears to have died after eating some poisoned file that was sprinkled on his food. Many people blamed Marie II for his death, just as they had blamed her for that of Doctor Jim, and gradually a groundswell of hostility was building up. Marie, however, seemed unperturbed.

Lafcadio Hearn

Marie II took plenty of lovers, one of whom was reputedly the writer Lafcadio Hearn, whom she had met in 1880. If there was a relationship between the two of them, it was not long-lived. Hearn himself described her as "a vampire" and distanced himself from her. Nevertheless, she remained a good-looking woman, even well into her fifties, and entertained a stream of paramours, many of them white. Both her sexual and political prowess in the world of Voodoo were now at their height and she was able to buy a small house on the banks of Lake Pontchartrain where she began to live and conduct her revels out on the Lake. She took a page from Doctor Jim's book and began to conduct some of her gatherings on boats and barges in the water.

There is some mystery surrounding Marie II's death in the latter half of the 1890s. There are many who insist that she was drowned. By this time, she had become "very wild" and her gris-gris had become extremely expensive. Her gatherings bordered on the darker side of Voodoo with Le Grand Zombi raised as an evil god for her followers to worship. There were rumours of blood sacrifice and it is known that the police were keeping a watchful eye on all her ceremonies. During one of these gatherings at Pontchartrain, according to old folk legend, a massive storm blew up out on the Lake and swept inland. It moved with such speed that the dancers along the shore were caught unawares and swept into the water. One of these was Marie herself. In another version of the same story, the storm blew up at night and swept inland, sweeping away the house on the shore in which Marie was sleeping. Her body was never recovered.

Other versions of her demise, however, claim that she was poisoned. It is known that Marie II had many enemies, and it has been suggested that she ate poisoned food, which they had tampered with. However, this version is problematic; it is known that Marie was extremely particular about everything she ate and drank, particularly because of the fear of poisoning. Skilled at the art of poisoning, she would have been well aware of the ease with which food could be doctored and would therefore be wary. Suspicion fell on Madame Legrand who at this time. was trying to make the Laveau family respectable and distance it from Voodoo practices and from the Voodoo queens. The woman, however, flatly denied any murder attempt and nothing really could be proved. Whatever the circumstances of her death may have been, it seems to have occurred around June 1897, as an inscription on the Laveau-Glapion tomb in St. Louis Cemetery No. 1 testifies:

> "Marie Philome Glapion, decedee le 11 Juin 1897. Agee de Soizante-deux ans."

A great many Voodoo followers still take this as the last resting place of the "real Marie Laveau," forgetting that there was one before her—the Widow Paris. There were some, however, who insisted that she was not dead at all, and that her "death" was a trick designed to throw the authorities off her scent. It was said that the police had been planning to arrest her and that she was "lying low" for a time before making a reappearance. She was allegedly "seen" in various parts of New Orleans—in shops, walking on the street, standing in the doorway of a house—but, even after some time, she failed to reappear. Besides, ever since the death of the Widow Paris in 1881, Marie II had a rival waiting in the wings for her Voodoo crown. This was Malvina Latour.

Malvina Latour: Marie III

Very little is known about Malvina Latour. At the time of the Widow Paris's death, she is described as a big, heavy-set, raw-boned woman, roughly in her mid-forties. Sometimes she claimed to be a daughter of Marie II by a black man, at other times she did not, and there is no evidence that she was. She was, however, extremely handsome, and carried some of the smouldering good-looks of Marie II and the Widow Paris. She had a sophisticated bearing and was unquestionably of high intelligence. It was whispered that she had been privately educated, unusual for a woman of colour. Indeed, it was claimed that she had a brother in the State Legislature but this remains unproven. After the death of the Widow Paris, she began calling herself "Marie Laveau" (making her, in effect, Marie III) though probably she had no intention of setting herself up as a major Voodoo queen.

Despite the fact that Marie II was still living, Malvina began to conduct a number of ceremonies in the city, the most famous being the one on St. John's Eve. These practices began to return towards the traditional practices of Rada Voodoo—the old religion that had been brought from Dahomey. She attempted to remove all of the Catholic trappings that had been introduced by the first Marie and to return the revels to their purest African state. She was a Catholic herself and looked at Voodoo as a profession, not as a religion. Therefore, her addition of Catholic imagery and ritual was considered sacrilegious in the

Voodoo world. However, her grip on the Voodoo world was not as tight as that of Marie II and the latter did not consider her all that great a threat. Because there was a slight chance that Malvina Latour was her daughter, she may have tolerated the revels on St. John's Eve and the limited gris-gris that Malvina sold.

In the meantime, Madame Legrand struggled to distance the Laveaus from the taint of Voodoo and to make the family name (and her own) thoroughly respectable in New Orleans society. She drew her family closer to the Catholic Church (she was a devout Catholic herself) and many of them renounced the Voodoo ways and denied that they had ever been associated with the African religion. Some of them may truly not have had any association with Voodoo at all. In 1903, the house on St. Anne Street was pulled down and with it: the last traces of the original Marie Laveau.

Acting supposedly as Marie III, Malvina Latour failed to bring any sort of cohesion to the New Orleans Voodoo cults, nor was she able to hold the existing worshippers together in any recognizable cult. After Marie II's death, voodoo in New Orleans began to fragment into minor cults and gatherings.

Leon Juniper

A group centered around Leon Juniper, a black man who had worked with the Laveaus and had, at one time, been a lover of Marie II. Juniper was not really a major Voodoo practitioner but his close associations with Marie II had given him some credibility in the Voodoo world. Each day, he would walk to St. Louis Cemetery No. 1, where Marie was buried, and perform a ritual known as the "four corners," which is still practiced today.

The person performing the rite enters the cemetery and goes to each corner in turn, making a wish as soon as he or she reaches the corner in question. Then the practitioner walks quickly along two blocks to the Church of Our Lady of Guadeloupe on North Rampart Street and says a prayer, kneeling before the stature of St. Expedite. During the performance of this ritual, Leon Juniper claimed that he heard the voice of Marie II speaking to him and in this way he was able to convey her instructions to her followers.

Miss Jackson

There was also a "Miss Jackson," a well-known black Voodoo queen who had learned her trade with Marie II and Leon Juniper. She made a great thing of dancing with a deadly python at some of the Voodoo ceremonies in a house on Roman Street. She also distilled liquor and sold it to the participants because nobody could bring in strong drink from outside. There was animal sacrifice (usually a goat or a rooster) at all her ceremonies.

Madame Augustine

Another figure of the time was Madame Augustine, a stately looking woman of colour. After Marie II died, she took over some of the surviving cult and held it together for a short while. She was considered to be very beautiful. After 1899, however, she disappeared for a long time but turned up again about the beginning of the 20th century. However, all her former beauty was now gone and she presented quite a terrifying appearance. This was not enhanced by the fact that her left eye was missing. She used this disfigurement to her advantage, claiming that the socket had supernatural powers. But even so, she was not to enjoy anything similar to her former prestige as a Voodoo queen.

Angele Lavasseur

Several of the queens referred to themselves as "Marie Laveau," which makes tracing the true inheritance of the name exceptionally difficult. One of these, Angele Lavasseur, certainly owned a cabin on the shores of Lake Pontchartrain, where she held weekly revels, mainly for white people. During one of her revels, a major storm swept the Lake and smashed her cabin, drowning all there, including Angele herself. This may be the origin of the drowning story concerning Marie II.

Marie Comtesse

The most celebrated of the New Orleans Voodoo queens of the early 20th century was known as "Marie Comtesse" although she also styled herself "Marie Laveau" or sometimes "Marie IV" (Malvina Latour, or Marie III, disappeared into relative obscurity) but who was, in fact, no relation to the Laveau clan. She was famous for her "revels" that were nothing more than orgies over which she presided. Her speciality was to provide shapely young girls who danced naked for customers attending her dances out near Bayou St. John. It was said that in the swamps, she buried an absolute fortune, none of which has ever been found. She was always very grandly dressed with a white shoulder bag in which she carried her gris-gris that she distributed to paying customers at various times during the night.

Her end was strange and sudden. During one of the revels, she leaned against a wooden post on the edge of a swamp. The post, which was partly rotted, suddenly gave way and she fell awkwardly, breaking her neck. "La Comtesse," as she was known, was buried in the Wishing Vault in St. Louis Cemetery No. 2. She was practically the last of the great Voodoo queens of New Orleans and no other would manage to hold the various cults that existed in the city together in the way that the old Voodoo queens had done. The era of the Laveaus and others would be counted as a kind of Golden Age of Voodoo in the city. After that it would fragment and splinter into a number of cults.

American Voodoo: Charleston

Conjure men and babalawo were to be found everywhere in Charleston, selling gris-gris, and allegedly commanding the dead whom they called from their tombs.

John Domingo

Although Marie Laveau was the most famous of all the Voodoo queens, and New Orleans was certainly widely considered to be steeped in African magic, there were other sinister practitioners in other parts of the country. Charleston, South Carolina was also viewed as something of a Voodoo city, and John Domingo, the Black Constable, was clearly a rival to Dr. John back in New Orleans. In the late 1800s, Domingo, who had formerly lived in the Carolina Low Country, was considered to be the greatest and deadliest sorcerer in the whole state since the days of Gullah Jack Pritchard, a notable conjure-man who had been involved in an uprising amongst the slaves around the time of the alleged Denmark Vesey slave revolt almost a century earlier.

He was considered to be more powerful than many of his contemporaries, such as Dicky Breaux, the black Voodoo king of Dorchester Road, or Cut-Bread Jack, who lived for a time on Charlotte Street. Domingo himself lived in a queer, shabby old house with a peaked roof on Magazine Corner where it led into Mazyck Street (although it doesn't bear that name now). The house has long since been demolished to be replaced by a stretch of waste ground and grass. The house had been formerly owned by a Dutchman who had been forced to flee from Holland for some blasphemous and unmentionable crime and who ran the place as a shop. The house had an ill name even before Domingo arrived, and it had an even worse one when he lived there.

John Domingo was an extremely dangerous man—a necromancer and a sorcerer of frightening power. He was a huge man, powerfully built, his body wrapped in a huge Union-blue greatcoat in the winter and with darkly glittering eyes and a massive nose, hooked like the beak of a predatory bird. His long, shoulder-length hair was tied in thick tufts with a shoestring along with several long and greasy strands hanging down the side of his face. He always wore a silver ring, shaped like a snake, on the fourth finger of one hand. He said that it had been made somewhere along the Congo River and that it held great power—the power of Le Grand Zombi.

The street in which Domingo lived had once been extremely respectable and had been the abode of many of the old Charleston families of quality—the Northrops, the Gasdens, and the Malones. Now it had a "run down" feel about it and had such an evil name that few decent people would even mention it. An old legend stated that it had lost its good name after John Domingo himself had cursed it, though why he did so is uncertain. People scoffed that nobody could curse an entire street, but one look at Mazyck Street could convince otherwise. It was dirty and filled with piles of rubbish where dogs rooted all day and was to remain so until around the end of the First World War, when part of it at least was pulled down. Those who had to travel through always hurried and did not delay, and the last of the quality folks, who still lived there because they had no money to move and nobody would buy their properties, seldom opened either their doors or windows.

The Black Constable as he was called, did not seem to be bound by white men's laws or the laws of Charleston. He made his own laws and his neighbours respected that. An old man who lived next door to him saw what Domingo kept in his back yard and it terrified him, but he was forced to shrug his shoulders and say nothing because he feared the Black Constable. Though the people of Charleston feared him, they still consulted him and bought his gris-gris—bags filled with goofer dust (dust gathered from a grave under a full moon or sometimes made with the powdered bones of corpses), lucky jacks, and Voodoo sticks. He could sell charms that would make any man a favourite with the ladies, no matter how ugly he was. There is a story that Domingo sold a hideous old man named Isaac Motte a charm that had the young girls tormenting him, even though he was elderly and ugly. He was supposed to curse individuals by simply shaking a poudre on the ground where they'd passed. He reputedly obtained some of his gris-gris from the old cemeteries on Ghost Island, a place that was rumoured to be very badly haunted. Indeed the popular story was that the Constable could raise the dead with a snap of his fingers and make them do his bidding. Some called him a "Zombi man."

His neighbours knew better than to cross him. Once he had a dispute with a man who lived across the road from him and who owned a well that gave sweet and pure water. The Constable sent a rainbow to suck the well dry and it never gave water of any kind again. Women were also fearful of combing their hair out of their windows or of sweeping in front of their doors, in case the Constable would collect stray hairs or some other personal item and use it against them. There was great rivalry amongst some of the women around Mazyck Street, and they consulted with John Domingo to do their rivals harm or to ruin their looks. At his height, he maintained a great number of wealthy clients, and was reputedly one of the richest men in Charleston, although he chose to live as though he were a pauper.

He had a curious thing, similar to a whirligig, on the top of his curious old house, by which it was said, he could control the wind and summon up storms. He also sold favourable winds to sailors and fishermen. There were many stories about this. In one, a fisherman named John Akiss sent his old mother to buy a favourable wind from the Constable, but she, being an elderly woman, forgot. John Akiss then bought a wind from another sorcerer—the best he could do before he put to sea. John Domingo heard about this and took it personally. He sent a storm after Akiss's boat so that it was driven aground and wrecked on the Drunken Dick shoal and Akiss and his crew of nine men were drowned. And all through a simple act of forgetfulness. This reminded people not to trifle when they dealt with John Domingo.

But it was for his dealings with the dead that Domingo was best known. He was a necromancer of the first order and his neighbours stated that the shadows that clustered around his doorway after nightfall were the spirits of the dead whom he had summoned to him. Others said that they were lurking corpses that he had brought from the tomb for his own ends and purposes. Many said that Domingo executed his own brand of law in the area—hence his nickname, the Black Constable—and that he used the shambling dead to enforce it. Those who crossed him or misbehaved badly within his area often found strange and unpleasant things happening to them. They claimed to have seen ghosts and walking dead men and they suffered from ill fortune, or simply sometimes disappeared. All this was attributed to the terrible necromantic powers of John Domingo.

The Black Constable's end came about in a sudden and strange way. He was at the height of his pride and power in Charleston and was pretty much acting as the law in certain quarters of the city. One evening, he pursued two robbers who had violated some residents in his district. The robbers tried to escape but Domingo cornered them in Mount Pleasant and brought them back with him by river to Market Street. Stepping ashore he held one on each side, each by the scruff of the neck.

"See!" he cried to the assembled onlookers. "I am just like Jesus, with a thief on either hand." He paused as if considering something. "Only I'm more powerful than Jesus!" Again he paused almost in mid-sentence. No one knew why, nobody saw anything, except the Black Constable. For a moment, he stood upright, as straight as a post, a look of baffled bewilderment crossing his face. Then foam started to run down from the corners of his mouth. He rose up onto his toes as if something were pulling him up with a kind of hideous strength and several by-standers swore that they saw the marks of long and inhuman fingers on his windpipe, even though there was nothing there. Letting go of the two thieves, who ran for their lives, Domingo began to claw at the area around his throat making sounds similar to a choked chicken as if somebody or something were squeezing the breath from his body. For a moment, he seemed to dangle in the air and then was thrown backwards to the ground. Before anybody could reach him, he had aged a good number of years, becoming an old man, and his face had turned the colour of a withered cucumber.

The onlookers bore the body back to the Market House and laid it out on a counter. A doctor came and pronounced John Domingo dead. Even as they looked at it, the body seemed to shrivel up until it was merely a withered representation of its former self. At this, many people fled out of the Market House, and so nobody really knows what became of the body. It is said that by the end of the day, it was completely gone. It certainly wasn't buried in any of the local churchyards or consecrated ground, and John Domingo was too wealthy to be buried out in the Paupers Field with the destitute of Charleston. Several times afterwards, he was reputedly seen walking down Mazyck Street but this was merely a legend put about by credulous people. However, his name lingered on in the area, always with a sinister taint.

The counter on which his body had been laid out belonged to a local butcher. Afterwards nobody in the area would buy meat from him—they were afraid it had been "touched" by John Domingo and with his business ruined, the butcher died in an almshouse as a pauper. John's oldest son hanged himself in the back of a cowshed at Gadsden's Green and his youngest son was poisoned in a house on Archdale Street. The Black Constable's house was pulled down and the man who bought the site had to rebuild, hoping to exorcise the ghost of John Domingo, but nobody would rent it and so he had to live in it himself until he died. He never had any luck from the day that he moved in—his wife left him and he was always in debt, the final curse of the Black Constable.

Doctor Antoine

Also in Charleston, another babalawo named Doctor Antoine was conducting similar gatherings at a place known locally as Payne's Old Field, at the upper end of Meeting Street. Here candles were said to flicker and drums to beat on the darkest nights—and the dead were said to walk.

Delphine Paysandu and Mother Go-Go

Doctor Antoine was aided by a Voodoo queen named Delphine Paysandu who was said to have come back from the dead several days after she had been buried. Whether this was true or not is a matter for debate, but the story caused fear and uncertainty all across Charleston. In fact, there was talk that Delphine Pasandu was, in fact, a zombie. A similar story circulated concerning the intriguingly named Mother Go-Go, who also operated in the Charleston area. It was alleged that she too had died, but had risen from the grave to become a minor Voodoo queen in the Trapman Street area of the city. In a kind of zombie state, she presided over gatherings that took place in an old narrow house and which were said to involve the drinking of human blood.

Gullah Jack Pritchard

Even as late as the 1920s and early 1930s, a Voodoo man and master of zombies who called himself Gullah Jack Pritchard (supposedly possessed by the loa of the original Gullah Jack) was operating in the area around Charleston. He was arrested and sent to jail for extortion after a lengthy trial that drew a fair amount of interest and publicity due to his alleged "possession." As well as these local magicians, Charleston even had its own equivalent of Marie Laveau—this was Marguarite Lagoux.

Marguarite Lagoux

Marguarite Lagoux was a milliner and mantuamaker (one who made cloaks for ladies) with a shop on the western side of King Street. No trace of it now exists because much of the street was destroyed by fire. She lived in a small house in a narrow alley called Lilac Lane, the location of which is now all but forgotten. She was very beautiful—a quadroon by colour—and was wooed by many of the wealthy young men of Charleston, all of whom she appears to have turned down. Many of her patrons were rich white women and it was whispered in society circles that Marguarite was a voodoo practitioner who ran small gatherings in a yard, just off Lilac Lane. And it was rumoured that she also sold gris-gris along with her hats and cloaks. In some quarters, she became known only as "Madame Margot, the Voodoo Queen."

Gradually, she seemed to lose her good looks; her face became thin and mean looking and the lovely looking girl slowly began to disappear. She seemed to age incredibly fast. It was rumoured that she was quite wealthy but she gave no evidence of this—she dressed respectively but showed no signs of grandeur that had, say, characterized some of the Laveaus back in New Orleans. Some people declared that she had a vast fortune hidden away somewhere in the city but nobody knew where. And there were suggestions that she trafficked with the dead—shambling shadows were often seen around her door in Lilac Lane—and that this had somehow had an affect on her beauty. By the time she was in her mid-thirties, she was a crone, slightly stooped as if with age and with a pinched and drawn face. She closed her shop in King Street and retreated into Charleston's back alleyways. The gris-gris that she sold became much darker and more dangerous—charms for casting curses or for causing lust and unbridled passion in the most reserved of hearts.

She had one daughter, Gabrielle, who married a wealthy gentleman in New Orleans, and became a great society beauty. On the day of the wedding, Madame Margot stood in front of a great mirror and looked at herself. It is said that a shadow, perhaps the shadow of the dead, passed between herself and the glass but only she saw it. She burst into wild and demonic peals of laughter that brought her neighbours running in to see what was wrong with her. Ever afterwards, she refused to have a mirror near her and consequently she became more and more dishevelled in her appearance. Her wits were never the same after that and from time to time she would cackle and laugh to herself for no reason. There are some who assert that the celebrated Charleston witch, rather eccentrically named Old Mother Go-Go, was none other than Madame Margot. Although she had conducted wild revels in Lilac Lane, these soon fell away and she became something of a fabled recluse, only sought out by those with evil intent or the desperate.

She seemed to fall in upon herself, withering slowly away. One night, the tailor who lived across the road from her in the little alley, reported that her house was filled with light, and the sounds of revelry as it had been in earlier days when she'd held the voodoo revels there. He assumed that there was a Voodoo party in progress and kept to his own house. At one stage, however, he did notice a tall black man going up to the door and rapping loudly. The visitor was grandly dressed, but, said the tailor, an unpleasant odour followed him down the street—similar to a charnel stench. At last, his loud knocking was answered and he was admitted to the house. Minutes after he had entered the house, the lights went out and the sounds of revelry ceased. A sudden and violent storm blew in, with lightning cracking around the chimney pots of the old houses of Lilac Lane and the wind threatening to rip the tiles from the roof. Then, just as suddenly as it had arisen, the storm was gone and the night was as calm as ever. Sensing that something momentous had happened, the tailor crept from his house to the building across the lane. The door lay wide open, as were all the windows and he peered inside. The rain had beaten in and laid in puddles as the tailor looked around the door. There lay Madame Margot with her head in the fireplace and her body as black as soot, completely dead. Some say that the elegant dark man who had called was none other than "Le Baron"—Baron Cimitiere, who had come to carry off her evil soul. Others say that it was "Le Grand Zombi" himself.

Largely because of her evil reputation, the bishop declined to have a Mass said for the repose of her soul and the local priest would not allow her body to be buried in St. Sebastian's church. She was therefore buried in the Potter's Field, where the poor were interred under a large magnolia tree. Some say, however, that she was buried in her own garden.

Even though her house in Lilac Lane was later pulled down, her malignant spirit seemed to linger on. After a woman had hanged herself at the end of the Lane, it was closed as a public thoroughfare, but even then people would not cross in front of it. There was an old story that any schoolboy who dared to cross before it would be soundly beaten at school that day.

The country around about Charleston also contained its fair share of Voodoo men and witches. This was the Carolina Low Country, the equivalent to the Bayou Country around New Orleans, that had once been the domain of the Rice Kings and contained many of their plantations. The slaves here were known as Gullah and came from Angola. Their magic was just as potent as that which came from Dahomey, and many sorcerers flourished amongst them.

DcotorBuzzard

The most famous of all the Low Country Voodoo men was Stephaney Robinson, also known as Doctor Buzzard. Part of his fame derives from his arch-nemesis, the High Sheriff of the Low Country, J.E. McTeer, who was not a mean sorcerer himself. Doctor Buzzard died early in 1947 as a very old man and was known throughout the Low Country as a "root worker"—a man who did not work in charms or curses but in poudres and potions, many of which were derived from roots. In 1943, Dr. Buzzard was described as an elderly and dignified gentleman "always soberly dressed in quality black," who might have been mistaken for a bishop in the A.M.E. (African Methodist Episcopal). According to legend, Doctor Buzzard's father may have arrived in America as a slave who had great "conjure power" which he passed on to his son.

EdMcTeer

Ed McTeer, who became High Sheriff of Beaufort County, by contrast, came (on his mother's side), from an established slave-owning Carolina family, the Heywards, whose forebears had signed the Declaration of Independence. McTeer also believed in the power of E.S.P. and he believed in the power of Voodoo. His maternal grandfather was a major rice planter and had witnessed first hand the activities of the conjure-men. His grandmother was said to have possessed the "second sight" and his mother was rumoured to have attended séances amongst the slave-folks. In 1926, McTeer's father who had served as county sheriff died both suddenly and his son, Ed Junior, succeeded him almost immediately. However, the new law officer soon began running into some troublesome cases. A number of people in Beaufort County and beyond began to sicken with some sort of unexplained illness, and strange individuals appeared in local courts and began to fix witnesses with a steely gaze, apparently causing them to "seize up" or change their testimony. There were stories that some of these strange visitors were actually dead. Mysterious white powders began to appear in various parts of the courtroom including upon the judge's desk. McTeer suspected the work of conjure-men or babalawo and resolved to make an example of one or two of them in order to bring the local Gullah community to heel under the law. The man he picked on was the most celebrated conjure-man in the Carolina Low Country—Doctor Buzzard.

By this time, the doctor was famous even beyond the boundaries of Carolina. He was now extremely wealthy and rode around in a large black Lincoln, dressed in the finest of clothes. Moreover, he was rumoured to own property all across Charleston, although nobody could rightly say where. Officially, he lived in some style on the prestigious St. Helena Island, but he was reputedly living in other areas as well. Several attempts had been made to bring him to trial, however Doctor Buzzard was a courtroom specialist and had eluded imprisonment many times, often on technicalities. It was known that he was well versed in the law. McTeer, nevertheless, targeted him for surveillance. Recruiting local cab drivers that usually handled the Doctor's out-of-town customers, he mounted a watch on Doctor Buzzard's St. Helena Island home. But as soon as he began to gather his information, it suddenly died away and stopped. Nobody, it seemed, was willing to talk about Doctor Buzzard. McTeer was personally convinced that the Doctor's "second sight" had warned him of the police surveillance and he began to formulate new plans.

Before these could be enacted, however, World War II broke out. When German submarines moved in offshore, torpedoing everything that came in and out of the harbours of Charleston and Savannah, there were rumours that German spies had come ashore and were in Charleston itself. The local Coast Guard set up patrols to look out for rubber dinghies landing along the coastline. As their Commander, McTeer had more pressing matters to contend with. However, Doctor Buzzard would soon come to his attention once more. The local Draft Board was sending scores of young Gullah men to Fort Jackson, just outside Columbia for induction into the armed forces. The Fort was sending just as many back with unexplained heart flutters and diarrhoea. McTeer suspected the conjure men and root doctors and began to investigate. He further sent a letter to the War Department alleging Voodoo practices amongst some of the Gullah. His response from the Department was both frosty and sceptical. They thanked him for his note, filed it away, and promptly forgot about it. But their minds were to be changed by an event on 26th October 1943. A group of draftees set out for Fort Jackson from Hampton, South Carolina. One of them, a youth named Crispus Green, had told his family to expect him home very soon. He wasn't going to the war because Doctor Buzzard had "fixed him up." Almost half the draftees on the bus had received poudres and tonics from various Voodoo men to cause flutters in their hearts—"hippity hoppity hearts"—or extreme nausea. Before the bus reached Fort Jackson, however, Crispus Green and another young man were dead, and half the others had to be rushed to hospital. The War Department suddenly became extremely interested and the FBI also became involved. McTeer was ordered to take leave of his coastal patrol and assist in the investigation. He was going to have a difficult time because none of the surviving afflicted would testify against a root doctor. However, McTeer was able to procure a sample of a "medicine" that had allegedly been given to some of the victims. It was nothing more than crudely made moonshine mixed with a small amount of lead arsenate. Through the poison, McTeer traced a conjure man—not Doctor Buzzard as he had hoped—but Peter Murray of the Laurel Bay Plantation, also known as Doctor Bug. Murray was arrested and brought to a rural hearing. Set beside the might of the judiciary and the law, he cut a pathetic figure—a shambling, dull-eyed old man who barely seemed to recognize what was going on. Doctor Bug made no real effort to defend himself. He admitted that he'd given the potion and pleaded guilty. The magistrates set his bail bond at a thousand dollars. Doctor Bug simply produced a battered trunk and counted out the money from a pile of wrinkled dollar bills. However, as he left the court, he was approached by officials of the Internal Revenue Service and fined another two thousand dollars for unpaid taxes. This last fine was too much for Doctor Bug—he could pay his fines for practicing Voodoo without a murmur, but it was a different matter when it came to paying his taxes—and, according to tradition, he died shortly afterwards.

Doctor Buzzard, however, remained free throughout the war and in 1946, in an attempt to use his own powers against him, McTeer donned blue sunglasses (blue being a predominant Voodoo colour) and began to shoot all buzzards nesting on the city's water towers. His shots were on target in many cases, however one of the birds seems to have fallen unnoticed into an open tower and, after lying undetected for several days, contaminated the entire city's water supply. It seemed that the Doctor was simply mocking the High Sheriff. However, a spiritual war had begun between the two men.

Once, when McTeer brought in a witness, whom he thought might testify against Doctor Buzzard, the Doctor was arrested at the same time. Although placed in a different interrogation room, Doctor Buzzard seemed to be aware of the questions that the informant was being asked and of the answers he was giving and when the Doctor donned his blue glasses, the witness in another room seemed to become confused and hesitant in his testimony. McTeer had to admit he was beaten. On another occasion, Doctor Buzzard showed up at a trial that McTeer was conducting and fixed certain witnesses with a steely gaze from behind blue glasses, making them falter in their evidence. McTeer spoke out.

"Doctor Buzzard!" he shouted. "I believe that you are trying to 'root' this court and if you persist, I will have you over for contempt." The Doctor never flinched.

"I hear you," he replied. But he was annoyed and left the courtroom shortly afterward. McTeer seemed now to have a slight advantage and his luck was soon to change for the better but under tragic circumstances.

Doctor Buzzard's son, who was famous for his hedonistic lifestyle, drove his car across one of the causeways that crosses Beaufort County's tidal marshes during a blinding rainstorm, drove off the road, and was drowned in a saltwater creek. He was allegedly drunk at the time. All the same, Doctor Buzzard believed that his death was the result of McTeer's hex and approached the High Sheriff to "cut a deal." He would stop prescribing potions if McTeer would stop casting spells. The deal was struck. However, it didn't last—Doctor Buzzard was soon prescribing potions and allegedly practicing Voodoo again and McTeer had him arrested once more for the crime of "practicing medicine without a licence." The doctor now hired a lawyer—a respected State senator who practiced privately—but it did him no good. He was found guilty and fined heavily. It appeared to knock the wind out of his sails and he took to his bed, refusing to get up even to see clients. Shortly afterwards, he was diagnosed with cancer of the stomach. Soon he was dead, but not before leaving a message, which reverberated around the Gullah community—no Voodoo man was more powerful than the white authorities.

However, despite his death, the legend of Doctor Buzzard lived on in the Carolina Low Country and in the Charleston area and both his stature and powers seemed to increase with every retelling of the tales about him. Some said that on one occasion, Doctor Buzzard had managed to escape from McTeer's custody by turning himself into a cat; another said that that he had sent dead men to intimidate prospective witnesses against him.

Ed McTeer remained as High Sheriff of Beaufort County for almost another twenty years. In 1960, however, he was challenged for the job by a South Carolina Highway Patrol sergeant. The campaign was a long and bitter one with allegations flying back and forth between the contending parties. McTeer was said to have used chain-gang prisoners for personal work on his Coffin Point plantation, his deputies took bribes from Gullah bootleggers, the sergeant was involved in smuggling and moonshining, and he had a number of alleged sexual offences against him—the whole debate became very messy and acrimonious. In the end, a Charleston television station agreed to host a debate between the two men—although separately, as things were now so bad between them that they would not appear together. McTeer made his broadcast but, when it came the sergeant's turn, the electrical power went down all across the Low Country and reception was patchy. Many said that it was McTeer's Voodoo powers that had caused the blackout. All the same, the Highway Patrol officer narrowly won the vote and Ed McTeer retired to write his memoirs. The new High Sheriff enjoyed a stormy career that culminated in his assaulting a grand jury member. He barricaded himself in his own home and threatened suicide but was eventually coaxed out, arrested, and placed in mental health care. Local wisdom said that McTeer had driven him insane through sorcery.

McTeer's memoirs, *Fifty Years as a Low Country Witch Doctor*, became a best seller even beyond South Carolina and made him a minor national figure. He was courted by a number of television and radio stations but refused to talk about Voodoo or about his feud with Doctor Buzzard. In the Carolina Low County, the old ways of the Gullah people slipped further underground and today forms a kind of colourful background to the day-to-day life of the area.

Santeria

Voodoo, however, is still alive and well in a number of forms in many parts of the world. It is the state religion in Benin, West Africa, and is practiced widely in other African, South American, and Caribbean countries. Aspects of it, such as divination and healing are sometimes known by other names—Santeria (divination by shells) and Mama Wati, but many follow the same patterns of belief and the term "Voodoo" is simply retained as a "catch all" description. The old gods still remain and are worshipped today. In New Orleans and Charleston today, it is still possible to buy gris-gris and poudres and many shops and Internet sites based there still sell Voodoo materials. There are a sizeable number practitioners scattered all across the world and, in many respects, Haiti is now its spiritual home—perhaps because of its connections with the Duvalier regime.

Le Grand Zombi

The most potent and recognized symbol of Voodoo is, of course, the zombie—the shambling dead man that rose from the grave controlled by the bokor, or sorcerer. Strangely, zombies do not generally exist is Voodoo tradition, although there is sometimes a tradition of creating mindless servants in some versions of gegbo—the darker side of the voodoo religion. Most of the zombies that appear on the screen or in popular literature are the creations of Hollywood and the Western mind. In Rada Voodoo, "Le Grand Zombi" is one of the incarnations of Damballa-wedo and takes the form of a gigantic python or serpent. This is generally regarded to be the most dangerous and unpredictable form of the loa, and is therefore not often summoned. Only a skilled and powerful magician can control it and it will take revenge upon the summoner if called inappropriately. In Petro Voodoo, however, the meaning changes slightly and refers to those who have been taken over by the loa, whether they are alive or dead. This may have given rise to the concept of the zombie, as we understand the term. The loa is then controlled by the bokor, who in turn controls the physical manifestation. Out of this basic idea has grown a number of zombie nightmares—most sensationally the lumbering, animated corpse who can attack the living at the behest of some evil bokor. The notion of the gris-gris (charm) is inextricably linked with that of the zombie, with the former serving as a beacon for the shambling dead creature, placed by the bokor to guide it to the victim. This is, of course, a dramatic invention of Hollywood and bears little resemblance to actual Voodoo belief.

The zombie was, however, a combination of a number of African and Caribbean folk terrors that wandered around in the tropical night. These were half-remembered bogeymen from the slave days, such as the Ghanaian Dodo, a shambling form that often hid in trees ready to drop upon the unwary traveller and devour him, or the Modulo, a humanoid creature from Zulu lore, who entered houses at night to drink the blood of sleepers through its incredibly long fingernails. Some of theses beings were simply known amongst the slaves as "cockroaches" (a kind of living dead thing) that would attack the "fowl-houses" (slave encampments or enclosures), silently creeping in as soon as the moon was up, with the intention of doing harm. Many of these elements coalesced into a common figure: the shambling nightwalker.

Zombification

Across the years, many explanations for "zombification" (the turning of individuals into zombies) have been advanced. Most of these concern living people who have "died" and seemingly come back to life, bereft of their will and purpose.

Poudre

The most common explanation is that a "poudre" (a toxic or mind-numbing substance) had been surreptitiously given to the victim, placing him or her under the control of a bokor. According to some toxicologists, the sorcerous medicine might contain elements of a stonefish or puffer-fish which slowed down the vital life-signs so much that the victim lapsed into a death-like coma from which only the bokor could revive him or her with an antidote, but at the expense of the individual's will. This theory has formed the basis of several academic papers on toxicology, as well as a number of books and stories such as William Seabrook's *Dead Men Working in the Cane-fields* and Wade Davis's *Serpent and the Rainbow* (which was subsequently made into a film, directed by Wes Craven). However, the *poudre* used by the bokors (if indeed such a thing actually exists) has never been discovered and any samples purporting to be the magic preparation have proved worthless under scientific analysis. If a zombie *poudre does* exist, then it still remains a secret.

Zombie Films

And of course, there is the shambling figure of the zombie, though this is perhaps owed more to European minds than it does African. Certainly there are stories of the restless dead amongst the Africans and Creoles but these are little different from those of, say, the marbh bheo (nightwalking dead) in Ireland. The connections between zombies and Voodoo ceremonies are largely constructed in the minds of sensationalist filmmakers. Movies such as George A. Romero's *Night of the Living Dead* (1968) and *Dawn of the Dead* (1978) and Lucio Fulci's *Zombie Flesh Eaters* (1979) had served to popularise the idea of the zombie and have added fresh impetus and folklore to the legend. More zombie films are allegedly in the pipeline—linked closely to several new books, linking the animated corpse with Voodoo practices—that may well propel the shuffling dead man to new heights amongst the elite of the Undead.

Ghouls and the Golem

...and they lived by the Red Sea, until Adam and his wife sinned. Then the Holy One sent her forth to ever after wreak her revenge on the children of Mankind.

—Zohar 1 19b

Middle-Eastern Folklore

Although less familiar to Western minds, the folklore and legends of the Middle East have nonetheless played their part in some of the night terrors that continue to haunt our imaginations. Elements of both Arabic and Jewish folklore have subtly woven their way into Western mythologies, creating a number of creatures that stalk and haunt the hours of darkness.

Sons of God

Arguably, these creatures are the oldest of such terrors—their origins shrouded in the mist of the early Middle East of pre-Biblical times. Many of them were born in the chaos that preceded the very foundation of the world and, although not truly chronicled until medieval times, have existed since then. According to some Middle Eastern legends, they were born out of interactions between the developing Universe and mysterious entities known as "the sons of God." (The Bible tells us that they found the daughters of Man fair, and mated with them.) Out of such interaction was born a race of monsters and devils that seemed to overwhelm the world. These were eventually destroyed in a great flood that God sent to cleanse and purify the Earth (a concept that appears in several myth-cycles, including the Bible). It was thought, however, that some of these beings survived the Deluge and persisted in the world, tormenting a new and developing Humankind.

Lilith

Another legendary source for these monsters and terrors was Lilith, reputedly the first wife of Adam. Although she has been discussed elsewhere in this book, it is perhaps worthwhile to make mention of her in this context. The Jewish Talmud describes her as a demon of the night, with long hair and a human likeness. It is also suggested that she had wings and was able to fly. According to the third century Palestinian scholar, Jerimia ben Eleazar, both she and Adam "begot ghosts, male demons, and female night demons" that were to prey on Mankind across the centuries.

Adam Kadmon

Very ancient legends tell of how Lilith, a demon born out of chaos, seduced Adam (or perhaps Adam Kadmon—the first prototype of Man created by God) into becoming his wife. Through her, it was said in rabbinical lore, the forces of primal darkness sought to gain entry into the world of men. She led the proto-Adam (or Adam Kadmon) to commit sinful deeds and she bore him many children—most of whom were monsters and night terrors. In the end, according to some versions of old rabbinical tales, appalled by the foulness that was being spawned on earth, God destroyed Adam Kadmon and his brood but, for some unspecified reason, did not destroy Lilith. Instead, He banished her into the mountains and deep caverns where she continued to mate with demons and raise more monstrous entities (later largely destroyed by the Great Flood). Adam Kadmon was replaced by the more familiar Adam, the father of Mankind, and was given a wife, Eve, made from his own flesh. However, this second Adam also sinned—although perhaps to a lesser extent than the first—and he and his partner were banished from the Paradise that God had established on Earth and into the wilderness where the monsters spawned by Lilith presumably still dwelt. These terrors would subsequently become the tormentors of Mankind.

Alphabet of Ben Sira

Lilith is probably first mentioned by name as a "night monster" in an ancient text known as the *Alphabet of Ben Sira,* a book of Talmudic magic, probably produced some time between the 7th and 11th centuries. This work also mentions Adam, describing him as the "father of ghouls"— referring to the awful children born to him by Lilith. The implication here is that the beings terrifying Mankind at the time may have had some element of human in them but, this was subdued by a supernatural evil.

Sefer Hasidim

Although the majority of such creatures were swept away in the Deluge, a number of them did survive into the Second Era of Man (that is, when he had re-established himself in the world after the flood) where they continued their dark work. Many of these entities were demons, either invisible or partially visible to the human eye, but were implacably opposed to Humankind and continually sought ways to injure or kill God's children. No one was exempt from their attack, and books such as the *Sefer Hasidim* or *Book of the Pious* (attributed to Rabbi Judah he-Hesid or Samuel the Pious, 1150–1217) are filled with anecdotes and stories concerning their wiles and maliciousness. These beings were subtle, seeking to subvert men and turn them from good and the worship of God through devious measures and stratagems. This was the original notion of such entities, although much later opinions on demons and monsters in Semitic theological thought became more divided. One unidentified early writer noted: "They are more God-fearing than men are…they harm no-one without good cause; if a man does not provoke them…he need have no fear." The suggestion here was that the evils carried out by such entities were no more than as a reaction to provocation by humans. This, however, was in no way to diminish their supernatural powers, and if they chose to strike out in retaliation, they would do great injury and harm in the mortal world. The prime provocation was considered to try and force them, through some form of formal conjuration, to do the will of a human individual or to try and subdue them in some way. Provocation could also come from ill-chosen words, deeds, or even glances that infuriated these spirits, entities, and forces. Uncleanliness in individuals or dwellings only served to encourage entities of a certain sort that would remain until purification. Whilst some were extremely dangerous, others were merely irritants that brought further discomfort to an already difficult life, or simply terrified individuals with their sounds or in some cases, appearances.

Two schools of thought were now rapidly developing—one stating that demons and monsters had been opposed to Mankind ever since the foundation of the world; the other asserting that they were no more than a response to man's desires—lust, greed, murderous intent, uncleanliness, and neglect of Godly worship. Stories supporting both views circulated widely and are recorded in a wealth of literature—stories of unprovoked attacks on travellers by evil spirits; of ill-luck dogging a family following some inadvertent act; of a subsequent illness, deriving from the evil eye, or of invocations for the lifting of a sickness caused by demons. All of these relate to the spawn of Lilith who, for whatever motive were determined to make human life difficult. Mankind was always in peril.

Gigul

Closely allied to the concept of demons was the concept of the *gigul* or "clinging soul." This Jewish folklore term is difficult to specify but may lie somewhere between the ghost of a dead person and an elemental force or demon.

These entities were known as "dybbuk" although the word itself did not appear in rabbinical literature until roughly the 17th century. In its earliest incarnation, the "clinging soul" may not have been all that threatening and may well have referred to a Presence that attached itself either to an individual or a dwelling, and refused to go away. It may well have possessed a person—indeed, one of the earliest references that we have to it is in the Bible

(1 Samuel 16: 1–4) where an "evil spirit" overtakes King Saul and hurls him into an unprovoked rage. Saul himself visited a woman at Endor (a "pythoness," probably some sort of medium) who summoned another "clinging soul"—that of the prophet Samuel himself (1 Samuel 28:3).

Dybbuk

In the 16th century, however, the idea of spirit possession by the dybbuk became extremely popular in certain Rabbinical schools, for example those of Isaac Luria (1534–1572) and his disciple Chayyim Vital (1542–1620). Through this school of theological teaching, the "clinging soul" assumed a demonic status, inimical to the welfare of Mankind. Its pedigree stretched back to the earliest times and it could only be driven out by a rabbi. Its mission was to tempt men away from the path that God had laid out for them and into lax and sinful ways. As the tales about dybbuks began to proliferate, they assumed greater and more dangerous supernatural powers in the popular imagination, adding to popular lore and fear.

The Old Gods

And just to complicate matters even further, there was the problem of the old gods. Prior to the birth of Islam under the prophet Mohammad (570–633), what is now known as the Middle East had been a cauldron of cults and deities. Many of these had their origins within the ancient civilizations that had flourished there—the Canaanites, the Hittites, the Phoenicians, and many others. From the earliest times, these ancient gods spoke to men, either through their own priests or through visionaries. In the 7th and 8th centuries, reference is made to a group of men known as *kahins,* which meant seers or oracle mongers. These were men who had been possessed by the gods (or emanations of the gods), taking them into ecstatic trances that enabled them to prophesy and foretell coming events. These men would continue well into the Islamic period, providing a link with the pre-Mohammedan past.

Hubaal

There may well have still been temples dedicated to ancient gods scattered throughout the Middle East even after the Prophet Mohammed died. One of the foremost of these deities was the moon god Hubal, sometimes rendered as Hubaal. The origin of the name is unknown, but it is thought to have derived from an Aramaic word for "spirit" and that this god was worshipped in Upper Mesopotamia from very early times. Some have argued that Hubal was a former incarnation of the god Baal, mentioned in the Bible, but this is unlikely because Baal or Baal'at was a god of the Phoenicians. A splendid idol of the god was placed above the Kaaba or inner mosque in Mecca where it was worshipped by pilgrims. Indeed, if accounts are to be believed, there were some three hundred and sixty idols in the temple or mosque. Some of these were thought to have been either connected to, or manifestations of, Hubal. For example, the deitie's emanation or "daughter," al-Lit (the name simply means "goddess" and she was believed to ensure fertility both in the land and in individuals); al-Uzza and Manat (the crone-goddess who, with her golden shears, determined the fate of every individual in the world), and many others. There were also supposed to be regional gods amongst the idols that determined the lives of groups of people by their merest whim. Mohammed overthrew these idols when he entered the Kaaba, starting a movement which would unify much of the Arab world under a single god, Allah. In his call to prayer, the muezzin announced to the faithful that there is "no god but Allah" and this may very well be reflective of these pre-Mohommedan times. And yet the influence of the ancient gods lingered on, in the form of elemental forces and distinct entities lurking in the shadows. It was on their powers that the kahins sometimes relied when issuing their prophecies and their powers might also be felt in other ways—against those who followed the developing monotheistic religion. Somewhere in the back of the Middle Eastern mind they continued to wait, and watch, and in some cases, act.

The emerging picture, then, is an extremely complex and conflicting one, comprising various strands of belief. On one hand, there was the notion of demons—the spawn of Lilith and Adam (or Adam Kadmon) that had existed since the foundation of the world and which had emerged from the primal chaos; on another there was the idea of the "clinging souls," not quite ghost, not quite demon, but enjoying supernatural power and yet another strand comprised the old gods, worshipped before the advent of Islam that hadn't quite gone away. Some of these entities might manifest themselves during the hours of daylight but, as darkness fell across the Semitic world, they assumed an even greater aspect of menace and power.

They might manifest themselves in many ways. Most of them were invisible—little more than shadowy, barely definable presences that brought sickness and disease in their wake; others might be more corporeal, capable of inflicting terrible injuries if they so chose. Some of the demons, though invisible themselves, chose to manifest their presence in very visible ways. The most common form, found in many rural areas of the Middle East were the djinn.

al-Haddin

Many youngsters and pantomime goers will be familiar with the favourite old story of Aladdin with its relatively friendly genies. Although the story is traditionally set in China, (as it is in Burton's translation of the collection of Arabic fables *One Thousand and One Nights*), it is perhaps based on a much more ancient Arab tale, featuring a hero named al-Haddin, who actually fought genii or djinn. The djinn were disembodied demons that made their presence known by kicking up small dust storms or whirlwinds in the deserts. They were creatures of air, but were supernaturally powerful and could tear a man in pieces by sheer force. They inhabited the lonely tracts of desert and deep, gloomy valleys that often lay between human settlements. In fact, they were sometimes known as "the Lords of the Wilderness" and travellers were extremely wary of them. Those journeying from city to city, town to town, or camp to camp, often carried protective amulets and charms against the ferocious attentions of such spectral creatures.

Iblis, the Lord of Jahannam

It was thought, in some quarters and according to some legends, that these entities might be fallen angels and that, similar to Mankind, they were organized in groups or tribes and had their own fearsome ruler—Iblis, the Lord of Jahannam (the Islamic Hell). When Allah had created Man from the dust of the Earth, he instructed all angels to bow down before His supreme creation. One of the chief angels, Iblis, being exceptionally proud, refused to do so.

Being a creature of fire, he would not bow to what he considered to be an "inferior" creature made from earth and, following his example, several other angels also declined to obey Allah. For this wilful act, they were cast out of Paradise and into the desert wilderness where they remained, brooding and vengeful, seeking to harm Man, who had brought about their downfall.

Shaitan

The story parallels that of the expulsion of the angel Lucifer that is to be found in Christian mythology and legend, and it is possible that the two stories have the same source. In Christianity, Lucifer becomes Satan and is cast into Hell. In Islamic folklore too, Iblis's chief angel is known as "the Shaytan" or "Shaitan," taken to mean "one born in anger." The idea of fallen angelhood gave the djinn increased status and powers and made them implacable opponents of Mankind. They had the power to destroy those whom they encountered, or to carry them away to Jahannam, never to be seen again. A far cry from the genies of Aladdin! The dangerous djinn were wily, but as with the pantomime fable, they could be trapped—usually in stoppered vessels or bottles marked with a powerful sigil or seal. An extremely powerful magician could only accomplish this. However, if the force were to be accidentally or deliberately released, it would be twice as violent.

Iblis therefore became Lord and Master of the djinn who were now seen as creatures composed of wind, fire, and smoke and who had an inherent affinity with all three. This made them incredibly dangerous, and Iblis himself assumed a powerful role in Arab mythology.

Afreets

The idea of disembodied and violent entities dwelling in the wastes gave travellers an added fear when passing through lonely or remote places. In many instances, the way between cities, towns, and campsites lay across lonely deserts, through gloomy gullies and ravines and bare mountain slopes. And travelling was always particularly difficult. Not only did travellers contend with groups of human robbers dwelling in these wildernesses, they also had to contend with storms, drought, and wild animals. This made any journey both an adventure and an ordeal. And with the djinn, demons, and other supernatural terrors, it seemed now even more fraught. Any swirl of wind out in the empty plain might be an evil or malicious entity stalking the traveller as he journeyed. As he lay at night in some isolated spot, sounds would drift to him out of the dark—the cry of a night animal or the sighing of the wind amongst the rocks—stimulating his imagination and terrifying him out of his wits. These were the voice of the djinn or of *afreets* (a similar form of entity or sometimes another name for the entity) that were always lurking close by. Vast stretches of wilderness, eerie sounds at night, legends of mysterious and hostile entities, coupled with fantastic travellers' tales all combined to create a context within which supernatural terrors could exist and within which belief in their existence was taken for granted.

Animals Associated With the Dead

Animals, too played their part in such a developing folklore—particularly those animals connected with the dead. Chief amongst these were jackals and hyenas. Both animals were scavengers, rooting amongst the rubbish tips and heaps of refuse that humans had discarded. But there was another side to their foraging. From time to time, jackals and other wild dogs were seen hunting amongst graveyards and other burial places in search of the rotting human flesh of buried bodies. The light sandy soil of some areas made it impossible to bury corpses at any depth and so they lay close to the surface, attracting scavengers. Human beings viewed such hunting with great abhorrence and repugnance. The very thought of consuming dead flesh was horrific beyond imagining. Admittedly, there were stories, often carried by travellers, of solitary hermits, far out in the desert, who dug up and devoured dead bodies, but, these were depraved and crazed individuals, perhaps driven mad by years of isolation. A series of ancient, Islamic tales told of groups of men, dwelling in deep and lightless caves, far out in the inaccessible desert, who worshipped foul gods, were completely naked, smeared themselves with ashes, and who ate decaying flesh and sometimes each other. Such cannibals and madmen were to be avoided. However, the wild dogs and scavengers that haunted the graveyards and cemeteries of the Arab worlds were another matter. They might be djinn, who as well as travelling invisibly, could take on other shapes and forms. Moreover, the sniggering cry of a hyena, heard in the darkness of the night, must have struck terror into the heart of many a sleeper, suggesting all sorts of evil entities lurking in the gloom outside their house.

Anubis

There was also the connection in the popular mind between the jackal and Anpu or Anubis, the ancient Egyptian Lord of the Underworld. In mythology, this sombre god was always depicted as having the head of a jackal, supposedly representing a close connection with the dead. He was seen as a stern judge, evaluating the souls of the dead before they passed on to their ultimate reward and as such was to be feared and treated with awe. It was his link with the dead, however, that made him especially feared. Anubis presided over the Kingdom of the Dead and had command of legions of cadavers who would carry out his instructions and take vengeance on those who failed to show him proper respect. He was also venerated as the god of embalmers—those who preserved the dead and who kept bodies intact. These beliefs only added to the grimness of the god and created an extremely sinister aspect around him.

The Ghoul

The combination of eerie noises, dogs foraging amongst graves, and the idea of demons gave rise to a new type of entity in the popular mind—the ghoul. The name was simply taken to mean "the grabber" because that was how the creature was supposed to capture its victims. Ghouls were an often-corporeal demon, rumoured to be one of the children of Lilith, who lurked in graveyards, sometimes attacking those who passed through them, and feasting upon the recently interred. They dwelt underground and only appeared as soon as it was night, as they were susceptible to strong sunlight and bright lights. In a sense, ghouls were the epitome of the demon world—they were unclean and grotesque to look at. They had hideous strength, coupled with supernatural powers, and their habits and diets were awful, to say the least. They feasted on rotting human flesh; they stank and spread diseases and pestilence wherever they passed.

In the public imagination, there was a strong visual connection between ghouls and the dead themselves. Some popular descriptions of them detail them as naked, though encrusted in earth and filth, pale skinned almost to the point of ghostliness, distorted human-like features but with a frightful and malicious aspect: red eyes—redder than any ruby or fire-opal. They had long and dagger-like teeth, sometimes curved like the blade of an Arab knife suitable for rending flesh, whether living or dead. But it was their hands that commanded most attention—these were said to be abnormally large, with long fingers, curved like birds' claws and sporting long and sharp nails that again, were suitable for rending flesh. Such shovel-like hands were also useful for digging up corpses from the light soil of their graves. Other depictions of them describe them as shrouded beings, darkly robed and cowled, which added to their sense of mystery and threat. They were said to be faceless, with only a dark emptiness where their countenance should be and with a sense of palpable menace about them. Because they were related to the djinn, some accounts described them as little more than glowing, disembodied faces, narrow and malicious whilst other, rather conflicting descriptions recount them as shambling figures, covered in soil and swathed in filthy bandages—almost similar to a mummy—moving with a slow and shuffling step. All these images coalesced into a frightening belief.

Underground Dwellings

Traditionally ghouls were said to live underground, emerging out of deep pits or holes in the earth, although they could sometimes simply materialize out of thin air in front of an astonished traveller. Consequently, deep gullies and cracks in the earth were to be strenuously avoided. The idea that the ghouls were almost a form of troglodyte may well have come from old travellers' tales (possibly exaggerated) of cannibalistic hermits and solitaries, dwelling in the rocks and caves deep in the desert wastes. Some of these anchorites were undoubtedly mad and either shied away from or else attacked those who passed by their abodes, giving rise to stories of ferocious ghouls, lurking in such remote places. Ghouls, it was believed, also dwelt in the shadows of large rocks and stones, well away from the sun. They would change their shape (it was believed that some ghouls, such as djinn, were shapeshifters) into the form of beautiful women in order the lure passers by into the shade where the creature would revert to its true form before feeding. They also dwelt in deep caves and in crevices in the rocks—the only indication of their presence being their eyes, which glowed and flashed red like coals in the darkness. Indeed, anywhere there was dark or shadow might be a habitation for ghouls in the Arab mind. Their main haunts, however, were graveyards and abandoned cemeteries where there was a ready supply of corpses upon which they were said to subsist. Crossing such place (particularly after nightfall) was therefore adjudged to be a particularly hazardous occupation. As the ghouls dwelt underground and were closely associated with dead bodies, anyone walking across a grave might suddenly find a seemingly withered hand grabbing and clutching at their ankles as the creature attempted to drag them down.

Ghouls and Disease

The connection between ghouls and the spread of disease was also extremely strong. Ghouls were said to be unclean and pestilence followed them as a matter of course. Because they were of the djinn-kind, and djinn were creatures of wind and storm, they were said to use such elements in order to spread plague throughout a community. Mixed with the storm and wind were fragments of organic materials that in some instances, may indeed have spread disease and this was directly attributed to the work of the supernatural. Even the very *touch* of a ghoul was said, in some instances, to be deadly and could carry pestilence amongst humans. In other cases, the very *passing* of the creature, with disease clinging to its robes, was enough to bring plague into a community. It was also argued that the spittle or saliva of the ghoul held poisonous properties—poisons that could be absorbed through the skin, or if something that the creature had spat upon or had left a trace of saliva were to be touched or stepped upon (remembering that many travellers often went barefoot). This was sometimes offered as the reason for the spread of epidemics between communities and for the transmission of certain diseases.

Ghouls also commanded great power. They had unquestionably supernatural strength but they had other powers, too. They could materialize and dematerialise such as turning to smoke, similar to a djinn, if threatened. They also had command of the mind, luring individuals with false visions or else confusing them so that they wandered into dangerous places. Moreover, they had the power to take on the shapes of birds and animals, particularly carrion creatures (those who ate dead meat) and sometimes had power over them, turning them against men.

Algol

The Arabic term for ghoul was "al-ghul," which was used both individually and collectively to describe them. The awe and fear in which ghouls were viewed is demonstrated in the star-studded night sky. Arab scholars were amongst the first to seriously study the heavens. Indeed, they are counted to be amongst the first real astronomers—and some of their folklore would appear to have left its mark amongst the celestial bodies. A star in the Beta Persis system, in the constellation of Perseus, may have originally been logged by Arab stargazers. They gave it the name of their most common demon—al-ghul, nicknaming it the "demon star."

Rhas al-Ghul

Another Arab name for the star was Rhas al-ghul, meaning "the demon's head," firmly establishing it in a dark and sinister context. Today, we know it as Algol and it is sometimes still rumoured to be a star of ill omen. Those born whenever Algol was in the ascendancy were destined to become robbers and murderers, or some unfortunate event would almost certainly befall them. The ascendancy of Algol was also a time when the powers of black magicians were at their height in the Arab world and when the greatest evil was wrought. In fact, Algol was so closely associated with dark sorcery that its name does not appear in many Arab astronomical texts in case they fell into the wrong hands.

Eye of Medusa

Curiously, the star was also known to the ancient Greek astronomers amongst whom it had a similar reputation. They knew it as "the eye of Medusa" (Medusa was a Gorgon—a monster whose very gaze could turn men into stone—who was killed by Perseus) or "the winking demon," because the light emitted by it appears to fluctuate from time to time. And it was also considered to be extremely evil in aspect. It was not until 1667 that it was formally "discovered" in the West by the Italian astronomer Geminano Montanari of Bologna, although its existence was well-known long before that. Even in early modern Europe, Algol was known as an "unlucky star." It is still sometimes known as such today and the evil reputation of the ghoul, seems to have percolated down across the centuries. The word itself lingered on in many European languages, including English.

Encounters with ghouls are to be found in many travellers' tales from all across the Arabic world. Those who ventured on lonely roads or near abandoned burying grounds returned with stories of shadows that moved, of voices that whispered, or of things, half-glimpsed in the twilight, that were not as they had originally seemed. Some travellers vanished in the desert wastes and their disappearances were often put down to the activities of ghouls.

One tale, from a collection of 12th century Middle Eastern stories, illustrates this:

> A certain merchant was travelling alone through a lonely, rocky place between two cities. As night began to descend, he made camp but he was ill advised to do so as he made it close to an ancient cemetery that had been long abandoned and that it was said had served a blasphemous city, now buried under the desert sand. This place was said to be the haunt of djinns and ghosts. Such tales, however, did not frighten the merchant, as he was a practical man and did not give much credence to such legends. Indeed, he was more terrified of the bandits and robbers that were said to prowl the area and who might well attack him. He lit a great fire in order to keep away thieves and wild animals and proceeded to settle himself down for the night. As he lay close to the blaze, the night seemed to be filled with noise—the cries of distant night creatures, and the movement of strange winds; the merchant began to feel a little bit afraid. He gathered his blankets around him and tried to sleep but sleep would not come. Gradually, he became

aware of a voice seeming to call to him from somewhere nearby—a voice that called him by name! It seemed to come from the abandoned cemetery well beyond the glow of the fire. Rising, the merchant walked a little way to the very edge of the firelight and looked out into the night. By now it was completely dusk and he could see very little. The voice, however, continued to call—softly, beguilingly. Fearful that this might be some trick of the robbers that dwelt in this wilderness, the merchant advanced no further.

"Who is there?" he called back. "Who calls me? Advance and show yourself for the night is dark and I cannot see you!" The wind stirred the sand about his feet but seemed to come no closer to his fire. Somewhere close by, a jackal howled.

"Alas," replied the voice mournfully. "I cannot come any closer to you but I am a friend and in need of help. I will do you no harm." The merchant was not convinced but the voice now had a strange, pleading quality about it that stirred his heart in pity. Though he was a merchant, he was not a cruel man and had no wish to see a fellow human in any distress.

"If you could come but a little closer," he urged. "I am afraid that you might be a robber who is seeking to lure me into the darkness." The voice sighed.

"I am no robber," it replied. "Only an old man in great pain and distress. I have not the strength to overpower you or do you harm. I only wish your help." Its pleading seemed so convincing that the merchant advanced a little more beyond the firelight. In the gloom, he could just about see the ruined wall that surrounded the abandoned graveyard and he thought that he also saw the shape of a man standing beside a gap where it had completely fallen away. He thought that it seemed withered and slightly stooped as if it indeed were the form of a piteous old man. It certainly did not appear to be a robber. All the same, fearing a trap, the merchant returned to his fire and lifted a burning brand before walking down towards the ruined wall.

"Put the light lower, I beg you," quavered the voice as he drew closer. "I have an affliction of the eyes and strong lights are not good for me. That is why I stay in the shadows, but don't let that deter you. Come forward my friend." The merchant lowered his burning torch but all the same, he kept it in front of him. He approached the place where he had seen the figure and, was it his imagination, or did he sense a shuffling movement as the other drew back slightly?

"How can I help you?" he asked. Away across the desert, the jackal howled again and the merchant was suddenly wary. The air near the ancient burial place seemed inexplicably chilly and he thought he detected a smell, rank and foul, similar to freshly turned grave earth. Nevertheless, he advanced, keeping the torched lowered in his right hand. "What is it that ails you?"

"I am injured," answered the other. "Come closer so that I can show you." The merchant took a few steps forward. He felt uneasy and suspected that this might indeed be a trap and that he would be set upon by desert bandits. And yet, as he drew nearer, the shadowy figure seemed impossibly thin and frail—not like a bandit at all.

"How have you injured yourself in such a lonely place?" he queried. The shape in front of him did not answer but shuffled forward a little.

"I beg you, keep your light lowered," it said. "My eyes…" As it drew a little closer, the merchant suddenly raised his torch, the feeling of unease almost overwhelming him. He gave a cry of utter horror as the light revealed the edge of the ancient cemetery.

The creature that stood in front of him was indeed shaped similar to a living man but there the similarity ended. The torchlight revealed it to be tall and thin to the point of emaciation, and dressed in rags that looked like the remnants of grave clothes. Its face was swathed in filthy bandages like a mummy, but through a gap, a single red-tinged eye peered out malevolent. The being was hung with clods of rancid earth from the graveyard beyond and as it moved slowly forward, it raised great hands that were more like shovels with extremely long and ragged fingernails, from which more earth fell. This, the merchant realized was no human being at all, but a ghoul that dwelt in the cemetery and that had tried to trick him so that it could feast upon his flesh. He thrust the torch out in front of him like a sword and the figure recoiled. Ghouls, he knew, were afraid of the light and even more so of fire. As he did so, part of the bandage that covered its lower face fell away and he saw great teeth and fangs, still hung with pieces of the rotting flesh of recently consumed corpses. With an invocation to Allah for His protection, the merchant scrambled backwards towards his fire whilst the ghoul continued to shuffle forwards.

Amongst his possessions was an amulet that had been given to him many years before by an Islamic holy man. It was said to be inscribed with a protective charm that would ward away djinn and other hostile supernatural beings. Although he had never really believed in it, the merchant still carried it with him and he was glad now that he had it. Setting aside the torch, he hunted frantically for it and, as he did so, he heard the ghoul drawing closer. It was moving very slowly as its kind could not, according to popular legend, travel very quickly, but moved with a halting step. At last the merchant found the amulet in a bundle of clothes. He held it up, protectively, in front of his face with his right hand—his left hand groping for the still-burning torch. The horrible figure was almost upon him. As it towered over him, it suddenly stopped and fell back with a shriek that resembled the howl of a jackal. Once again, the merchant evoked the name of Allah for his own protection and when he looked again, he was alone beside the fire and entangled in his own blankets. As he rose to his feet, he first though that the whole incident had been no more than a bad dream but as he looked down, he saw that in his right hand, he held the amulet and a little way from the main fire, lay the burning torch that he'd carried, now turning to smoke. The episode had been real and the ghoul was now gone. He offered a prayer of thanks to Allah for his deliverance.

The next morning, he ventured down to the ancient cemetery, which, he imagined, had once served a part of the now vanished city. Walking amongst the funeral markers, he noticed that more than a few of the graves had been disturbed and in one corner, close to a large, shadowy stone, there was a deep hole, that emitted a foul and acrid smell. He did not bother to investigate this for fear of what he might find in its dark depths. Leaving the cemetery behind he packed his things and continued his journey to the city, but from then on he was much less sceptical regarding the existence of the supernatural.

Material Objects

Tales such as the previous example were quite common in parts of the early Middle East. Many travellers often carried amulets and charms about their person in order to protect them from the attentions of such horrid entities as ghouls. Some of these protections might have been what are now called material objects: a fox's tail, for example, was a particularly potent protection against djinn, or a series of interwoven crimson threads might protect the carrier from the gaze of a demon or ghoul. Necklaces made of coral or certain semi-precious stones were also used as charms to ward away evil. In some cases, a wax or metal tablet bearing a sacred word or holy name might be used, although these were much more common amongst Jews than early Arabs. For example, a metal plate inscribed with the letter *heh* (a sign for the mystical Tetragammaton) would drive away demons of every kind, including djinn and ghouls. A cake of unleavened Passover bread hanging in a house would keep away foul spirits and ghouls from the door. The same charm, carried in a pouch, would also protect the traveller on his journey. Those charms were especially favoured by the Hebrews and had their roots in the Talmudic faith. And these wayfarers needed all the protections they could carry, for who knew what form the ghoul would assume if they were encountered as this story, from a very early period demonstrates:

The son of a prince was travelling through a wide and rocky valley at one time. No one lived in this place, save only a few ancient hermits who shunned all contact with the world. It was a barren and lonely place, especially when the sun began to go down. Yet, it was in the cool of the evening that the prince's son chose to cross it—riding alone, for he feared little upon the road.

On his way across the valley, he encountered nothing, for the caves of the anchorites were distant and they would not come close, even out of curiosity. Not even an animal lived or moved in this dreary waste. The very air stank of death and emptiness. The evening grew colder as it does in the desert, but the prince's son did not halt but kept on travelling. Then, in the shadow of a great rock, he saw a woman. She was young and beautiful and she was dressed like a princess. She sat, part in shadow, on a great flat rock near to the centre of the dead valley. The prince's son slowed his horse, for her had never seen such a beautiful creation and wondered what she might be doing in this arid waste. He drew up his mount close to where the woman sat.

"Who are you?" he asked her. "And what are you doing in this miserable place? Your clothes show that you are highborn but I see no one with you—no servants nor protectors. So I ask again, why are you here?" The woman lowered her eyes as she answered him.

"I am a king's daughter who has been expelled from her royal palace by her hateful stepmother. She had strong men carry me away to this terrible and lonely place where she hoped that I might be eaten by the wild beasts or poisoned by the crawling snakes. She hated my beauty and the love that my father—her husband—bore me. She wanted me cast out from his court so that she could pollute his mind with her evil. She is a witch! She wishes me dead!" The prince's son reined in his horse.

"This shall not happen!" he declared, for he was already smitten with her. "Not whilst I live shall it be so!" The girl only laughed and the prince's son thought that he detected a hint of madness in her tone.

"Brave words," she replied almost mockingly. "But I have been cast out here too long. The world will have forgotten me. My father will already have mourned my passing and I will be but a memory to him now!" The prince's son was not to be turned however.

"I will take you to my father's kingdom," he declared. "There you will be safe from whatever evil that has threatened you." The woman smiled wanly.

"Then lift me up onto your steed," she said, "and I will surely come away with you, beyond the reach of my stepmother." The prince's son leapt down from his horse to the ground in order to help her. As he did so, however, the ground around the rock where the lady stood seemed to heave and move as though it were being badly disturbed. The earth began to split and crack and hands began to emerge, clutching at his legs and feet. A horrible stench filled the air, an awful stench that made it almost impossible to breathe. A filthy claw with long and ragged nails grabbed at his ankle and held him fast and, as he looked, the beautiful woman in front of him slowly began to change into a creature you would only see in nightmares. To his horror, he realized that the area around the rock was the abode of ghouls! He had been tricked by creatures that now sought to devour his flesh. He had almost hoisted one of the evil tribe onto the saddle of his horse! Kicking the clutching hands away, he rushed back to his horse, which was itself already whinnying and drawing back in fright. Although he was not superstitious, he had a framework of red threads tucked away in his saddlebag as a precaution against evil. And it was as well that he did! The ghouls were close behind him, rising from the broken earth similar to emerging corpses. He opened the saddlebag and drew out the magic thread. Spreading it between his fingers, he held it up in the fading light. Calling out a certain charm that was known mainly to the Hebrews, he drew his fingers amongst the thread. The ghouls paused in their mad rush. Even as he watched them, they seemed to disintegrate, their essences being drawn into the patter of thread between his fingers. One followed the other until they were all gone, absorbed into the lattice before his eyes that he then crumpled up and thrust back into his saddlebag. On his way through the valley, he came to a deep ravine and into this he threw the crumpled ball of thread, watching it fall away into the darkness. Then he continued on his journey and was troubled no more, but he had a narrow escape. His father, the prince, gave strict orders that the ravine in question be sealed forever in the name of Allah and ordered that travellers should avoid the valley. So it is, to this day. The prince's son, however, became ill due to his close contact with the terrible creatures and died of a fever soon after. Let this be a warning to all travellers.

Stories such as this demonstrate how widely held the belief in ghouls was throughout the ancient Middle East and how widely they were feared. They also demonstrated to travellers that the monsters could be defeated. Even so, this did not seem to lessen the popular terror of them and they still assumed a central place amongst the terrors of the night throughout the Middle East.

Gehenna

Although ghouls were supposed to infest remote places such as isolated valleys and deserts, this was not always the case. Sometimes they lurked close to cities as well. The Valley of Hinnom (also known as Gehenna), for instance, just beyond Jerusalem, was allegedly their abode. This was a place where all the rubbish of Jerusalem was dumped and which burned. Indeed, Gehenna became an early Christian name for the Fiery Pit or Hell into which Satan had been cast. It was associated with filth and disease in the Semitic mind and was thus an excellent dwelling place for ghouls and afreets. Few people dared to venture too deeply into it.

Resurrections

The idea of the ghoul also remained alive in the European mind. The word itself was to resurface in the English language during the Victorian period, and in a specific sense; it referred to a new breed of criminals who were connected to the developments and advances in surgery and medicine. These were the Resurrections or "Sack 'em ups"—men (and sometimes women) who gave dead bodies to medical institutions that were then used for both surgical and medical experimentation and demonstration purposes. The crime involved grave robbing and the clandestine digging up of freshly interred cadavers that were then passed on to the medical halls. It was a dark traffic and those who practiced it were sometimes referred to as "ghouls." Their behaviour was said to be "ghoulish"—a word that has remained in the English language and is still in use today. The most famous of all these

"Resurrectionists" were the Edinburgh body snatchers, William Burke and William Hare who are frequently referred to as the "Irish ghouls" (both of them were of Irish birth), and indeed the year 1828, when both men were at the height of their murderous intent, is often referred to as "the year of the ghouls" because of this.

Ghouls in Film

Although never as successful in a cinematic sense as vampires, werewolves, or even zombies, the ghoul did spawn at least one film of note. Filmed in England in 1933 at the height of Universal Pictures' monster mania, *The Ghoul* was directed by T. Hayes Hunter and was released through Gaumont-British Pictures.

The Ghoul

The Ghoul featured Boris Karloff, fresh from his success in *The Mummy* and Cedric Hardwicke, both British actors. A rather uneven film, it nevertheless holds the distinction of being the first film to be awarded a "Certificate H" (for horror) by the British Board of Film Censors and some of its showings in the United Kingdom were severely limited. It later became a minor "cult film" in the United States with several re-releases—the latest onto DVD in 2003.

Night of the Ghouls

Another film that "established" the ghoul in the public consciousness, though for very different reasons, was "Night of the Ghouls" directed by Edward Wood Jr., more famous for his "Plan 9 from Outer Space"—possibly one of the worst movies ever made. "Night of the Ghouls" runs it a close second. Originally shot in 1960, it was not actually released until 1983, largely because Wood could not afford to have the negative processed. Because of its sheer awfulness as a film, it became something of a "cult classic" and once more brought the terrifying figure of the ghoul to the forefront of human imagination. In the wake of the film's release, a number of books (many of them badly written) began to appear, bearing the word "ghoul" in their titles.

Golem

From the earliest times, the ultimate goal that was pursued by magicians was the creation of life itself. However, it was suggested in Talmudic commentaries that the best that sorcerers could hope for was to create the more unthinking life forms: camels, oxen, and so on—whilst the much more refined and complex forms, such as men themselves, were far beyond the ability of humans. This sort of creation was reserved for God alone. Other religious thinkers believed that whilst men or man-like beings might be created through a knowledge of sacred words and signs used by God in the Creation of the Universe, they would lack the intelligence and subtlety of thought that only the Divine could give them. Early rabbis, therefore, preoccupied themselves by trying to create entities such as a three-year old calf or an ox using a process that was known as "Name magic"—special names that Jehovah had uttered in order to create the world—that were to be found in various obscure editions of books such as the *Talmudic Laws of Creation*. This was not to be considered as forbidden magic for "the laws of God were brought about through His Holy Name." Letters and sounds were juxtaposed in an attempt to emulate God, often without much success.

Homunculus

The process of creation both fascinated and obsessed the thirteenth century *Hasidim,* a group of Pietists and Mystics. It is thought that they were among the first to use the word *golem,* which they used to denote formless matter that had no life in it. It was simply stuff out of which life might be formed and which God had used in order to create Man. Through the invocation of certain special Names, these men sought to create a homunculus—a small, primordial representation of a human being that would enjoy some form of animation. Some of them claimed that they had discovered texts, which were the secret words of God, given to Moses on Mount Sinai along with the Torah and the Talmud. These were the invocations that God had used to create Adam Kadmon, the prototype human who ultimately became the partner of Lilith and had to be destroyed. It is possible that the earliest legends concerning the Golem come from this group of thinkers.

Rabbi Samuel

The earliest known of these thinkers is said to have been Rabbi Samuel, father of Judah the Pious (d. 1217, author of the *Book of Angels*, a collection of theological and esoteric works) who is said to have constructed a homunculus that accompanied him on his travels and which could apparently think and move of its own volition but could not speak. Some of those who saw it described it as a small, grey-skinned manikin that the esteemed Rabbi kept in a jar or container.

It was amongst the German Jews, however, that interest in the creation of homunculi flourished. Here, many Rabbis heavily influenced by the thinking and writing of the *Hasidim,* contemplated the creation of life from shapeless matter. Others warned against the sin of attempting to emulate God, but the urge to create even the basest form of life continued to thrive and grow.

Joseph Delmedigo

The writer Joseph Delmedigo stated in 1625 that there "are many of these legends (concerning the creation of life) current, particularly in Germany." During medieval times, the area, which now constitutes large parts of Germany and Austria, seemed to be awash with mystical texts—many of which were said to date back to the early Middle East.

Kaballah

The vast majority of these were said to be portions of the *Kabbalah,* or *Q'balah*—a sect of mystical texts that had been supernaturally revealed to Moses, either when in Egypt or when he was on Mount Sinai.

Sefer Yetzirah

Of course, there were many versions of this magical text, one of which was known as the *Sefer Yetzirah* or *The Book of Creation* (sometimes translated as *The Book of Formation*) that contained the various names which God had used to create both Adam Kadmon and Adam. This work, which is said to have been revealed by God, emerged around the 16th century and is usually credited to Isaac Luria—generally regarded to be the father of the modern Kaballah.

Through this text a rabbinical magician could form a living, man-like being out of shapeless clay. However, the creature thus created would have no real will of its own—no Divine spark or soul because these were the specific gifts of God. These entities were known as golem.

Rabbi Elijah of Chelm

There are a number of tales concerning rabbis who created such beings. The most famous legend concerns Rabbi Elijah of Chelm, a 16th century mystic. He is reputed to have created a being out of clay using the *Sefer Yetzirah* and breathing life into it by inscribing the Name of God on its forehead. Although it lived and moved and performed small tasks, the creature had no will of its own, behaved similar to an automaton, and could not speak. However, it grew to almost gigantic proportions and became increasingly destructive so that the Rabbi, appalled by the potential of what he had created, removed the name from its brow, whereupon it crumbled to dust once more. This is probably one of the earliest stories concerning the golem but there were others.

Rabbi Eleazar ben Judah of Worms

One of these stories concerns the German magician, Rabbi Eleazar ben Judah of Worms (1165–c.1230). Rabbi Eleazar was considered to be one of the last of the mystical *Hasidim* and is generally credited as being the author of the *Sosei Razavya*—"The Secret of Secrets"—a tome that was based on the *Sefer Yetzirah.* A German himself, born in Mainz, Rabbi Eleazar had distilled much of the swirling mystical lore emerging in 12th century Europe. He dared to record, for the first time, a formula for creating a golem, which took up twenty-three folio volumes, emphasizing the formidable nature of the project. The image of a man was to be made from "virgin soil" which was to be taken from a remote, mountainous place where no man had ever dug earth before; over this image was to be intoned "incantations of the 221 gates." This specific incantation had to be recited over each individual organ in turn.

Emeth

Various combinations of names and letters were to be used in the formation of the figure and on the forehead of the image was to be placed either a secret Name of God or the word *emeth* (meaning "truth"). The destruction of the golem might be accomplished by removing the initial character of that word, leaving *meth* (meaning "dead or devoid of life"). In other instances, the utterance of other incantations might be used to destroy the creature that some rabbis described as "a reversal of laws of creation."

Judah Loew ben Bezalel

The most famous of all the rabbinical magicians associated with the golem however, was Judah Loew ben Bezalel (1525–1609) also known as the Maharal of Prague. The so-called "Frankenstein of Prague" was credited with creating a golem, which, it is said, may still be in existence today.

In an increasingly Christian Europe, Jews were struggling to hold onto their identity and culture. Increasingly, in the Christian mind, they were becoming closely associated with sorcery and witchcraft—probably because many Jews were rich and prospering more readily than their Christian counterparts. This, of course, led to allegations of evil magic against them and the tales of various rabbis seeking to create life (which, in Christian eyes, only God Himself could do) only added fuel to the prejudicial fire. Jews were now regarded as black magicians, poisoning wells and water supplies and summoning up demons for the purposes of destroying the Christian religion. These views were taught as fact by a number of early modern Christian clerics. There were attacks by Christian elements on Jewish homes and businesses throughout Prague and beyond. Local politicians, seeking popular approval, spoke out against the Jews and, subsequently, the community in Prague increasingly felt itself under pressure. The Maheral, Rabbi Judah Loew, was becoming extremely concerned about the situation, especially the inflammatory speeches given by Christian leaders, which only stirred up violence.

The Golem of Prague

In 1580, he is reputed to have asked God for some way in which he could protect the Jewish community (and especially the Jews of Prague) against the "blood libel" that was being perpetrated against them. God allegedly gave him the formula by which he could create a powerful golem that would serve as a Jewish protector. It is said that Rabbi Judah used the formula to give birth to a strong and violent creature, which he kept well away from human eyes in an attic of the *Altneuschule,* the principal synagogue in Prague. Said to be immortal, the golem was allegedly transferred to Warsaw in Poland, during World War II and the Nazi occupation coupled with the persecution of the Jews in that city. There, it is supposed to have attacked and killed several Nazi soldiers before being hidden away again. It was reputedly returned to Prague where it may still be located. The idea of a huge figure lumbering through the fog-bound streets of a European city is enough to fill anyone with dread.

It is perhaps worth noting the Rabbi Loew's grave in the Old Jewish Cemetery in Prague's Jewish Town is one of the most frequently visited tourist sites in the city. Many of those who visit it are well acquainted with the legend of the golem and many also visit the *Altneuschule*, convinced that the creature is still there. Perhaps it is, although the Jewish authorities in Prague do a good job of convincing the curious that perhaps it didn't exist after all. And yet, there are still many who search for it, convinced that it still exists, hidden somewhere in Europe.

Descriptions of the golem vary. Some accounts state that it was simply the size of an ordinary man but with a blank, lifeless face and unable to speak. Its arms seem to have been longer and more muscular than that of an average human. Other descriptions state that it was much bigger than any regular human, gray skinned, and with a narrow, bland face with dark and slitted eyes. It positively oozed a sense of menace as it lurched along with a lumbering walk, which in no way resembled that of a human. This was a monster in many senses of the world—a soulless entity that knew neither right nor wrong and which could be commanded for good or evil.

There was much discussion amongst the rabbinical schools as to what actually *motivated* the Golem, whether it was a dybbuk or evil spirit, or whether it was the Breath of God Himself. Few could agree. Some rabbis claimed that it was a sin for a man to take on the role of Creator and that any such creation must be evil. Some even connected the creature to Iblis, Lord of the Damned, and denounced it as a minor demon. It was generally agreed, however, that the creature could only be dismissed or destroyed by a rabbi, using a special formula that could only be passed down within the Jewish clerical tradition. This was to be done in the form of an exorcism, which, certain rabbis argued, did not necessarily mean that the creature was evil. Others insisted that it did. At the same time, there were further arguments concerning the *intent* of the golem. Because the creature had no will of its own, it had to be directed by its creator and whilst most of these seem to have been holy rabbis or clerics who were interested in mysticism and alchemy, there were also suggestions of "false rabbis"—evil sorcerers with a knowledge of the sacred rabbinical texts, who might manipulate the golem for their own ends. For example, the golem would often be used to settle feuds or intimidate wealthy Jews. Some theologians insisted that merely by creating the golem, a rabbi had exposed himself to sin and might become evil in his ways; some argued that no sin had occurred because the act of creation was carried out with the express approval of God, otherwise they would not have been successful. These debates raged mainly between the European schools of Jewish thought and, although the golem was known in Middle Eastern demonology/mythology, it maintained a relatively peripheral role amongst the night terrors there.

Golem Lore

Ironically, it was a German language collection of Jewish lore that brought the story of the Golem and of Rabbi Loew to the fore in 1847. It was picked up by Czech literature almost immediately and was used as a source by the writer Alois Jerasek in his "Old Bohemian Legends." The Czech writer and poet, Jaroslav Vrchlickys, also composed a poem about the creature "Golem" in which Rabbi Loew is punished for his presumption against God in actually creating a living being. The main literary work concerning the Golem was written at the end of 1914 and was published in 1915. This was Gustav Mayrink's novel *The Golem,* which has become something of a minor classic of

European Jewish literature. In 1982, the foremost Jewish writer and laureate, Isaac Bashevis Singer, wrote his own English version of the golem legend—also entitled *The Golem,* which is still available

Some students of literature have argued that the motif of the golem, the living creature formed out of unloving clay, provided the basis for Mary Shelley's classic novel *Frankenstein,* in which a living creature is made out of the unliving parts of dead men. Whether Mary Shelley actually knew of the golem legend is unknown though it is quite possible, given her own outlook and the tastes of her husband and companions that she may well have.

Golem Films

Like the ghoul, the Golem remained on the periphery of horror cinematic representation. It was, it was argued, too obscure to occupy the status of the werewolf or vampire in the minds of the movie going public. This is not to say that no films were made about it. Indeed, a rather classic film, *Der Golem*, was made in Germany in 1914, directed by Peter Wegener, with an updated version (again directed by Wegener) released in 1920. These black and white films were mainly adaptations of Mayrink's novel and are counted as some of the foremost movies of the German Expressionist cinema. Another film concerning the creature, *Golem*, was made in 1936 under the direction of Julian Duvevier. But as a monster, the golem was not considered to be sufficiently terrifying—or else far too obscure—to take on the might of the Universal monsters. From time to time, the golem has peripherally featured in other films and tv series—most notably in an episode of the popular supernatural/sci-fi series *The X Files.* Even so, the creature has not gone away, but lurks somewhere in the back of the human psyche, ready to emerge again as soon as night falls or the cloying fog rolls in. The shambling, shadowy figure still holds the power to frighten us all. Part of that fear must surely lie in the secrecy and mystery that still surrounds it, even today.

Golems in Comic Books

The figure of and the mystery surrounding the golem enjoyed something of a brief resurgence during the early 1960s, as the comic books of the day began to pick up on it. In the developing world of comics literature, golem-like figures began to appear albeit bearing fanciful names such as *It: The Unliving*, *Attack of the Clay Man*, *The Thing that Stalks in the Mist*, and *Nightmare Stalker from Hell* to name but a few. Representations of the creature were also fanciful and owed more to artistic interpretation than to any folkloric tradition. Many were portrayed as something between a Caribbean zombie and a bandage swathed Egyptian mummy. There was even a short-lived attempt to establish the golem motif as a type of superhero. The obscure and equally short-lived *Mystic Comics* (1963/64) created a character named *Colosso the Clay Man*, which was loosely based on Golem lore. In this, a young man could transfer his consciousness into and therefore animate a gigantic clay figure that had been stored in a secret place, for the purposes of fighting crime. This series does not appear to have been a success and quickly vanished into obscurity along with the comics company that produced it. Another thankfully brief series concerned a man who transformed into an unthinking and violent golem-like creature in a parody of the Incredible Hulk after touching a meteorite that had fallen from outer space. It, too, disappeared without trace. Nevertheless, the golem (and also the ghoul) continued to resurface as peripheral characters in some of the later comics publications from such major companies as Marvel and DC.

Both the ghoul and the golem may well stem from the oldest traditions that we know of—from amongst the extremely ancient legends and folklore of the Middle East. Both have undergone a number of perceptual changes across the years. The golem, for instance, did not enjoy any widespread notoriety as a monster until the 16th, century although tales about it had certainly been in existence long before that. But the basic core of their terror is very much the same as it was in early times. Tales about them are often fragmentary, but they blend together into a rich tapestry of terror, that has still the power to startle and alarm both Middle Eastern and European minds.

Hints of ancient books and texts that have the power to summon and control demons and monsters have filtered down over the years and, as we will see elsewhere in this book, have influenced some of the darker aspects of our more modern literature.

Although we tend to largely ignore them or else treat them as lesser terrors than vampires and zombies, the ghouls and golems—those terrors of the night—still remain with us, lurking in the furthest corners of our mind and ready to emerge at the slightest provocation. We would do well not to dismiss them too lightly for they are reputedly far older than Mankind itself and represent extremely ancient powers that have lingered with us since the foundation of the world!

The Terrors of H.P. Lovecraft

That is not dead which can eternal lie,
And with strange aeons even death may die.
—H.P. Lovecraft
The Necronomicon

Arguably, no single modern writer has had more influence upon today's horror fiction than H.P. Lovecraft (1890–1937). Many writers in the genre from all across the world, from Britain's Ramsey Campbell to America's Robert Bloch and Stephen King, openly acknowledge their debt to him. His work has been reprinted over and over in novels, various anthologies, collections, and in magazines ranging from formal commercial publications to small, narrowly distributed fanzines. Commentaries on his work abound, each assessing various aspects of his life, outlook, and contribution to an overall horror fiction. For a man whose largely reclusive lifestyle often mirrored that of some of his characters, this is no mean achievement. His fiction, upon which many subsequent writers have based their own work, is a rich tapestry of ancient, slumbering evils and menacing monsters, seemingly drawn in detail from the traditions of the past. His fiction is crammed with "eldritch rites" that stretch back into "time immemorial," "inhuman entities," "blasphemous texts," and "shunned places," described so meticulously that commentators have often wondered if there were not some factual basis to them. Was Lovecraft privy to some corpus of arcane and horrendous knowledge to which the rest of us remain mercifully oblivious? This suspicion is borne out by hints and inferences in the work of some other writers—for example, the Welshman Arthur Machen (1863–1947)—but Lovecraft is perhaps the best known. Does his work contain germs of truth masquerading as fiction? Before considering this, it is appropriate to give a brief biography of H.P. Lovecraft himself.

Lovecraft's Early Life

Howard Phillips Lovecraft was born on 20th August 1890 at 454 (then numbered 194) Angell Street in Providence, Rhode Island. He was the only child of Winfield Scott Lovecraft, a travelling salesman, and Sarah Susan Phillips Lovecraft—a descendant of an old Rhode Island family. He was to remain in Rhode Island for all of his life with the exception of two years spent in New York. He was a sickly child, subject to colds, flus, and infantile ailments that perhaps made his mother overly protective of him. Long periods at home and in bed suffering from illnesses, either real or imaginary, made him brooding, introspective, and dependent upon his mother.

When he was eight, Howard's father, Winfield Lovecraft, died. In reality, he had been incarcerated in a sanatorium for the previous five years suffering from paresis (insanity and paralysis brought on by syphilis). This left Howard in the care of his high-strung mother and two aunts. The Phillips side of the family had been well-established in Rhode Island and had intermarried amongst each other—cousins marrying first cousins—and, it was suggested, weakening the line. A constant theme in Lovecraft's work was the notion of inbreeding amongst "degenerate families" and this may be a fearful reflection of the circumstances amongst his own kin. A number of his stories begin with the narrator suggesting that he might be mad. The thought of hereditary insanity must have haunted Lovecraft like some gibbering spectre. Allied to this, some of the "curious inbred families" that are scattered through his work and that usually gave birth to monsters, have names prevalent in his own family, which may be suggestive of his fear.

Decline of the Family

When his grandmother died, (two years before the death of his father), the family went into a kind of decline that culminated in his mother's illness. Young Howard certainly experienced the most appalling nightmares. The later death of his grandfather, Whipple Van Buren Phillips, produced even greater problems—this time financial ones. Much of the Phillips family fortune had been leeched away in unprofitable business deals and by unscrupulous business associates and, by the time of the death, the estate was near bankruptcy. The Lovecrafts were practically destitute and had to give up their home in order to share a house with another family. For a proud clan, descended from an old Rhode Island family, this was hard for Sarah Lovecraft to swallow. She lavished all her attention and invested all her hopes and ambitions on Howard, a situation with which the boy may not have been fully able to cope. The suffocation of his mother's affection may have placed an unbearable burden upon him and may have damaged his relations with women, and indeed many people, for the rest of his life.

Leaving his birthplace had also affected Howard greatly, and the reduced circumstances in which he now found himself afflicted his mind. He would take long bicycle rides to the Barrington River where he would simply stand and look into the swirling waters. It is thought at these times, he was seriously contemplating suicide. But somehow, his resolve overcame such urges and he always returned home.

A shy, bookish boy, he spent much of his early years reading texts in his grandfather's library—particularly classics of ancient Rome (Ovid, Plato, and Horace) and volumes on ancient and vanished civilizations. He learned some Latin and was able to translate at least some of Ovid's work. This led his mother to believe that he was destined for Brown University, one of Rhode Island's premier educational establishments. She told everyone that her son would one day be a respected University academic. This, however, was not to be the case and probably for the rest of his life, Lovecraft may have felt a sense of humiliation and held the view that he had somehow let his mother down. His fiction throngs with references to "Miskatonic University" and some of the people who taught there—perhaps betraying a deep longing for the formally recognized academic life. His own attendance, first at Slater Avenue School and then at Hope Street High School had always been erratic, and Lovecraft frequently quoted "ill health" as the cause. There seems little doubt that he did have ill health, including a serious nervous breakdown in 1908, but it is possible that he stayed with his mother, who was already experiencing some mental health difficulties. It is also possible that as a solitary, morbid boy, he was loath to face the tumultuous world of college life.

In 1921, Sarah Lovecraft, his mother, died in the Province sanatorium where she had been a patient. The cause of her death was actually due to a badly managed gall bladder operation, but she had been mentally ill for quite some time before. Her death had a profound effect on Howard—she had been his closest companion whilst he was growing up—and it's thought, not for the first time—that he contemplated suicide. Losing both parents in this way induced in Howard a constant fear of hereditary insanity to which he believed he was prone.

First Publishings

Instead of academia, he turned his attention to poetry and writing fiction. At the age of seven, he had already produced a poem, based on the readings in his grandfather's library, entitled "The Poem of Ulysses," but his first actual published work was a letter to the *Providence Sunday Journal* in 1906 on astronomy (a subject that was starting to interest him). However, he appeared to be making no headway as a writer in these early days. He was also becoming more reclusive, staying close to his over-protective mother, and preferring to contact friends by extremely long letters. He also wrote juvenile treatises, mainly for amateur magazines and usually concerning astronomy and science. Most of these were simply crude speculations but they were to lay the foundations for at least part of his future writing.

The Alchemist and *Argosy*

In 1908, he wrote the short story *The Alchemist* but, in truth, he was not writing much fiction, and for five years was to remain in a kind of productivity drought. In 1913, however, he wrote a series of letters to the magazine *Argosy*, attacking the "insipid love stories" of the then-popular writer Fred Jackson. They were written in such a clever way—a parody of Alexander Pope's *Dunciad*, that they evoked much literary interest and the United Amateur Press Association invited Lovecraft to join their ranks.

Short Stories

The letters marked a turning point in his career. He began to correspond with like-minded writers and to produce drafts of stories almost ceaselessly, some of which were to eventually surface amongst his recognized works. In 1917, he wrote both *Dagon* and *The Tomb*; in 1919 he was producing *Beyond the Wall of Sleep*, *The Doom that came to Sarnath*, *The Statement of Randolph Carter*, and *The White Ship*. In that same year, he discovered Lord Dunsay, whom he described as his "greatest literary stimulus…since Poe." (He had presumably read Edgar Allan Poe in his grandfather's library.) Through 1919 and 1920 he maintained this same creative streak, writing both poems and short stories.

Sonia Green

Sarah Lovecraft's death freed Howard a little and he was able to travel a bit more, particularly to amateur literary gatherings. For instance, on July 4 1921, he was able to travel to the first Amateur Journalist Convention in Boston and there he was to meet a woman who was to temporarily change his life: Sonia Haft Green.

Sonia Green was a progressive and self-assured woman. She was a New Yorker and a businesswoman, owning a milliner's shop on 5th Avenue. She was also seven years older than Lovecraft and of Russian-Jewish descent. Howard Lovecraft was impressed with her devotion to letters and, superficially at least, they seemed to have a similar outlook on the world. However, this was no whirlwind romance; it took three years before the two decided to marry.

In all that time, Lovecraft never informed his two aunts—his mother's sisters—of the relationship with Sonia, only writing to them after the marriage, which took place at St. Paul's Cathedral in New York. Perhaps he feared that his wife's ancestry would scandalize the elderly and genteel New England ladies. He resolved to leave Providence for the first time in his life and set up a home with Sonia in New York. A happy future seemed to lie ahead of them.

Nevertheless, the marriage seemed doomed from the start. Sonia herself was unwell and several times had to leave the marital home in order to seek recuperation in various rest homes. Her business collapsed shortly after they were married and she had to give up the milliner's shop, which was their main source of income. Moreover, Lovecraft himself found it extremely difficult to get a job in New York. Besides, he had a growing horror of the city—there seemed to be groups of "aliens" (foreigners) on every street corner; the pace of life was much faster than he had been used to back in Providence; the people there seemed too greedy, grasping, and commercially-minded for his liking. At the same time, he was still writing and was developing his stories into a kind of mythical framework, which would later become known as his Mythos. The couple were now struggling financially and the relationship appeared to falter. Lovecraft continued to write but the money that came in for his published pieces was not sufficient to meet their bills.

Return to Providence

On 1st January 1925, Lovecraft moved into a "bachelor apartment" (no more than a couple of rooms) in a squalid area of Brooklyn whilst Sonia travelled to the Mid-West in order to find work. She would only return intermittently and the marriage might well have been counted as being over at this stage. However, during this time Lovecraft was most prolific, turning out a good chunk of his most interesting work. He was, nevertheless, finding New York increasingly oppressive and was becoming more and more withdrawn—seldom venturing out for days at a time. He was also negotiating, with his aunts, the possibility of a return to Providence. The arrangements were complicated and involved Sonia, Lovecraft's aunts, and several friends, such as the writer Frank Belknap Long. In April 1926, Howard Lovecraft eventually returned to Providence. He would not leave again.

Where did Sonia figure in these arrangements? It seems that she may have had only a peripheral involvement in the central decision. She is thought to have implored Howard to return to New York but he steadfastly refused. The solution would seem to have been for her to come to Providence and open a milliner's shop there, but Lovecraft's aunts stepped in. Under no circumstances would a "tradeswoman" who claimed a kinship to them be allowed to operate in the town where they lived. Though they were in "reduced circumstances" (virtually poverty-stricken), they were still people of quality and had an old and established name throughout Rhode Island. This was the final nail in the coffin for the marriage, and although Lovecraft still professed to love Sonia, the relationship drifted towards an inevitable divorce in 1929.

Feelings Towards Foreigners and Women

Some commentators have suggested that Lovecraft may have held anti-Semitic sympathies; indeed some have gone so far as to suggest that he might have secretly held proto-Nazi views. Lovecraft dwelt in Providence, a town that he seldom left throughout his life and that he remembered in his early boyhood as a genteel old Colonial place. However, as the 20th century advanced, Providence was beginning to develop and change. Migrant workers were arriving there as they were doing all over America, and with them came unfamiliar ways and ideologies. It was thought that evil crept into communities through foreigners—those who brought in sinister ways and odd religions. Again, with regard to Lovecraft, this suggestion is not so clear-cut. Howard Lovecraft saw his boyhood home change from a grand old edifice of the Colonial period into a more multi-cultural city where people from other parts of the world mixed freely with the descendants of the Colonists. It was a microcosm of what was happening all over America and it somewhat alarmed him. The values he had grown up with—which his mother's family had espoused—were changing or being swept away. Thus the "insidious foreigner"—the Pole, the Jew, the person from the South Sea Islands—appears throughout his fiction as

an "undermining influence." Although she did not eradicate such a viewpoint entirely, Sonia may have changed it only slightly.

It has also been suggested that his attitude toward women was ambivalent and that he deliberately sought out male company because females scared him. This may not be completely true. Certainly he was very shy and awkward around women—his mother's suffocating nature had seen to that. But there is little doubt that he carried on voluminous correspondence with women and even helped a number of them with their own fiction. The names of Hazel Heald and Zeliah Bishop, with whom he conducted a lengthy correspondence, spring immediately to mind. And it is thought that Lovecraft was developing an attachment to the amateur poetess Winifred Virginia Jackson, although extremely little is known of their relationship. Lovecraft's marriage to Sonia put a stop to any such burgeoning romance.

Creation of Cthulhu

The years 1925 and 1926 were arguably Lovecraft's most creative period, during which he began to develop his Mythos, with tales such as *Pickman's Model*, *The Horror at Red Hook*, and the classic story which was to firmly establish his work in the popular mind—*The Call of Cthulhu*. He returned to the genteel, reclusive lifestyle that he had enjoyed before meeting Sonia—spending his days writing lengthy letters (some amounting almost to small books) to friends and writing colleagues. He also wrote new fiction and by 1927 produced *The Case of Charles Dexter Ward*—his only Cthulhu novel—as well as *A History of the Necronomicon* and the genuinely chilling *The Colour Out of Space*. In 1928 he completed *The Dunwich Horror* with its theme of remote New England communities, ancient and "blasphemous" rites, and nonhuman monsters. It seemed that his time in New York had somehow changed him and had made his imagination darker and more brooding.

This morbidly became even more pronounced in his following major work that was written in 1930—*The Whisperer in the Darkness*, followed in 1931 by *The Shadow Over Innsmouth* (in which he extended and enlarged the Mythos), and *At the Mountains of Madness*, two of which are regarded as some of his best work. It has been suggested that he based the decaying coastal village of

Innsmouth with its peculiar inhabitants, on the then rather run-down fishing town of Cohasset, Massachusetts although there is no evidence of this. Many of these stories were published by the developing "pulp" market, which was to characterize the 1930s horror and science fiction genres. He was already a regular contributor to the magazine *Weird Tales,* edited by Farnsworth Wright, but he also wrote for such publications as *Amazing Stories,* which enjoyed an equally wide readership. Gradually, his reputation as a "master of horror" began to grow, although he does not seem to have particularly relished this. He still mainly communicated by letter and was now becoming widely known as "the Rhode Island Recluse," which only seemed to add to his mystery and eeriness. It also led to much speculation about who he was and about the sources to which he might have had access.

In 1933, Lovecraft moved to what was to be his final home in Providence—66 College Street. The house must have appealed to him because of its age—it had been built in 1825 and was believed to be haunted. All the same, Lovecraft settled down there to write *The Thing on the Doorstep* and *The Shadow Out of Time*. But he was ill once more.

Death of Lovecraft

At first, it was believed that he was suffering from Bright's Disease—an inflammation of the bowel that had been caused by drinking copious amounts of black coffee (one of his favourite drinks). But it is more probable that he had a form of intestinal cancer. He started to deteriorate quite alarmingly and his output slowed down. On 10th March 1937, he entered the Jane Brown Memorial Hospital with his condition dangerously advanced. He had resisted medical advice for almost two years—perhaps out of the memory of his mother's botched gall-bladder operation—and it was now too late. There was little that could be done for him and he died ten days later. He had left behind a dark and monstrous legacy.

Other writers in the genre who also wrote for the pulp magazines—such as August Derleth, Frank Long, and Robert Bloch—hailed Lovecraft as their inspiration and extolled his undoubted contribution to macabre literature. Many more—from authors of established fiction to those writing for small fanzines—

would draw upon his Mythos for their own work, producing pastiches, which reflected Lovcraftian themes and settings. Indeed, if we include people such as Clark Ashton Smith, Donald Wandrei, Ramsey Campbell, Robert M. Price, and Brian Lumley, Lovecraft spawned an entire genre of horror all his own. In order to accommodate this developing corpus of fiction and commentary, his friend and correspondent August Derleth established Arkham House Press (based on Arkham, the principal city in Lovecraft's Mythos which, in fact was no more than a thinly-disguised Providence) on 15th March 1937, several days after his death. This publishing house is still going strong and has reprinted a number of volumes of Lovecraft's own work as well as books by authors working in the Lovecraftian vein. A few other publishers have also dedicated themselves to printing Lovecraft-type works and a number of films have been produced centred around Lovecraftian themes.

Scholars, too have closely examined his work and one question emerges time and time again amongst academics, other writers, and fans alike. There is no doubt that Howard Lovecraft created a unique universe in which immeasurably ancient gods watched the menial activities of Mankind with an antipathy bordering on outright hostility and in which ancient books and texts, locked away in mouldering attics, often acted as a doorway to some other bizarre and unclean dimension in which foul things lay in wait for unwary and the naive. But we are entitled to ask, did all of this hold some element of truth? Did Lovecraft perhaps somehow have access to a body of knowledge, which was unavailable to most humans? Were the horrors that he created simply the meanderings of an isolated and morbid mind or did they have their origins in some separate and terrifying reality? And if so, what was the *source* of theses nightmares and how did it make itself available to Lovecraft? Did he unearth something—as did many of his protagonists—in the library of a relative, in this case his grandfather Whipple Phillips? Or did he find such dark knowledge from another source? This is the question that his intrigued many of his followers and devotees for almost a century.

The Influences of H.P. Lovecraft

It is probably true to say that what became known as the "Cthulhu Mythos" can be divided into two aspects—what might be termed "the scientific Mythos" (deriving out of his interest in astronomy) and the "folkloric Mythos." The two are not mutually exclusive but generally speaking, in the former, the horror comes from the stars, whereas in the latter it emerges out of myth and legend, and research by the protagonist of the tale or by someone closely connected to him or her. It is this aspect that has intrigued investigators of Lovecraft's work. The folkloric element hints at incredibly ancient practices that have somehow been preserved and to the vanished peoples who carried them out. It also suggests dark and powerful deities that were worshipped by these peoples and which might still be able to intervene in the world. These ancient entities might be accessed by mortals through arcane (and "blasphemous") texts—written on scrolls, books, and even pottery fragments, all spelled out in a sinister language that needed translation, the utterance of which was sufficient to damn the soul. Could there be an actual, factual basis to any of this?

Ancient Civilizations

The folkloric Mythos as developed by Lovecraft (and others) draws on a number of legendary strands. Arguably, two traditions stand out—that of prehistoric America and that of the ancient Middle East. Fragments of other legends have been tagged onto them—the legend of Atlantis for example, and obscure tales from the South Pacific. But essentially, Lovecraft and those who came after him were especially fascinated by cultures that had emerged out of the very dawn of time.

And there were indeed evidences of early cultures in America, which were beginning to be examined around the time in which Lovecraft was writing. Archaeology was an up and coming science that was attracting interest even outside academic circles.

Howard Carter

In 1922, for instance, a team led by the archaeologist and Egyptologist, Howard Carter had discovered and entered the tomb of the boy-king Tutankhamun in the Valley of Kings in Egypt, finding wonderful treasures but also statues of strange and exotic gods and goddesses, then barely known in the West. There were also widespread tales of a curse, which beset members of the team who had gone into the tomb and which had followed them even beyond the borders of Egypt. Several members of Carter's team, it was widely rumoured, had succumbed to the "curse of the Pharaohs." The dark gods of that ancient civilization, it seemed, cast a long shadow. Intrigued by the notion of such slumbering, arcane powers, the people of the 20th century—in America in particular—began to wonder if there were other ancient peoples, perhaps with similar exotic and ferocious gods who might have existed elsewhere.

Mound Builders

Indeed, for the Americans, there were evidences of an equally old and even more mysterious civilization on their own back doorstep. Scattered across the American Mid-West and into New Mexico were the awesome traces of a civilization which was probably just as old (if not older) than the Egyptians, the last vestiges of which had been glimpsed by Spanish explorers in the 16th century. These ancient people are almost as much of a mystery today as they were in Lovecraft's time. They were the Mound Builders who constructed massive earthworks—cones, hillocks, terraced platforms, and pyramids. Prehistoric America had more pyramids than there were in Egypt. (One, still standing in the state of Illinois, has a much larger base circumference than that of the Great Pyramid of Khufu.) Around the 1100s, massive beehive centers, known to have existed in the lands to the west of the Appalachian Mountains, were studded with deep caves in which these vanished people dwelt and formed the centre of massive earthwork "cities" comprising it is thought of no less than 12,000 inhabitants—a little more than the city of London at that time and with links to other such centers well beyond the earthen walls and wooden palisades. These people traded with each other—working in copper and silver, but also in obsidian, a hard, black, volcanic glass, which was turned into knives and weapons. They adorned themselves in various "barbaric" yet, exotic artifacts, moving them along the various waterways that were the lifelines of their civilization—alligator teeth and conch shells, brought from the Florida coast, up the Chattahoochie River to Tennessee; mica brought down from mines in the Smokey Mountains of North Carolina; grey pigment (pulverised lead sulphide) was brought from the area of present-day St. Louis; red and grey pipestone (for making pipes) was brought from the territories around the Ohio River. And of course obsidian, mined in Idaho and Wyoming, travelled all over the continent, causing archaeologists to consider that it was not only used in weaponry but also ceremonial rituals as well.

The Adena, The Hopewell, and The Mississippi

The era of the Mound Builders falls into three distinct archaeological periods: the Adena, which was centred around the Ohio River valley from roughly 500 B.C. to 100 A.D. (although these people may have had an even older hunter-gatherer pedigree) and the Hopewell (named after Cloud Hopewell of Chillicothe, Ohio on whose farm their artefacts had first been found). Their culture seems to have peaked between 50 B.C. and 400 A.D. They were also centered in Ohio but had spread to other areas including Pennsylvania and Mississippi which existed from about 800 A.D. onwards until the European invasions of the 16th century. This latter civilization appears to have been the most highly developed and stretched as far south as the Mississippi River, building great temple mounds as they went. It was the last remnants of the Mississippi culture, the third archaeological period, that the Spanish conquistador Hernan de Soto (1500–1542), as he entered the Mississippi River area in 1542. But by this time, they had been decimated by diseases that they had contracted through the Europeans, mainly French traders and trappers who were already in the area. In fact, de Soto's death on the banks of the Mississippi has sometimes been attributed to his interference with some of their shrines, which he had allegedly desecrated. All through the territories were "effigy mounds," which were shaped or bore the shape of various animals, birds, and serpents. Others seemed to suggest odd geometric shapes—octagons, circles, and squares—all of which aroused the curiosity of the early settlers.

The Mississippi culture would seem to have a highly developed religious aspect to it. It has been suggested that its religion was primarily Shamanistic, and if this is so, the evidence suggests that connections between the human world and that of the spirits may have been very close. When excavated, some of the mounds and tumuli were found to contain layered tombs, lined with logs, where the remnants of bodies resided, perhaps still somehow involved in the world around them.

Ephraim J. Squier and Edwin H. Davis

Between 1845 and 1847, Ephraim J. Squier and Edwin H. Davis, both working under the auspices of the American Ethnological Society, dug in to a large earthwork known as Mound City located in south-central Ohio, and found that it was in fact a necropolis—a city of the dead—which covered 13 acres and contained over 23 burial tombs. Squier and Davis published their findings in 1848, as the first of a series of books on natural science and archaeology sponsored by the recently established Smithsonian Institution. Their writing was to set the tone as to how these early people might be viewed. They spoke, for example, of "sacred enclosures" devoted to obscure religious functions and surmised that the builders were skilled engineers, well versed in geometry and mathematics. This led others to speculate that the alignments of such constructions were somehow connected to the stars and might be used for mysterious purposes. Their book, *Ancient Monuments in the Mississippi Valley*, proved to be a best-seller and won such widespread attention that, in 1849, the newly-elected President Zachary Taylor appointed Squier, a political activist, to a diplomatic post in Central America, where he continued to develop archaeological theories and interests. Attention was now paid to other great mounds, such as Monk's Mound near Collinsville in central Illinois. It was said to be the biggest man-made earthen mound north of Mexico, which contained four terraces and provoked much speculation. This speculation was already taking strange and unnerving turns.

Manasseh Cutler

In 1788, an astute clergyman from Massachusetts named Manasseh Cutler arrived at the new town of Marietta on the Ohio River. He found trees being cut down to make way for a new building and as they did so, a massive 40-acre earthen settlement was revealed. Assuming that the felled trees had flourished after the settlement had been abandoned, Cutler decided that the age of the trees could be determined by counting the number of annual growth rings in a cross-section of the trunk. Using this method he determined that the earthworks was anywhere between four hundred and over a thousand years old. However, apart from being mathematically astute, Cutler was also a little fanciful and concluded that this was the central structure of a powerful, advanced, and religiously orientated civilization that had flourished along the Ohio before the coming of either Indians or Europeans.

Cutler's ideas, coupled with the discovery of ancient necropolises such as Mound City, couple with Squier and Davis's emotive language (they had referred to many areas as "sacred" or "taboo" ground—the home of ancient and terrifying gods), set the scene for much of early 19th century thinking. By the early 1800s, fables connecting the Mound Builders to a vanished prehistoric "super civilization" had taken root in the American imagination. The mythmakers evoked theories of an advanced prehistoric race, which had worshipped extremely ancient and powerful gods dwelling amongst their earthen temples. These people were now gone from the plains and river valleys, leaving only behind these monuments as testament to their existence.

Caleb Atwater

This theory gained fresh credence as an amateur archaeologist, Caleb Atwater, a postmaster from Circleville, Ohio, began to take an interest in the earthworks. Although sometimes fearful of such places, many of the farmers showed no great respect for them and began to systematically pull them down. Before they vanished completely under the plough, Atwater began to measure them and record details of their structure, publishing his findings in 1820. He found, to his astonishment, that many of them, no matter how far apart, conformed to a similar construction. This led him to believe that some widespread "super race" of engineers had built such structures. Although he was meticulous and methodical in assessing the mounds, Caleb Atwater was also a romanticist. He believed these people (more advanced than even 19th century

Americans) had come from somewhere in the East—possibly India—in order to establish ritual sites to ancient Eastern gods on the banks of rivers and in remote places. His theories might appear ludicrous today, but in the early 19th century they were taken seriously, especially as they appeared to be backed with such meticulous empirical research. Atwater was lauded by no less than an expert of the day: Stephen Williams, a professor at Harvard, commended him on the detail of his work and the excellence of his deductions. For many people, the mythology of a prehistoric "super race" somewhere in America was becoming a reality. A number of "scholars" trawled through numerous ancient texts as well as their own imaginations, attributing the mounds to a wide variety of ancient peoples—Celts, Vikings, Anglo Saxons, Greeks, Romans, Persians, Assyrians, Phoenicians, and ancient Chinese. Some even suggested they had been built by the Ten Lost Tribes of Israel and there was a suggestion that they may have been constructed by survivors from the vanished continent of Atlantis. Later the imposing academic figure of John Wesley Powell—a Civil War veteran, famous for his epic journey down the Colorado River and through the Grand Canyon in 1869, which lead to his appointment as director of the U.S. Geological Survey in 1879—was to assert that these works had been raised by the forerunners of the Indians themselves. The idea was now too deeply ingrained in the popular psyche to completely disappear.

Abelard Tomlinson

Not even the exposure of a massive fraud, perpetrated by a farmer named Abelard Tomlinson at Grave Creek Mound, West Virginia in 1838 shook this belief. Tomlinson claimed that whilst digging near the Mound, he had unearthed a small oval sandstone tablet bearing a 25 character inscription written in a mysterious language. This tablet generated 35 years of research and controversy as University-based experts variously identified the inscription as Canaanite, Numidian, Celtic, and Phoenician. Later, the tablet was declared a fraud, designed by Tomlinson himself, but it had already led to a burgeoning tourist industry which still continues today with the establishment of Grave Creek State Park.

Effigy Mounds

If their enclosures were sacred, what sort of gods did these early people worship? It is widely thought that all the Mound Builder civilizations—particularly the Mississippi culture—had a highly developed priestly order that conducted and guided their worship. This is suggested by the elaborateness of their burials, which are indicative of some form of intensive ritual. The shapes of the "effigy mounds" also seems to indicate that most of their deities were animistic—serpents, wolves, and eagles. But there are others that are suggestive of no living thing. Manessah Cutler declared that the geometric shapes of some of the hills denoted ancient formulae for contacting spirits (later archaeologists derided this, stating that they were simply gathering places for various clans), whilst others have interpreted other mounds in entirely different ways. For instance, one mound in Illinois is said to resemble a hump-backed dwarf, which may have been one of their gods. Others have a definite shape but are said to resemble something inhuman. It is also highly probable that the priests of the Mississippi and even earlier cultures practiced human sacrifice, using obsidian knifes for the purpose. Obsidian knives appear from time to time in Lovecraft's work, always suggestive of extremely ancient ritual. Ceramic bowls, unearthed in some mounds, bore odd faces that, said scholars, might have represented the gods they worshipped. The fact that many of these may be funerary urns, as they have been found beside the crouching cadavers—the Hopewell culture seems to have buried its noble dead in sitting positions—signalling some sort of transition to another world. It is surmised that the deities worshipped by all these people were intensely barbaric and fearsome—perhaps a suitable template for some of Lovecraft's ancient entities.

What became of the Mound Builders and why did they vanish? The common theory is that they were completely wiped out by epidemics. By the time de Soto encountered them on the banks of the Mississippi, they were already suffering from European diseases such as smallpox and typhoid, which must have eventually extinguished them. However, such explanation did not readily satisfy the followers of the "super-civilization" theory. If these people did indeed worship powerful old gods perhaps these deities, coupled with their own scientific prowess, would enable them to survive. The fact that many of these Mound Builders had lived in caves within their structures gave rise to another theory—that they had gone underground to avoid the advance of the Europeans and were still down there, waiting for a chance to return to the surface. This was given further credence by the fact that the folklore of some of the local Indian tribes—for example the Choctaws—made references to underground races living in the lightless realms under the earth, emerging only at night to steal away maidens and horses. The notion of a subterranean super civilization of Mound Builders together with its ghoulish gods, still extant and perhaps hostile towards Mankind (whom they wished cleared away from the surface so that they might return to the light once more), was gaining in popularity throughout the early 19th and 20th centuries.

Subterranean world

The idea of a subterranean world, of course, was not new. From earliest times, it had been surmised that the earth might, in fact, be hollow and that various races had fled into its interior in order to avoid certain instances on the surface. For example, an ancient tale from the Middle East suggests that the terrible spawn of humans and demons had fled into the Underworld in order to avoid the deluge (flood) that God had sent to cleanse them from the upper world. But there were also tales about vanished Roman and Greek cities, the inhabitants of which had fled underground to avoid some natural disaster, such as volcanic eruption, and continued to live down there, either as they had been at the time of their flight or else developing separate cultures and technologies.

Athansius Kircher, Mundis Subterraneus

In 1665, the scientist Athansius Kircher was speculating in his *Mundis Subterraneus* concerning "great cavities" under the earth's crust in which a civilization might establish itself. The idea was taken up by others—including Edmund Halley in his *Theory of Magnetic Variations* (1692). It was not long before writers began to speculate what some of these "inner worlds" might look like, and fanciful accounts soon began to appear "from those who might have visited them." Early tales, reputedly taken from those who had been accidentally swept into the inner worlds, usually by the sea (as in Edgar Allen Poe's *Descent into the Maelstrom* which Lovecraft must surely have read in his grandfather's library), speak of lightless caverns where strange creatures dwelt, such as pale and bizarre-looking fish. The walls of the caverns were covered in mysterious inscriptions.

Charles de Fieux

In 1735, the French writer Charles de Fieux, the chevalier de Mouhy, penned a now-forgotten classic, which involved subterranean travel—*Lamekis, ou les voyages extraordinaires d'un Egyptien dans la terre interierure*. The story is set in the distant past and the characters are centered around the "hero" Lemakis, who moves from ancient Egypt through a number of fantastic countries in which he encounters a prince and princess who have been banished to a subterranean world upon the death of their father. The chevalier de Mouhy explains that he received the story from an ancient and mysterious Armenian who arrived at his court and told him the tale, which he declared to be true.

Ludvig Holberg

One of the earliest and most detailed accounts, however, must be that written by Ludvig Holberg (1684–1754), often referred to as "the father of Norwegian and Danish literature." His *The Journey of Neils Klinn to the World Underground* describes a complex and fantastic world lying far beneath our feet. Although this was thought to be a satire on the religious and political life of his time, "the Moliere, or the North" insisted that it was based on real accounts given to him by Norwegian fishermen.

John Poltrack

The English, too were beginning to consider the possibility of an underground world. John Poltrack's *The Life and Adventures of Peter Wilkins* contains many elements of *Gulliver's Travels,* but provides details of "underground Utopia." In the story, Wilkins, a Cornishman, is wrecked somewhere near the South Pole (long considered as being an access to the subterranean world), and accidentally falls into a strange land existing under the earth's crust. There he finds the kingdom of Doorpe Swangeanti, to which he was borne on a chair, held aloft by several winged beings. He discovered a thriving civilization of "ingenious and industrious" people. He introduces them to technology and whilst they are happy, perhaps they were more so before the coming of the civilizing stranger. In many ways similar to *Gulliver's Travels,* the story is an allegory and owes much more to the writer's imagination and satire than it does to fact, but in the world of the 18th century, it was thought to be a truthful account.

Jules Verne

Following in the steps of *Peter Wilkins*, a number of other such tales appeared (some portraying the inner world almost as outer space in which near-dead planets orbited around dark stars), including (in 1864), Jules Verne's classic *Journey to the Centre of the Earth.* By this time, of course, the theory of the hollow world seemed to have been backed by at least some scientific evidence. Following the War of 1812, a veteran of the conflict and gifted amateur scientist, John Symmes, made a number of calculations concerning the North and South Poles. His conclusion, which was submitted with full mathematical and astronomical calculations, deduced that neither pole existed but, according to magnetic movements, their alleged sites were actually entrances to the subterranean world. This entrance became known as "Symmes Hole" and the concept of it caused great excitement. In the late 19th and early 20th centuries, it fired the imagination of a number of writers of fiction, especially in America and Britain. The Chicago-born writer, Edgar Rice Boroughs (1875–1950) described a number of fictional adventures set in an inhabited underworld.

Edgar Allen Poe

Lovecraft, however, may have been more familiar with the work of two other celebrated writers who had either dabbled in or had made reference to the hollow earth in their fiction. One was the American, Edgar Allen Poe, whose *The Narrative of Arthur Gordon Pym of Nantucket* (1830) drew a great deal of attention when it was first published. Although it starts off as a conventional sea-tale with Pym enlisting on the whaler *Grampus,* it soon turns into a story of shipwreck, cannibalism, and darkness, ending with the hero being swept into a hole leading (apparently) to the core of the world. In this, Poe had clearly been influenced by the work of Symmes, and the yawning vortex into which his hero was plunged is undoubtedly a "Symmes Hole." Much more detailed and fantastical was Edward George Bulwar-Lytton's *The Coming Race*. Bulwar-Lytton (1803–1873) was a novelist and poet, widely known for his historical novels such as *The Last Days of Pompeii*. But *The Coming Race* firmly established him in the genre of fantastic fiction. In the story, the narrator and his friend descend into a deep chasm, when the rope securing them to the surface breaks, trapping them in a terrifying Underworld. His friend is devoured by "a monstrous reptile. The narrator then encounters the Vril-ya, an extremely ancient race of advanced beings who fled the surface countless millennia before. They resemble humans, although they are clearly descended from frogs. The account is very detailed and may have inspired Lovecraft in some of his own creation.

Arthur Machen

Another influence on his work may well have been that of Arthur Machen. Born Arthur Llewellyn Jones (he would later change his name for writing purposes) at Caerton-on Usk in rural Wales in 1863, Machen was fascinated by local folklore and by stories of fairies living under hills. America, of course, was not the only country to boast strange mounds and to have legends and folktales associated with them. Ireland, for example, had a rich and detailed history concerning ancient earthworks (ringforts) and standing stones. Here, too were the ancient tumuli of former races that had dwelt on the island in prehistoric times. These were the paces of the Sidhe (pronounced Shee), that translates roughly as "the people of the mounds." Although they'd been consigned to earlier times, remnants of their race were still said to exist underground, close to tumuli, standing stones, and lone trees. Such places, together with the remains of ancient earthworks which dotted the Irish countryside, were often considered to be supernatural sites and are usually avoided by local people.

Fahr Ree

Similar geographical features occur in Wales and, as in Ireland, were attributed to supernatural elements, particularly fairies (the word "fairy" is believed to have originated from an old form of Gaelic—*fahr ree* meaning "the spirit race"). Stories concerning them circulated widely throughout the Welsh countryside, and Machen certainly picked up on these and incorporated some of the themes into his stories. Throughout the Celtic world, the fairy race was not considered as being terribly friendly towards Mankind—indeed, they were often believed to be hostile and not to be crossed. As in Ireland, the Welsh fairies dwelt underground—a subterranean race—and their places were to be avoided if at all possible. Much of Machen's horror fiction therefore deals with a small "primordial" race, living beneath the Welsh hills and secretly seeking to overthrow Mankind or to do harm to humans. Machen's portrayal of a hidden race, well away from Mankind's gaze and inimical towards humanity was at once both terrifying and fascinating. It preyed on many people's deepest nightmares. What if such a proposition were actually true? Lovecraft himself must have picked up on this, as he also hinted at dark races living in remote areas of rural America, (and remote areas elsewhere in the world) together with their dark and hostile gods, who were ready to attack Mankind at a moment's notice. The idea translated readily to America where there were still sparsely inhabited places and areas that had dubious reputations, such as the "balds" (hilltops on which no vegetation would grow) in Missouri, the Devil's Tramping Ground in North Carolina, or indeed the Devil's Hop Yard in East Haddam, Connecticut (note that the same name is used in Lovecraft's *The Dunwich Horror*). In some legends, these were connected with either mysterious and elemental forces or the worship sites of cults who communed with such forces or with rumoured weird races of underground people. These were areas in which people were said to vanish, queer lights were said to be seen, and strange noises heard. They were places best avoided and they are featured in many of Lovecraft's stories.

Pale Underground-Dwellers

Such beliefs were "fleshed out" by old Indian tales of subterranean worlds. The Choctaw Indians for example, spoke of mysterious pale-skinned people who lived far underground, away from the light and who only came up to the surface in order to hunt by moonlight. They were deemed to be the descendants of the Mound Builders; their interior world was highly dangerous and no surface dweller should seek it out. In effect, the Choctaw tribe sought to avoid any form of contact with them and often referred to them as "ghost men." Some of them were reputed to be giants with an appetite for human flesh, dwelling in deep river caves and ravines. But it was not only men who inhabited these interior worlds. There were stories of monsters dwelling in great caves under the earth—particularly monstrous insects.

Tsul-ka-lu

The most famous of these monstrous tales were to be found amongst the Cherokee Indians of the North Carolina area. They told tales of a particular monster known as Judaculla that lived in a deep cavern at the head of Tuckaseegee River. Descriptions of this creature vary—at times it was a huge wasp-like insect, bigger than an eagle, that could carry away full-grown horses or a full-grown man to its lair; at other times it was a massive slant-eyed giant, sometimes referred to as *Tsul-ka-lu* (the name translates from the Cherokee tongue as "Great Lord of the Hunt")—the last of a monstrous breed of ferocious hunters who had lived in the area in prehistoric times.

Judaculla's Rock

In Jackson County, North Carolina, just outside the town of Sylva, a 3,000 year-old soapstone boulder known as Judaculla's Rock stands. Deep in what is known as Cullowhee hill country, the stone is almost overgrown by the surrounding vegetation and is difficult to find. However, it appears to be covered in indecipherable pictographs, said to be the unknown language of a vanished race. Others have claimed that they are nothing more than the traces of microscopic creatures, first observed in the 1500s by European explorers. Some historians state that they are an ancient battle plan, drawn up in 1755 by the early Cherokees but nobody is really sure. What is known is that the Cherokees still consider it an extremely ancient site and have held rituals there from very early times. There were certainly mysterious ceremonies held there between the years 1850 and 1880. Local legend says that there are at least two other similarly marked stones in the area but the location of these has been lost. The Judaculla Stone is said to bear the mark of the giant's seven-fingered hand as he leapt from hill to hill, but these lines may in fact be part of the ancient pictographs. Judaculla was also allegedly able to change his form and so in some instances is depicted as a massive human, and at others as a gigantic wasp. In this form it descended on sleeping children and carried them off. According to Cherokee myth, the creature could not be destroyed, except by fire.

The Devil's Courthouse

Close by is an area of bare rock known as the Devil's Courthouse, that lies just off the Blue Ridge Trackway, near Pisgah. Cherokee legends say that this eerie spot is Judacullah's dancing ground, both in humanoid and insect form, and is even today widely avoided by locals. Some say that somewhere amongst the bleak rocks is an entrance to an underground world that is Judacullah's kingdom, and that certain people have been carried off. There are rumours, too, of scattered pictographs in the area, but no one is quite sure where they are to be found. Incidentally, The Devil's Courthouse is noted for its high instances of unusual plants and strange insects that can often deliver a deadly bite.

Spearfinger

The Courthouse was also believed to be the home of Spearfinger—a ghastly witch-like being whose skin was supposed to be as hard as the rock. She lived in the area far beyond the memory of any human and had the power to take on any shape including that of a wasp or bee. It was said that she could even take on the form of the rocks and could only be recognized when in human guise, by the first finger of her right hand, which was long and sharp like a pick or awl. In her human form she would attempt to lure away Cherokee children by imitating the voices of those whom they loved—especially that of a grandmother. When the child drew close she would pounce upon the child and carry it away to her underground world beneath Whiteside Mountain (on which the Devil's Courthouse is to be found). She was said to be the last of an ancient race that once lived on the mountain and that was incredibly hostile towards humans. Despite this sinister reputation, extensive developments have been made to turn the area into a tourist attraction. The place is nevertheless suggestive of a monstrous elder race of giants, witches, or insect creatures (or else shapeshifters who can assume attributes of all of these).

Nanthala Gorge

Similar tales relate to Nanthala Gorge, which runs along U.S. Highway 19 through Swain and Macon Counties in North Carolina. The bottom of the Gorge is a very dark and forbidding place and is heavily lined by trees and foliage. It is also said to be the entrance to the home of Ulagu (the word in Cherokee means "boss" or "leader"), a giant Yellow Jacket or wasp.

Ulagu

In appearance, Ulagu is said to be as big as a house with a massive wingspan, which creates a roaring wind wherever it goes. Ugalu has a taste for human flesh, particularly that of young children, so the stories say, and will drop without warning on a settlement to carry the unsuspecting humans off to its lair. Most victims are quite simply paralysed with the speed of its descent and the ferociousness of its attack. The creature can travel and manoeuvre in the air quickly so that when Cherokee infants were carried off screaming, it was difficult for the hunters to keep up. They managed to trace it to its hideout by tempting it with a whole deer, to which a long string—the thickness of a rope—had been attached. In this way they could track Ugalu to its hideout in the gorge. The hunters made their way down into a great cavern that was filled with thin papery material. Many yellow wasp-like creatures, all slightly smaller than the Ugalu itself but vastly bigger than human beings, lived in these chambers. Fearful that they would be stung to death, the hunters fled the terrible place. For all we know, Ugalu and his insect followers may still be down there to this day, watching and waiting to strike against Mankind.

Clingman's Dome

Again, similar stories exist around Clingman's Dome in the Great Smokey Mountains. Named after Thomas Lanier Clingman, a Confederate general during the Civil War and later a United States senator, the highest point of the Great Smokey Mountains National Park overlooks Newfound Gap at the heart of the mountain chain. Somewhere on its slopes is a well-hidden entrance to another world, possibly underground. It is a place where the two worlds cross. The Cherokee call the spot Kuawa-Hi, which means "the Mulberry Place" and at one time considered the entire mountain a place to avoid, lest they should accidentally stumble into it and be transported to another world, never to be seen again

Stull, Kansas

In the village of Stull, Kansas, a similar spot is said to exist, possibly on the edge of an ancient graveyard. This is supposed to be an entrance to Hell and has gained Stull some notoriety over the years. Evil forces are said to emanate from the place, reputedly from far underground. Indeed there is a popular urban myth that when the last Pope, John Paul II, visited the United States, he had his plane specially rerouted so that he would not overfly Stull and be exposed to such evil.

The idea that lost races—whether human or insectoid, perhaps more advanced in some ways than us, may be living underground in the dark and waiting to attack humanity—was an extremely powerful one that appeared in many cultures from rural Wales to rural America. Mankind shuddered at the thought of something monstrous and shadowy lurking just outside the limits of our vision and of our knowledge, on the periphery of existence. And who was to say that it was not true? Fragmentary evidence suggested (and, for some, continues to suggest) that there might be *some* element of truth behind it all. This terror was to form the very basis of Lovecraft's work and lend it an immediacy. The very idea of the Great Old Ones and of an Elder Race, waiting to strike against Humankind, must have filled the hearts of his readers with a fear that resonated throughout the modern psyche.

The Vanished Continent

There was yet another element to be considered—the legend of a vanished continent. The most famous of these was, of course, the doomed continent of Atlantis, which has given its name to the Atlantic Ocean. Legend states that the advanced civilization was overwhelmed by a volcanic eruption, causing the entire continent to sink beneath the waves and disappear. But did such a place in fact ever exist?

Atlantis

The notion of Atlantis is, in fact, a very old one. It appears around 355 B.C. when the Greek philosopher Plato mentioned it in a series of dialogues (philosophical treatises). Plato located a fabulous and highly civilized island continent in the Western Ocean somewhere beyond "the Pillars of Hercules" (which have been identified as the Straits of Gibraltar)—a long distance away from Ancient Greece. Atlantis, argued Plato, was similar to a Paradise on earth, with almost every luxury that Man could dream of or that civilization could bring. Unfortunately this wonderful lifestyle made the people there complacent and greedy and the gods decided to punish them. They created a massive earthquake that disturbed the sea so greatly that it overwhelmed the entire island, consigning Atlantis to the ocean depths. This occurred, Plato said, nine thousand years before his own lifetime. Since then, the myth of an advanced and vanished civilization in the West has persisted, but a central question has also arisen amongst commentators. Was Plato simply using the legend of Atlantis as an allegory—a warning commentary on the Greek civilization of his time—or was he referring to an actual destroyed culture about which he had heard?

The myth of a sunken continent has appealed to the popular imagination throughout the years and many attempts have been made and theories put forward to suggest that Atlantis might have existed. Similar to the Mound Builders, the idea of a prehistoric "super civilization" was, and still is, an immensely exciting one. Various locations have been given for its location—from the Arctic Circle, to the Eastern Coast of America, to New Zealand. Perhaps the most convincing argument for the lost continent came from Professor K.T. Frost of Queen's University, Belfast, who suggested that it might have been part of the Minoan civilization based around the island of Santorinas (north of Crete), the majority of which appears to have vanished almost overnight around 1500 B.C. Seismology seems to back up Frost's theory, detailing a massive volcanic upheaval in the area—on a scale of that of Krakatoa—around that time. Shortly afterwards the relatively advanced Minoan civilization collapsed. Could this have been the Atlantis disaster to which Plato referred?

Atlantean Civilization

Descriptions of the Atlantean civilization vary. There is a common thread throughout all the accounts that it was advanced for its time. Some descriptions portray it as a place of towering spires—futuristic even by our standards; others as a Classical Greek culture in the midst of a savage and primitive world. Still, other accounts show it as a more barbarous place, where its people, though technically advanced, still worshipped old and monstrous deities. Human sacrifice was said to have been carried out on a regular basis. Outraged by this unseemly behaviour, the god Zeus condemned the entire continent to volcanic destruction. Not only do the accounts fail to agree on the religious make-up of Atlantis but few can agree on its political make-up either. Some describe it as an "island city state," making it very small in size, whilst others call it a "confederation of kingdoms" (some of these accounts speak of "seven kings") stretching over an entire continent.

Hyperborea

The notion of Atlantis was further confused by some ancient Greek legends concerning another semi-mythical land—Hyperborea. Amongst the Greeks, there dwelt a number of "foreigners" who allegedly had come from somewhere in the Northwest. The Greeks referred to them as Hyperboreans (from the word *boreas,* meaning "the north wind") and claimed that they came from a country far beyond the Pillars of Hercules. Pliny makes reference to them as coming "from the North." It was said that the sun always shone in that country, which was a peninsula from a much larger frozen continent, and that Apollo often wintered amongst these people. It is thought that the Hyperboreans who dwelt amongst the Greeks were either slaves or captured mercenary warriors and that their "country" might have been a geographical mixture of Britain and the Scandinavian lands. The idea of Hyperborea was to appeal, not so much to H.P. Lovecraft (although he did make mention of it), but to one of his contemporaries, Robert E. Howard, creator of Conan the Barbarian. The Hyperborian lands, home of a tall fair-haired people, bordered on Conan's own native land of Cimmeria, and the Hyborian Age in which many of his adventures are set, holds overtones of an ancient land. During World War II, the Nazi party were deeply interested in Hyperboria as the possible home of the Aryan race from which Hitler claimed that all true Germans were descended. It was the home, the Nazis decided, of ancient occult mysteries and powers and therefore was located by German occultists as being somewhere near the North Pole, perhaps within a "Symmes Hole." Hitler believed that this ancient land had been inhabited by a race of fair-haired giants who were physically perfect in every way and this became the prototype for his ideal of the Master Race.

Lemuria

Of more interest to H. P. Lovecraft perhaps was another vanished land. This was Lemuria which, similar to Atlantis had sunk beneath either the Indian or the Pacific Ocean. Tales of a lost island kingdom had featured heavily in the legends of the Tamil peoples of southern India and Ceylon (now Sri Lanka) but such a place was called Kumerinatu. It was the land of their origin from which they had fled when the oceans had overwhelmed it. The name "Lemuria" (deriving, it is said, from "lemur," although another rather dubious definition gives it as a Tamil word meaning "old red ground") was given to it by the anthropologist Philip Sclater in 1864. This was a time when the Darwinian Theory of Evolution suggested that land bridges to explained the dispersal of various animal types throughout the world. They drew on old legends of sunken landmasses to describe how certain creatures of similar strains were found hundreds of miles apart, and in doing so popularized these tales once more. For example, this was the time when the theory of the lost land of Lyonnaisse (which was reputedly an early medieval kingdom said to lie between the south of England and the French coast—now the English Channel) enjoyed a new surge of popularity. The idea of Lemuria allowed for the spread of various species in the East and fitted in well with evolutionary theory.

Theosophists

What would have been of interest to Lovecraft, however, was the fact that, in the 1880s, the vanished continent attracted the attention of an occult group known as the Theosophists, led by the eccentric Helena Petrovna Blavatsky.

The Society of Theosophists had been founded in New York in 1875, by Henry Steel Olcott, William Quan Judge, and H.P. Blavatsky. It was initially set up to investigate, study and explain mediumistic phenomena (Blavatsky herself claimed to enjoy certain psychic powers) but very soon it extended its remit to explore Eastern religions. Both Blavatsky and Olcott travelled extensively in India, and Blavatsky claimed to have visited Tibet (which was then practically inaccessible to foreigners) several times. She claimed to have made contact with the "Great Masters," ancient, mystic lamas who had powers well beyond that of normal humans and who were in constant contact with beings on another plane. She also claimed that she was their representative in the world (they never left their mountain fastness) and that they regularly communicated their will to her. In order to convey their wisdom to Mankind, the Masters instructed her to write a series of "truths" which she did in her first major work—*Isis Unveiled*. The Masters also revealed to her the location of the Garden of Eden which they said lay in a "great lost continent" stretching south from Asia to Tasmania and which served as the birthplace of all occult sciences.

The Book of Dzyan

From this continent had emerged a mystical work known as *The Book of Dzyan* that outlined the true history of the world. It revealed that Mankind was only the Fourth Race of creatures that had lived upon the earth, and that previous races had been imbued with many occult and psychic powers. This intelligence was communicated directly with H.P. Blavatsky, so no original version of that work can be seen, although many subsequent versions of it have been published.

Blavatsky's theories stirred up a great deal of interest, particularly as she followed *Isis Unveiled* with further Theosophical works such as *The Secret Doctrine* and founded a journal on Theosophical matters, which was widely circulated. Indeed her notions concerning vanished Lemuria intrigued other people who soon emerged with theories of their own. One of these was Frederick Spencer Oliver.

Frederick Spencer Oliver

In 1894, Frederick Spencer Oliver arrived at the startling conclusion that survivors of a psychically advanced race, fleeing the destruction of Lemuria, had arrived on the West Coast of America. (This echoed earlier theories that remnants of the Atlantean civilization had also reached the American coast and that the rise of the Mayan and Aztec civilizations was due to their influence.) Oliver suggested that these survivors had made their home beneath Mount Shasta in California where they lived underground in subterranean cities and influenced events on the surface world, particularly in America, through their supernatural powers. From time to time, they made themselves known to ordinary humans with whom they communicated telepathically as did the Great Masters in Tibet with whom the people beneath Mount Shasta were in contact. More recently, followers of the theory have claimed that the survivors of Lemuria have also been in contact with extra-terrestrial beings which accounts for the seemingly increased UFO activity along the Western American coast.

Mu

There was one other "lost land" that appealed to many followers of the mystic and occult. This was the vanished continent of Mu, although many of the theories concerning this place seem to replicate those concerning Lemuria.

Mu was first identified as a "lost world" by the 19th century traveller Augustus Le Ploageon (1826–1908) and was said to be located somewhere in the Pacific Ocean. He had conducted some research amongst ancient Mayan ruins in the Yucatan Peninsula and advanced the theory, once again, that Mu might be the home of the Mayan race. However, the idea of the vanished continent did not grip the public attention until James Churchwarden (1852–1936) wrote a series of books on the subject, closely identifying it with the development of early America. Since then, other theories concerning Mu have emerged, most owing more to the imaginations of the theorists rather than solid fact. For instance, it was suggested that this might, in fact, be the home of the Chinese and Japanese races and survivors of the catastrophe that had swamped it brought that advanced scientific and occult practices from the drowned continent. Mu was therefore added to the catalogue of mythic "lost lands" and its people to the index of "super civilizations," whose knowledge is now mostly lost to the present world.

Dagon

There was also the question of the gods, whom such peoples worshipped, some of whom were said to be exceptionally ancient. Little is known about the worship in places such as Atlantis or Lemuria, but the deities there were said to have been "blasphemous," having existed "since the foundation of the world." At least some of these primal gods seem to have filtered down into later civilizations where they continued to be worshipped in various forms. One of these is thought to have been Dagon, although the original name of the deity is thought to have been something else. The name "Dagon" is, in fact, Semitic, coming from the root "dag" meaning "little fish." The name indicates a fish-shaped god that swam in the primordial chaos. Later it was represented as an ambiguous deity—half-man/half-fish. There was reputedly a temple to Dagon in the city of Azotus, mid-way between Gaza and Jaffa, that was eventually cleared of idols by Judas Maccabeus. Nevertheless, the cults of Dagon continued (some historians argue that the deity was later transformed into a fertility god) and that it was known to the Phoenicians during early Biblical times. Dagon was probably not the only deity that passed down across the years—others older and just as dark may have featured in the early mythologies of many ancient peoples, forging a connection with what were perhaps the earliest days of Humankind. The thought that ancient gods were also waiting, still worshipped by the survivors of lost continents, was an even more terrifying prospect for many people. Such gods are both monstrous and inhuman in physical shape—writhing masses of tentacles; towering misshapen beings with pseudopodic extremities hanging from their bulbous heads and with bulging and malevolent eyes, reflecting Blavatsky's assertion that all previous races on the earth before Mankind did not even *look* vaguely human.

Funan and Angkor Wat

As stories of lost cities and speculation regarding the civilizations that built them began to proliferate from around the mid-19th century onwards. For example, the discovery of the Khmer kingdom of Funan and the city of Angkor Wat deep in the Cambodian jungles by the explorer Henry Mahout in 1860, as well as tales of other lost cities hidden by the Amazonian rainforest (so interest and excitement about ancient cultures began to develop). Far from being something on the fringes of science, the idea of these mysterious cultures was now moving to the centre of the human imagination.

The Great Old Ones

The heady mix of sunken continents, vanished kingdoms and civilizations, subterranean worlds, ancient gods, and slumbering powers inflamed the imaginations of dreamers and writers all across the world. Many of these themes surface in Lovecraft's work. The Great Old Ones, beings that once dominated the earth, lurk just beyond human consciousness waiting for a time when they can return such as "when the stars are right." Given his interest in astronomy, Lovecraft would have been aware of celestial movements and could have incorporated them into his fiction. One of the times when these ancient deities were at the height of their powers was when the star Algol was in the ascendancy. Lovecraft would also have known that the name Algol derives from the Arabic *al-ghul* and that it was widely known as "the demon star." These incredibly ancient beings were worshipped by degenerates living in remote rural areas or in squalid quarters of the larger towns, who could from time to time contact them or whom they could control (usually through dreams) to do their bidding. Knowledge of their ways was usually too much for the human mind to cope with and those who trafficked with them were usually rendered insane by the contact.

R'lyeh

In Lovecraft's tales, Atlantis or Lemuria becomes the sunken city of R'lyeh, submerged somewhere under the South Pacific. Here, amid the ruins of an incredibly old civilization, the great god Cthulhu lies slumbering, waiting to be awakened. This powerful deity contacts its devotees—amongst whom are those already mad or weak-minded—through the power of dreams and visions as they sleep. Cthulhu is also related to the ancient god Dagon, of Semitic antiquity, and controls the Deep Ones—strange half-man, half-fish creatures who inhabit the decaying town of Innsmouth on the New England coast. Other Great Old Ones lie further away in the deeps amongst the stars or in another reality *between* the stars, making their presence known in oblique ways to those who seek them. Yet others dwell in the recesses under the earth, hidden away in deep woodlands or below crumbling churches, appearing only briefly from pits and gloomy cellars to terrify the narrator of the tale. Throughout many of the stories, these entities are served by degenerate inbred families, perhaps reflecting Lovecraft's personal concerns about his own family. Many of these are the descendants of ancient peoples who initially worshipped such beings in times long past and who are carrying on that tradition into the present day. The idea of mysterious races, working to destroy the reasonable, sane world is central to Lovecraft's fiction.

The Necronomicon and Other Magical Texts

Another major element in Lovecraft's work is the books that are from time to time consulted by characters throughout his stories and one in particular—*The Necronomicon*. These ancient tomes, which are sought by the followers of ancient gods and by scholars alike, contain terrible histories of the world as well as rituals and incantations for directly contacting these Elder beings. Foremost of these was *The Necronomicon*—the Book of Dead Names (although this can also be rendered as *The Laws of the Dead*), which was apparently a Latinised translation of an older work originating in the Middle East. The title of this volume first appeared as a reference in the short story *The Hound* (published in 1923) but later resurfaced as a major work in many of his other, much longer tales—for example, *The Dunwich Horror*. So central to the growing Cthulhu Mythos was this "abhorred and blasphemous tome" and so detailed were some of the quotations from it that many readers began to wonder if indeed such a book actually existed, and how Lovecraft somehow had access to it. Indeed, certain publishers have produced "facsimile" editions of a book purporting to be *The Necronomicon,* which have been eagerly bought by fans and followers of the Lovecraftian tradition. Copies of this text were supposedly held by various respected bodies across the world—always locked away in their "forbidden books" section—from the British Museum to the Vatican Library. But did such an "abhorred and terrible" book actually exist? And if not, what were the sources for the idea that it did?

Abdul Alhazerad

In its original form, the book is attributed to Abdul Alhazerad (born around 712 in the city of Tabez), a poet from Senna, Yemen and was allegedly penned during the time of the Ommiade Caliphs, around 730 A.D. Alhazarad supposedly journeyed into the Roba al-Khaliyeh or, Empty Quarter of the Southern Arabian Desert. There he found a nameless city (sometimes given as Irem of the Pillars) built by a vanished race and housing unimaginable horrors, which drove his mind over the edge of sanity. When he returned to civilization, he attempted to set down much of what he had seen and learned in a text that he entitled Al-Azif. The name comes from the sound made by nocturnal insects which, in Arab folklore, is also thought to be the conversations of (or the howling of)demons and spirits. An alternative title which has sometimes been accorded to it is the *Revelation of the Djinn* or *The Secrets of Demons.* After penning this terrible work, Alhazarad was allegedly torn to pieces in the marketplace of a bustling town in full view of everyone, by unseen and hostile demons. His text, however, survived and passed through various hands until it was translated into a Greek edition by Theodorus Philataes of Constantinople.

Olaus Wormius

The name *Necronomicon* was not given to the book until its translation into Latin by a figure whom Lovecraft identifies as a 13th century Dominican monk named Olaus Wormius, who also added a preface displaying a deep occult knowledge. Here, Lovecraft makes a slight error, because he is writing of an actual historical person who was most certainly not a monk nor did he live during the 13th century. Although certainly an antiquarian, Olaus Wormius wrote on medical matters during the 17th century when he spent his time as a student, attached to the Danish court. Actually, he is thought to have had absolutely no interest in the occult and so to name him as a translator of the darkly magical *Necronomicon* is something of a mistake. According to Lovecraft and several other writers following in his wake, the book was formally banned in 1232 by direct orders of Pope Gregory IX (1227–1241), founder of the Papal Inquisition and a fierce and implacable opponent of heresy. The idea that the

Pope would denounce a book compiled by a Dominican friar (or indeed that Wormius would *be* a Dominican) seems a little odd. The Dominicans were staunch protectors of religious orthodoxy and although Gregory favoured the Franciscans, he was also sympathetic to the Dominican Order, making them the chief Order of the Inquisition. Their nickname in this role was "Domini Canes"—the "Hounds of God." It therefore seems slightly strange that a Dominican should be so readily prepared to translate such a "blasphemous book"—but this is a minor issue.

Dr. John Dee

Using the Wormius translation, several other editions of the book are alleged to have appeared in Europe. One, said to have been circulating in the 15th century, was a German "black-letter text" whilst the other, supposedly dating from the 17th century, was probably Spanish. Some writers have also alleged that the celebrated Elizabethan magus, Dr. John Dee, possessed an English copy, which he kept well hidden. Most copies of the text, however, were said to have been destroyed—the last of them perishing in a fire in the studio of the crazed artist Richard Upton Pickman, in the story *Pickman's Model.* Lovecraft's friend, Frank Belknap Long, was said to possess a copy of it, from which he reprinted fragments (his copy was said to be incomplete) after Lovecraft's death. But was there even a book that might closely approximate the terrible volume lurking somewhere in the world? Or did the entire volume simply emerge from Lovecraft's fevered and brooding imagination?

From earliest times, ancient texts with magical overtones had been circulating in the scholarly world. A number of these had initially come from Egypt and, although supposedly Christian, had distinctly Pagan overtones. Most of them had to do with magic and the summoning of spirits for either healing or protection from harm. Some were charms designed for transcriptions to amulets. Other texts, originating in the Middle East, concerned themselves with astrology and astronomy. Some were the utterances and lore of the pre-Islamic kahins who often linked the destiny of individuals to the movements of celestial bodies.

Poeticon Astronomicon

It is thought that Lovecraft actually derived the name *Necronomicon* from the *Poeticon Astronomicon,* a poem concerning the stars written by the Roman writer, historian, and astronomer, Gaius Julius Hygiaus who lived in the first century B.C. This was a star atlas, detailing the constellations in their relation to mythology and showing the positions of certain individual stars. Its first known printing was in 1475 and was attributed to "Ferrera" about whom nothing is known. It was later reprinted in 1482 by Erhard Ratdolt in Venice, Italy. A mysterious and esoteric book, it may well have formed the basis for the idea of the *Necronomicon.* But there were others, too.

The Great Magical Papyrus of Paris

The Great Magical Papyrus of Paris, dating from the fourth century A.D. and housed in the Bibliotheque Nationale in France is one of the more terrifying manuscripts, which date from earliest times. It gives instructions for the drawing out and control of demons and is one of the earlier documents of exorcism. Certain paragraphs have been added to it in Coptic Egyptian in order to add a more Christian element—the Names by which the Divine can be addressed for instance—but the entire document has a Pagan feel to it. There are also references, contained therein to astrological and astronomical "houses" detailing a connection with the celestial spheres. It provided a codex of the names of demons and the utterances by which they should be called. It was widely regarded as a "dangerous text."

Yao Sabaoth

Intriguingly, the Papyrus gives a list of names, which can be used in the commanding of demons. Some of these names are echoed in other papyri from later periods—most notably a magical papyrus attributed to *Diokoros of Aphrodos* (also an exorcism and protective spell), held in the Cairo Museum. One of the Names, which occurs in many of the Coptic manuscripts, is that of that of "Yao Sabaoth" or "Yao Sabao" which is used as both a summoner and protector. It is unclear exactly who or what this entity was—it may be a secret Name for God (and there is every indication that it may have been amongst the later Egyptian Copts) or it may have related to another being entirely. However, its seemingly close connection to Lovecraft's *Yog Sothoth*—the Opener of the Way (Who is the Gatekeeper *and* the Gate) cannot be ignored. Indeed, the names of some of Lovecraft's gods—especially Yog Sothoth and Nyarlathotep (servant of the blind, idiot god Azathoth)—have an Egyptian "feel" to them and are suggestive of some of the ancient entities which emerge within the early Egyptian Christian and Coptic literature.

The Book of Black Earth

Legends concerning extremely ancient and blasphemous books were not, however, solely confined to the Middle East. Some tomes were featured in the folklore of Western Europe as well. The most persistent of these legends came from Celtic lore and referred to a fragmentary volume known as *The Book of Black Earth* that seems to have surfaced in Scotland. Exactly what this text was is not altogether clear, but variants of it seem to have appeared at certain times throughout Scottish history. For example, a version of it was supposed to have been copied down from the lips of Highland chailleachs (witches), by the Wolf of Badenoch Alexander Stewart, (1343–1405) at some time during the 14th century. It was transcribed either at Lochindorb, the Wolf's castle in the Highlands, or in the great stone circle at Kingussie in Speyside (now demolished). Although dating from the 14th century, *The Book of Black Earth* was said to reflect a much older and extremely dark knowledge, which had been passed down orally since prehistoric times. It mentioned dark gods worshipped amongst the early Celts but whose names had been practically forgotten, even in the medieval period. Disputes arise, however, as to the format of the text or as to what happened to it after the death of the Wolf. Some authorities state that the volume was only a fragmentary manual (there are even assertions that at least part of it was written on portions of flayed human skin) and that the majority of it was destroyed during the "reign" of the Wolf's brother, the self-styled Robert IV of Scotland (who acted as Regent for the infant James I of Scotland who was in captivity in England at the time). Other sources claim that portions of it formed the basis of the most celebrated of all Scottish grimoires *The Red Book of Appin* that was reputedly held by the Stewarts of

Appin until the 1800s. Fragments of it also allegedly surfaced in Scotland during the late 17th and early 18th centuries, during the period of the persecutions of the Covenanters. They referred to it as "The Wicked Bible" and placed it in the possession of one of their chief persecutors—John Graham, Earl of Claverhouse and later Viscount Dundee. There are assertions that portions of it exist, somewhere in Scotland, even to this day.

Crom Cruach

Scotland was not the only part of the Celtic world to have such an allegedly vile tome. In Ireland, too, fragmentary texts reputedly existed, allegedly dating from shortly after the arrival of St. Patrick on the island. Most of these were said to deal with the worship of a specific god, supposedly embodied in some of the standing stones which dotted the landscape and which was being increasingly overthrown by the followers of the Saint. This was the Crom Cruach, the Bowed God of the Mounds. The Crom was a particularly bloodthirsty god, who regularly demanded human sacrifice and who was reputedly originally worshipped by the Sidhe (the People of the Mounds) and later by certain druidic factions amongst the Celts. Some accounts describe him as an exceptionally powerful wizard who met with Patrick shortly after the Saint landed in Ireland. Others describe widespread and gory sacrifice to the god during the reign of a legendary Irish pre-Christian king—Tigernmas—during whose reign the Druids flourished and stones were worshipped.

Magh Sleact

The central place of worship was believed to have been Magh Sleact (or Sleaght)—the "Plain of Adoration or Prostration," now Tullyhaw in County Cavan. Here a central stone, sheathed in gold, was surrounded by a circle of twelve lesser stones. This suggested a solar connection and, there is a legend that, The Crom originally came from the stars with twelve helpers, each one a bloody and ferocious god in its own right. When the Blessed Patrick arrived at the site, however, legends state that the Crom Cruach sank into the ground before him. In other versions, he smote the stone circle with his crozier, destroying most of the twelve surrounding stones. The central Cruach, however, he was unable to destroy. As Christianity began to spread throughout the region, the stone was removed and supposedly disappeared. It was carried across Lough MacNean and stands today in a corner of a field outside the village of Belcoo in Southwest Fermanagh. The stone is actually just over six feet in height with a concave top and long incisions in its sides. Local tradition says that the Crom was a fertility god and into the top of it was placed the first-born of the year, where it was ritually decapitated and its blood allowed to run down the sides of the idol and into the earth to ensure plentiful crops for the following year. The barbarous Crom Cruach was widely known throughout Ireland and appears under a number of other names—the Bloody Crescent (symbolized by the horns of a crescent moon, again emphasising its solar connections), as *rig-iodol-hEireeann* (the king idol of Ireland), and as the Cenn Cruaic (the Bloody Head) in the *Tripartite Life of St. Patrick.* In this incarnation—of a bleeding head—it is supposed to have divulged ancient secrets that were written down and passed into a corpus of knowledge that formed the basis of a blasphemous tome.

Culdees

An ancient legend tells of how certain sections of the Culdees (an esoteric and aesthetic Celtic Order of monks formed in the 8th century by St. Mael Ruaine of Tallaght near Dublin. The name is an Anglicised corruption of the words *Ceili Dei*—the Friends of God) had in its possession, the Bleeding Head of the Crom that uttered strange and terrible accounts of the origins of the world and about pre-Christian Ireland that the monks dutifully wrote down. This lore they kept hidden from the eyes of mortal men. The legend was probably no more than malicious rumour, introduced by the English monks who supplanted the Irish Order after the 12th century but there are stories of ancient texts, dating from that time and attributed to the Culdees in both Irish and Scottish folklore. (Many of the Culdees eventually fled from Ireland to Scotland, where they founded a monastic settlement near Dunkeld.) The stories of their mystical literature survived long after the last of the Order had died out in Ireland, around the 16th century.

Druid Library

Although the early Celts wrote very little down, there were also Irish tales of infamous collections of works, which stretched back into early times. One of these was the rumoured Druid Library. In 1186, a famous Irish preacher and exorcist, St. Ambrose O'Coffey, came to the monastery of St. Columcille's Seat at Magilligan in North Derry to die. With him he brought a collection of extremely ancient manuscripts that was reputedly the greatest collection of works on witchcraft and evil worship anywhere in Western Europe. Some texts were allegedly written on tree bark, others on dried human skin. A number were copied by the monks onto parchment for storage in the monastery. After St. Ambrose's death, the library was kept at Magilligan to prevent it from falling into the wrong hands. St. Columcille's Seat was destroyed in 1203 by Donnell McLaughlin—a chieftain of Donegal—and "certain foreigners" (probably half-Viking raiders) but there is no mention as to what became of the library.

St. Columcille's Chest

Tradition says that the library was split up and hidden before the attack. Indeed a connected legend says that part of it was secreted in a chest—known as St. Columcille's Chest—and hidden in a cave somewhere along the coast. What became of the remainder of the Library is unknown. In the late 18th century, the legend continues, workmen building the Mussenden Temple on the estate of Frederick Hervey, the Earl-Bishop of Downhill, discovered the chest and brought it to Hervey himself. He managed to open it and found part of the contents still intact. What he read there disturbed him so greatly that he left the area, and afterwards could not sleep in a house for more than two consecutive nights. He died in 1803, reportedly a broken man. The chest was removed to Derry (where Hervey was Bishop) and has disappeared from the annals of history. That is the story, although there have been mentions of fragments of the Druid Library surfacing elsewhere. The ground on which the monastery stood is now a field—no trace of the structure remains—but is still treated with suspicion by some locals.

Viking Magic

As well as these ancient Celtic texts, the folklore of the West was also dominated by stories of books of Viking magic. In Celtic thinking (and in the thinking of other ancient peoples) evil and darkness resided in the North and so it seemed logical that the Scandinavian countries should be home to some of the blackest magics. The ferociousness of Viking attacks on Celtic settlements, of course, did not help matters much and it was thought that the lands to the North were frozen, bleak places in which the Devil and grim old gods still dwelt. There were rumoured to be Black Schools existing amongst the Viking communities in places such as Iceland where sorcerers were schooled in enchantments and witchcrafts of the vilest kind. Curiously, many of these schools were reputedly attached to Christian establishments.

Jon Arnason

The Scandinavian folklorist Jon Arnason, who published a collection of folktales on ghosts and magic in Iceland in 1862, mentions a particularly nefarious Black School that existed somewhere in the country (although he gives no specific location for it) that circulated a number of ancient books and grimoires throughout Scandinavia. There are also many tales from Ireland, England, Wales, and Scotland concerning Runebooks and Omenbooks which were said to contain witchcraft "of the darkest kind" in circulation throughout much of Western Europe and which hinted at gruesome deities that had been worshipped in the Northern lands since earliest times.

Could any of these books—Middle Eastern, Celtic, or Scandinavian—been a basis for the "abhorred" *Necronomicon?* It is impossible to know for certain but at least some of them *might* have served as the inspiration for that tome.

Apart from the *Necronomicon,* a number of other titles continue to surface within the confines of the Cthulhu Mythos. The *Book of Dzyan* transcribed by H.P. Blavatsky has already been mentioned but there were others—many of which were added to the Mythos by writers other than Lovecraft himself. A number of these may have had their origins in the literature produced around the medieval as well as in the early days of the Enlightenment as scholars were trying to replace these beliefs with myths of former days.

Malleus Malificarium

From the late 15th century onwards, the interest in witchcraft began to reach new heights. The reason for this was, arguably, the writing and circulation of one book which enjoyed the seal of Papal authority. This was the *Malleus Malificarium* (*The Hammer of the Witch*), which had been commissioned by Pope Innocent VIII (1484–1492). Similar to previous Pontiffs, Innocent was concerned about the continuance of "heresies" in remote rural areas—particularly in parts of Germany—which still contained elements of old Pagan worship. Although essentially a relatively weak Pope overall, Innocent was determined to deal with these heresies as soon as he took up Papal office. Almost immediately he convened a Council, which appointed two respected Dominican theologians to investigate the problem in the Hertz, Mainz, Trier, and Treves areas of Germany and Austria where it was considered that such heresies were at their height.

Jacobus Sprenger

The first of these investigators was Jacobus (James) Sprenger (1430–1494). Sprenger had been born in Basle and had joined the Dominican Order there, showing early promise as a scholar. In 1480, he was appointed as Professor of Theology at the University of Cologne and was later appointed Inquisitor Extraordinary for the Province of Mainz, Treves, and Cologne. His investigative partner was Heinrich Kramer (1430–1505) who had been born in Schletstadt in Alsace. In 1474, he was appointed as Chief Inquisitor in the Tyrol, where he earned himself something of a reputation as a "hardliner" against alleged witchcraft, but he also worked in Bohemia and Moravia. His appointment was to "give teeth" to the investigation because Sprenger had no real experience in legally persecuting Witches. And there is little doubt that Kramer had a deep interest in witchcraft, for in 1485, he drew up a damning treatise on the subject, which afterwards was incorporated into the *Malleus*. Kramer had also worked as an Inquisitor in Innsbruck but had been banished from the city by the local bishop who referred to him as "a bigoted old fool." Nevertheless, he was the person that Innocent wanted and so was appointed to investigation with Sprenger.

The book that the two Dominicans produced was to complement a Papal Bull entitled *Summis desiderantes*, which Innocent issued on 5th December 1484. In it, he attacked the heresies in Germany and instructed the German Inquisition to condemn and punish alleged instances of witchcraft with the utmost severity. The book that Sprenger and Kramer produced became a witch-hunters manual, detailing all sorts of horrors, which the Ungodly could commit. This book, with its Papal backing, was to set the tone for many other such volumes.

Demonoltria Libri Tres

There is little doubt that the French Catholic priest Nicholas Remy (1534–1600) was influenced by this terrible work. He published his own text *Demonoltria Libri Tres* (*Demonology Book III*) which for many years, became a textbook for those persecutingwitches and the main source for the study of the works of Satan on Earth. Nor was it only officers of the Catholic Church who produced these monstrous tomes on witchcraft and on the persecution of witches.

Jean Bodin

The Calvinist French witch-hunter Jean Bodin (1530–1596) also penned several treatises on the matter, advocating the use of torture, even in the cases of invalid persons and children. In order to justify such horrendous views, such people detailed the rituals and blasphemous incantations, used by alleged witches to fulfil their evil designs. Such horrors presented in manuscript form, terrified and sickened those who read them and some of these treatises were to perhaps establish the basis of some of the terrible volumes of the Cthulhu Mythos.

Compendium Malificarum

It was a relatively unknown priest from Milan, however, who was to produce the most terrible book. In 1608, Francesco Maria Guazzo produced a catalogue of terrors, which he entitled the *Compendium Malificarum* (*A Compendium of Witches*). This would give, in graphic and terrible detail, the powers and practices of Witches and depraved people who had sold their souls to the Devil. It shocked the early modern world with its explicitness. Guazzo's work has never really been equalled for the sheer terror it created in the minds of

European scholars and it firmly established what was to become known as the "witch craze" in the religious mind of the day.

This was a craze that was to last throughout the late 17th and early 18th centuries until the birth of what became known as the Age of Reason or the Enlightenment, when science came to the fore and the old superstitions began to fade away. Even then, the interest in the occult did not appear to die out. The thinkers of this time were anxious to explain away some of the superstitions that had gripped their ancestors or to place them within a new scientific context, so as to better understand them. This led to a plethora of books, combining what had formerly been considered to be witchcraft with science.

Alchemy

In a sense, magic always had its scientific and philosophical side. Alchemy—the art of transforming or creating matter from other elements—had always been considered as a magical operation. It would, however, form the basis of recognizable science. Philosophy, too, was connected into magical thought. From earliest times, the Gnostics had taught salvation through knowledge.

Gnosticism

The origins of Gnostic belief are unclear and are still a matter for research and debate. Nor was there any single universal doctrine in Gnosticism—the term was used to denote disparate groups of thinkers who shared a generally common philosophical outlook—but the basic tenets of the belief contended that human salvation lay not through faith and obedience of God's Laws (as the Christian Churches taught) but rather through an understanding of the underlying mysteries and secrets of the Universe itself. This drew the seeker closer to the Monad (the One), which lay at the centre of all things surrounded by lesser emanations known as Archons. Those who gained such knowledge became beings of considerably greater power than those who did not. Lovecraft's fiction mirrors some of the Gnostic beliefs.

Azothoth

In Lovecraft's books, at the centre of the Universe, the mad, blind god Azathoth seethes and bubbles whilst around him, lesser entities come and go.

Certain individuals attempt to make contact with some of the lesser brings and ultimately with the central deity itself, which usually sends them mad. The fits in with some Gnostic thinking that the Monad was essentially "unknowable" and that seeking out too much knowledge about it would ultimately destroy the seeker. The finite minds of mortals were not equipped to handle the infinite.

Gnostic writings influenced many seekers during what became known as the Age of Enlightenment. The pursuit of esoteric knowledge was now closely linked to the Divine and those engaged in such pursuits used this as a justification for their researches.

RaymondLully

No man embodied such a quest more than the medieval figure of Raymond Lully (Ramon Lul) whose thinking enjoyed something of a renaissance during this period. Lully seemed to successfully combine the scientific search with that of the supernatural journey—combining the scientific with the mystical—and this appealed to many of the Enlightened thinkers.

Born in Palma, Majorca somewhere between 1232 and 1236, Lully (Lul or Llul) became heavily involved in the Christian Church as a missionary in the Middle East. However, he was also a man with a curious and philosophical mind and the writings and debates of the early Arabs fascinated him. He became interested in the writings of the early Christians, particularly Gnostic branches of them that were to be found in the Arab lands. He also became interested in alchemy and astronomy. In these times alchemy was considered a sin because, through experimentation (and the supposed creation and transformation of substances) it was deemed to tamper with the order of things that God Himself had established. Astronomy, too was considered as a sinful practice because it was thought to query and explain the order that God had created in the Firmament. In order to protect themselves from Church attention (this was the age of the Inquisition) many alchemists and astronomers wrote down their experiments and findings in code, usually in some mystical or quasi-religious format. Thus the alchemist's literature is littered with accounts of strange journeys, of bizarre landscapes and encounters, unnatural births and of "alchemyical weddings," all seeking to conceal research and works that individual practitioners had carried out. Lully was no different. Some of his works—treatises, books—are couched in obscure terms . It was the fashion to try and "decode" some of these writings in order (it was thought) to discover and understand esoteric truths. Lully took his theories one step further. Greatly influenced by the astronomical and mathematical works of the Arabs (he had intently studied and learned Arabic), he was convinced that knowledge could be "created" using mathematical and scientific formulae. In order to prove this, he constructed a set of machines, that could "create" permutations of ideas which were fed into them and which were then supplemented by Lully's own thought and mathematical equations.

Ars Magna

The result was a massive work known as the *Ars Magna*, which was reputedly Lully's greatest work. It is a set of combinations of ideas linked by philosophical and mathematical equations—many of them in diagrammatic form. Some of these were said to represent stellar constellations and a few of them bear a resemblance to ancient symbols found amongst the Mound Builders of America. This led to a fevered speculation that perhaps Lully had discovered arcane secrets of the Universe which were known by some other more ancient peoples and, as late as the 1930s, he was still being hailed as a great alchemist and occultist, almost as a forerunner of Madame Blavatsky—even though it appears that he had always opposed the occult and saw himself more as an early scientist. When Lully died in Tunis in 1315, he was reputed to have left behind a series of treatises, which were filled with esoteric knowledge and claimed to describe the ultimate secrets of Creation. A number of these were believed to have turned up during the Age of Enlightenment but have been subsequently proved to be forgeries. Nevertheless, the idea of an ancient civilization that had some kind of advanced knowledge and which was connected to certain other cultures in the world gained widespread interest, mainly through his work. Books, interpreting his work and the work of other alchemists and philosophers—including the works of the English alchemist, occultist, and follower of Johannes Kepler, Robert Fludd (1574–1634)—proliferated throughout the 18th and early 19th centuries. Such works were highly popular in respected circles—almost the *Da Vinci Codes* of their day.

The interest in ancient magic, however, hasn't gone away. Indeed, if anything, the emerging new scientific philosophies had increased investigation into it—particularly into ritual magic and the use of incantations. In the 17th, 18th and into part of the 19th centuries, grimoires (books of spells and ritual) began circulating widely in Western Europe. Many of these claimed great antiquity, stretching back to the early Middle East.

The Key of Solomon

The greatest of these books was allegedly, *The Key of Solomon*, which was later split into two books—*The Greater* and *Lesser Keys.* This was attributed to the celebrated Biblical king who was famed for his wisdom and also for his command of demons and reputedly dated from the 1st century A.D. From this single source, many other grimoires had their origin as students copied what were supposedly fragments of the original work. In 1350, Pope Innocent VI certainly ordered a volume known as *The Book of Solomon* to be destroyed but whether this was indeed the *Key*, as some students claim, is open to question. A text named the *Book of Solomon* was condemned by the Church around 1559 but copies of it were widely circulated amongst scholars in Europe at the time. A Greek version of this work dating from somewhere between 1100 and 1200 is said to be housed in the British Museum in London. Excerpts, directly copied form the *Key*, would form the basis of another grimoire in wide circulation during the 18th century—*The Secret of Secrets.*

The Sacred Book of Abra-melin the Mage

Another celebrated grimoire was *The Sacred Book of Abra-melin the Mage* which gained some credibility in the late 19th century when an allegedly 14th century copy of it was "discovered" in the Biblioteque de L'Arsenal by the occultist S.L. McGregor Mathers, a member of the famous Order of the Golden Dawn (which was to gain some notoriety by including Aleister Crowley in its ranks). According to McGregor Mathers, this was a translation of a work of "potent power" which had been written by an ancient Hebrew magician named

Abraham ben Simeon. This volume was widely circulated in Paris and London during the late 19th and early 20th centuries and still enjoys a certain status amongst many occultists.

Grimoire of Pope Honorious

A third major grimoire was perhaps incorrectly attributed to Pope Honorious III who occupied the Pontificate from 1216–1227. There is little to connect this old and frail Pontiff with the occult—most of his Papacy was concerned with the Fourth Lateran Council and proclaiming the Fifth Crusade. Nevertheless, the *Grimoire of Pope Honorious* was believed to be a potent and terrible book, directly transcribed either by the Pope himself or under his direction, from ancient Semitic texts, which formed part of the *Kabbalah* (a body of mystic Jewish literature that featured heavily in rabbinical magic). Its alleged Papal connections seemed to give it added status and so it circulated widely amongst scholars of the occult during the 18th century. It is still considered to be something of a magical text today.

Others were added to these main allegedly magical tomes. These additions were simply portions of the books which had been copied or which had been combined with portions from other works. Many of them contained incantations and recipes, couched in quasi-mystical language and augmented by geometric illustrations, which resembled ancient symbols found elsewhere in the world, which seemed to give them an added authenticity. Many had fanciful names—*Le Grand Grimoire, The Red Dragon, The Black Pullet, the Book of Secrets*, all claiming great antiquity which stretched back as far as ancient Egypt and beyond. Most of them were fraudulent, put together by lively and imaginative minds and their pedigree was extremely questionable.

Lovecraft and his correspondents would, in all probability, been well aware of the existence of such books and many others like them, both quasi-mystical and scientific. They fitted in well with the notion of esoteric knowledge left by former civilizations and avidly pursued by the Gnostics and those who came after them, as late as the 18th century. The creation of a corpus of ancient and blasphemous lore was in many ways, central to the Cthulhu Mythos with its emphasis on vanished gods and lost civilizations.

Lovecraft and others picked up on some of these books and several of them also created their own in order add to the Mythos and to give it credibility beyond the confines of horror literature. Each one was a "terrible and blasphemous" volume, full of arcane secrets, which could only be correctly interpreted by those with a certain knowledge. This held echoes of the scholars of the Enlightenment as they tried to break the hidden "codes" of the alchemists. Many of his correspondents would send their ideas for "new" books to Lovecraft in his Providence retreat, and from time to time, he would incorporate them into his own fiction.

Book of Eibon

The most sinister of these additions, according to Lovecraft himself, was the sinister *Book of Eibon,* although no details about such a monstrous volume are available. This seems to be some sort of "fragmentary" work although no real detail about it is given. The title of the book was actually dreamed up by one of Lovecraft's writer-correspondents, Clark Ashton Smith, although it was rumoured to have been based on an actual book. In the last years of his life, Lovecraft declared that there were two versions of this work—the Norman-French *Livre d'Eibon* (*The Diary of Alonzo Typer*) and a slightly later translation—the *Liber Ivonis* (*The Haunter of the Dark*). The translation from Latin into 13th century French was, according to Smith, completed by a monk named Gaspard du Nord. Smith was to make reference to the work himself in his tale *Ubbo Sathla* and was to refer to Eibon (who allegedly initially compiled the text) as a Hyperborean sorcerer in his story *The Door Into Saturn.*

Cultes des Ghoules

Another of the "abhorred books" was *Cultes des Ghoules* by the Comte d' Erlette. This volume arose out of a connection to Lovecraft's friend August Derleth, whose ancestors were French and were named Erlette. No specific details are given about this volume, but several alleged "pages" of it have been published as part of the materials for role-playing games in both Europe and the U.S. They seem to reveal a book, which is little more than a traditional French grimoire of possibly an 18th century printing.

De Vermis Mysteriis

A further addition to this catalogue of horrific books was Ludvig Prinn's *De Vermis Mysteriis* (*Mysteries of the Worm*), which is mentioned several times in Lovecraft's work. Prinn was reputedly an elderly occultist who was burned at the stake as a witch after compiling the volume. In fact, the title of the book—*Mysteries of the Worm*—and its author are creations of Lovecraft's correspondent Robert Bloch. Lovecraft, however, gave the book its Latin title and used it in his stories *The Shadow Out of Time, The Diary of Alonzo Typer*, and *The Haunter of the Dark.*

People of the Monolith

Another of Lovecraft's correspondents, the famous Robert E. Howard (creator of Conan the Barbarian amongst others), created the book of poetry *People of the Monolith* and its insane author, Justin Geoffrey. Geoffrey was a Baudelairean poet who had travelled across Europe and had seen many strange things, especially in the area surrounding the Balkans, the knowledge of which had driven him mad. He died confined in an asylum. Howard was to make reference to the book and to Geoffrey in his short Lovcraftian story *The Black Stone* and was to quote from one of his poems in best Lovecraft tradition:

They say foul beings of Old Times still lurk,
In dark, forgotten corners of the world,
And gates still gape to loose, on certain nights,
Shapes pent in Hell.

Lovecraft himself was to briefly mention Geoffrey in one of his own stories—*The Thing on the Doorstep.*

Unaussprechlichen Kulten

Howard, who corresponded regularly with Lovecraft, is also credited with the creation of yet another volume. This is the *Unaussprechlichen Kulten* of the alleged German occultist Fredrick von Junzt. Not much detail is given concerning von Junzt except that he had made a study of ancient and terrible cults, which had survived since earliest times. He had catalogued them into a volume, which he called *Nameless Cults*. Shortly after its completion he was strangled and mauled by an unseen demon whilst in his locked chamber. The work is probably a creation of Howard's (although some scholars state that this volume more than any other might have its origins in reality) although Lovecraft balked at his original suggestion for its title—*Ungennte heidenthume*. It was August Derleth who came up with the title, although his command of High German leaves something to be desired (the name literally means Unpronounceable Cults. Lovecraft, however, liked the idea and gave it at least three editions—Dusseldorf (1839), Bridewell, and a heavily expurgated version published by the Golden Goblin Press in 1909.

The Pnakotic Manuscripts

Last but not least amongst the texts was one of Lovecraft's own creations—*The Pnakotic Manuscripts*. References to these texts were widely scattered throughout his stories—indeed they were second only to *The Necronomicon* in their number of mentions—although it is unclear as to exactly what they were. They are described as "fragmentary" but it is not clear as to whether they were scrolls, chapters of a single volume, or pieces of pottery. What is known is that they were pre-human and, according to Lovecraft, "inconceivably ancient." They had existed, he went on, since "before the advent of Man." He further describes them as being "mouldy" but gives no indication as to what form or material they might be.

The Seven Cryptical Books of Hsan

To this basic corpus of foul literature, Lovecraft's other correspondents and followers have added further blasphemous works. These were such terrible creations as *The Eltdown Shards,* the creation of Richard F. Searight, which have appeared in numerous Lovecraft pastiches as well as a couple of Lovecraft's own tales—*The Shadow out of Time* and *The Diary of Alonzo Typer*. There are also a one of Lovecraft's own creations—*The Seven Cryptical Books of Hsan* briefly mentioned in *The Dream Quest of Unknown Kadath*—together with the *R'lyh* text which has appeared in a number of Lovecraft-related fictions. Amongst this was mixed a good number of actual literature on Witchcraft and the supernatural. For example, Cotton Mather's *Magalia Christi Americana*

(Picture in the house, Pickman's Model, The Unnameable, The Case of Charles Dexter Ward), and *Wonders of the Invisible World, Pickman's Model;* Giovanni Batista della Porta's *De Furtivis Literarium Notis (The Dunwich Horror)*, Robert Fludd's *Clavis Alchemae (Case of Charles Dexter Ward)*, and Joseph Glanville's *Saducismus Trumphatus (The Festival)* amongst others. The inclusion of actual devil books leant extra weight to the text and caused the reader to wonder whether any of the other grimoires might indeed exist. Indeed, many still wonder if there is not a grain of truth in the supposed existence of some of these books and perhaps there is. The inclusion of such tomes, whether real or imagined, has added a certain scholarly gravitas, which has characterised much of Lovecraft's work.

American Degenerate Communities

A third strand of Lovecraft's frightening fiction was drawn from American history. Much of his horror derives from the "degenerate, inbred families" who dwell in the remote areas of the New England landscape. Even the old stately families had their "decayed" branches with whom they seldom spoke and had little contact. Some of these ideas may, as already noted, have arisen from his mother's family—the Phillipses, but there may have been more. It was not for nothing that he chose rural New England as the setting for the majority of his most horrific tales. Even in the 20th century an air of degeneracy and decay underlay some parts of East Coast society.

The American East Coast had largely been settled by the British and the Dutch, two countries that were not always exactly friendly towards each other. Therefore settlement had been extremely patchy. Today we think of bustling cities and busy freeways all along the coast—the New England of the 17th, 18th and early 19th centuries was extremely different. It was largely a wilderness of forest and swamp into which people might venture never to be seen again. There were a number of thriving cities to be sure—New Amsterdam (now New York) and Boston—but in many cases, settlers lived away in squalid and (by present standards) primitive settlements in the rural wilds. The isolation and insularity of such settlements produced a reclusive and suspicious people and sometimes allowed strange practices and beliefs to flourish, relatively unchecked.

Salem Village

For instance, in the largely Puritan Bay Colony in Massachusetts centred on Salem Village, a witchcraft hysteria was able to take hold during 1692. In the narrow, "pressure-cooker" atmosphere of the Salem community (now a part of Danvers, Massachusetts) nineteen women were to be hanged on the bare Gallows Hill outside the village, whilst one elderly man was crushed to death between stones on the say-so of a number of frightened and hysterical girls. Although it has attracted a great deal of interest, Salem was not unique amongst the introspective and often claustrophobic communities along the New England coast. Indeed, many were more bizarre and stranger beliefs and ideals flourished there. Scattered all across the Eastern American seaboard and away from the main settlements, were communities of what we today might call "peripheral people"—those who were driven out of the main settlements for various reasons. For example, there were communities of Quakers, shunned by the Puritans who dwelt on the edges of the major towns or in the forest. But we also have accounts of some even stranger communities, well beyond what constituted "civilization." An example of these was the community of Dogtown.

Dogtown

On a grassy plateau overlooking Gloucester, Rockport, and Ipswich Bay in Massachusetts, a disparate and extremely motley collection of individuals had made their home in the mid-to-late 1600s. The settlement of Dogtown was reputedly found sometime in the 1660s by a number of widows of Gloucester seamen who had perished in the ocean. With no men to look after them, they had become a burden on the Gloucester society and were therefore cast out into the wild. Some of them were rather strange individuals and presumably this didn't help their case. They were to be joined by the widows of soldiers who were lost in the various campaigns along the coast and soon the settlement began to grow. It was named Dogtown because of the amount of feral dogs which wandered about the "streets" of the community unhindered. The place became a magnet for the strange and the peculiar—both women and men—who were not wanted or who did not fit into a recognizable society.

Many of them were either Irish or Scottish. Some of them were mentally unbalanced. They lived in sod huts or in falling wooden cabins along the side of a single track, which formed the community's main "street," or around an open patch of grass that served as Dogtown's main common. Contemporary accounts speak of old beldames sitting on this green, cackling or talking to themselves in a most alarming manner. The smell of the place, according to commentators, was nauseating. This strange settlement would continue for almost two hundred years and was only finally cleared out during the 1830s when the last residents had left. What evidence of the place that had been left was swiftly demolished.

Local people from the Gloucester, Newbury, and Ipswich areas, had already branded Dogtown as a "witch village" and categorically stated that the Black Arts were worked there under public gaze. It may be that some of these old women earned a meagre living telling fortunes for the sailor-folk of the area, or that they may have issued curses against their neighbours, and this was essentially equated within the wider community as a practicing of the dark sciences. The majority of the village's inhabitants were described as "crones" (evil-looking women)—some very old, some deformed, some generally hideous in aspect—and were strenuously avoided even when they ventured beyond Dogtown's limits. In her book *Romances of a Nonagarian (1897)*, Newbury's Sarah Anna Emory conveys at least some suggestion of the eeriness with which the place was viewed:

"Dogtown was two miles distant from Crane-neck," she wrote. "After passing Dale's Pond, the road ran through thick woods. This, on some dark and stormy nights, was rather bug-a-booish." Dogtown, she goes on, was a place that most people tried to avoid, even during daylight hours, for fear of the raddled hags that dwelt there. In his *History of Dogtown* (1896), Charles Mann mentions several of them: Judy Rhines (Ryan), a fortune-teller who allegedly met with the Devil in the surrounding woods (she had a queerly deformed mouth—"teeth like a dog"—and went about mumbling to herself); Cornelius Finson or "Black Neil" (who had long teeth protruding from his upper lip); Tammy Younger (with a long beard similar to a man that stretched almost to her waist and a very "choice vocabulary"), and Juliet Hawe or

Hawthorne who walked about as if in a daze, cackling and shrieking with laughter (whilst in this state she claimed to see visions of the future). There is also reference to an "Old Mother Pike," a massive, aggressive elderly woman, "filthy in both body and speech," who brewed potions for ailments and to induce love of a discharged soldier, Nathaniel Bourke—"Hellish Natty"—who had part o his face blown away, leaving a side of it little more than a skein of scorched and twisted flesh. He made hooch for a living and seems to have been continually drunk. Dogtown, Mann continues, was "a resort of buccaneers and low men" that only added to its queer and supernatural reputation. There were also stories of connections between some of the settlement's inhabitants and "strange societies" (usually connected to the Freemasons in some way), that had grown up in neighbouring communities such as Wellfleet (originally called Billingsgate) and Ipswich. The village may well have been America's first "witch colony" and its inhabitants were both feared and shunned because of their strange and frequently grotesque appearances and unacceptable ways. They were often linked to the demonic and primeval powers that dwelt deep in the forests and swamps.

Little Piney Fork Country

Similar settlements to Dogtown existed in other parts of America as well. In remote mountainous areas in North Carolina, Tennessee, Kentucky, and West Virginia, isolated communities with equal reputations and equally strange inhabitants might also be found. Some of these areas were very remote and isolated such as what was to become known as the Little Piney Fork Country in Kentucky. This was an area around Rutherford Mountain, near the Tennessee border—a region lying between the valleys of the Bear and Little Piney Fork rivers and which was, until as late as the 1940s, virtually inaccessible. This region formed part of Brake and Trundle Counties but few officials ever made their way up to the remote county seats. One traveller, passing through in the 1930s, described the region as being "nothing short of a wilderness." And yet, this "wilderness" was home to many families who had lived there, pretty much in isolation, since Revolutionary days—the Talbots, Nesbitts, Baylanches, Parrigans, and Panningeses amongst many others. Many such families claimed a direct and unbroken descent from Revolutionary veterans who had settled deep in this relatively inhospitable region. There is no record of many of these people because few census takers ventured into the Piney Fork Country in order to count its inhabitants and few births or deaths were registered at the county seat. In fact for the year 1910, no real census records exist for the families living between Squaw Creek and the Mount Gilead area and there are no accounts of the formal establishment of a school at Coonsfork although one certainly existed "at the end of a dirt road that was too narrow for any vehicle except a horse" in the 1930s.

Waterfall

The main settlement in the area seems to have been Waterfall, a small town, but there were allegedly other villages hidden away in hollows and valleys, which considered themselves to be "self sufficient" and had little dealings with the outside world. These were communities that had "their own ways," where shootings and murders were common but which dispensed their own form of "folk justice." For example, the brutal murder of Jarvis Trunk and his sister Mary Ellen at their remote cabin at Bat Cliff Mountain in Brake County in 1886 was "solved" by the "folk hanging" of Bronston Nesbitt—who was quite probably guilty—without formal recourse to the authorities. This was also a place of intense superstition and supernatural fears. As late as the 1940s, few people would pass near an old hog wallow known as the Devil's Hollow for fear of encountering a "headless" man-bat who lived there. Others avoided certain dirt roads and trails for fear of "boogers and haints" and an area of Rutherford Mountain was widely known as the "Booger Hole" because of *something* that dwelt deep in a cave. This was said to be a fearsome creature that grabbed passers-by on the lonely mountain tracks and was said to have existed there since earliest times. The more cynical stated that it was no more than an old story, designed to keep folks away from illegal moonshining operations up on the mountain. There were however, also tales of "Indian stones"—great rocks that might have been moved by glaciers or volcanic upheavals but which had a certain mystery and awe about them. These, it was said, had been raised by spirits back in the Indian times and that certain tribes had worshipped there, revering old gods, which had once lived in the forest and mountaintops. Such stones were also places to be avoided.

Nor was the Piney Fork region of Kentucky unique. Other remote and self sufficient communities existed all through various mountain areas. In the Smokies for example, there were many tales of communities which shied away from general contact and which maintained their own laws and ways. This was the country of the granny women—mountain midwifes and healers who served as local doctors but whose powers actually bordered on witchcraft according to the mountain folks. There were a few famous instances of supposed witchcraft amongst them.

Granny Bacon

In 1923, an elderly woman whose name was given as Granny Bacon (a local woman from Black Mountain) was reputedly brought to court in Asheville, North Carolina for poisoning a youngster with "deadly yarbs" (herbs) in an attempt to cure a fever. The judge actually ordered the jury to acquit her, as he was unsure as to whether it would reach an unbiased decision concerning a granny woman on whom so many people depended. This was also a region that tried for many years to resist the Mann Act in 1910 (a piece of legislation—the White Slave Traffic Act, but more commonly known as the Mann Act after James Robert Mann—to standardize a legal age of consent independently of the various Sates because in many mountain communities young girls were often married before they were 14 years of age). Whilst we may stand aghast at this today, such things were considered to be "mountain ways" and not to be interfered with by legislators. This opposition led to rumours and legends (most of them completely unfounded) regarding the mountain people and their societies—the most common one being that such places fostered and encourage inbreeding as the limited numbers of families, locked away in their mountain fastness, bred amongst each other. There were tales too of mental retardation and physically hideous monsters, which resulted in such unions. Whilst most of this might have been untrue, the stories were extremely widespread and in many cases, were accepted as absolute fact.

Yarb Doctors and Conjure Men

In the early 20th century, such areas remained steadfastly superstitious. These were areas where the granny women, the "yarb doctors," and "conjure men" still held sway. In the Dutch and British settlements in places such as Pennsylvania, such people were known by the German term *hexmeister*. Such practices were a hodgepodge of Indian spells, Biblical or "Hebrew" incantations, and beliefs that had been brought from Europe. Many of these were collected into a single volume by an itinerant preacher who travelled through various mountain regions, speaking with hermits, hexmeisters, and the inhabitants of isolated communities and writing down their charms and spells. His name was John George Hohman and he was active in many mountain areas between the years 1802 and 1857.

Der Lange Verborgne Freund

In 1820 he published the book under the title *Der Lange Verborgne Freund* (*The Long Hidden Friend)* which became translated into *The Long Lost Friend.*) This became one of the main Bibles of "powwowing" and was extremely popular in many parts of New England during the 1920s when Lovecraft was writing. The book was a collection of charms and incantations, which were said to cure and protect against all kinds of ailments and fevers that afflicted the mountain folks. Although *The Long Lost Friend* is considered to be one of the most important of mountain magic books, there were others. Two others of equal importance were the *Sixth* and *Seventh Books of Moses*, which allegedly traced their origins back into Biblical times.

Sixth and Seventh Books of Moses

The Sixth Book was a conglomeration of incantations and spells, calling upon angels and ancient Hebrew powers, whilst the Seventh was a series of drawings and signs, all of them set in both Hebrew and "Egyptian" styles. These were to be used in the preparation of amulets or "himmel briefs" (heaven letters) which would protect against sicknesses and evil spirits. Some argued that the geometric drawings contained in the Seventh Book resembled some of the structures left by the Mound Builders.

The Wondrous Tablets of Zion

Of lesser interest was a work entitled *The Wondrous Tablets of Zion* that was said to be a fusing of "Egyptian" knowledge with European spells and charms. Like the other books used by the mountain magicians, it was a "secret" book, the contents of which were not for unbelievers and much of it was couched in quasi-Biblical phraseology. And like the others, it dealt with both black and white magics—it contained incantations and rituals for healing as well as for cursing. Other tomes circulated widely—*The Book of Enoch*, *The Book of the Magus*, and *The Testament of Esau*—which, similar to the grimoires of early modern England were usually copies of permutations of other works. The contents of most of them bordered on what we might view today as witchcraft.

The circulation of such dark and eerie materials both deepened and added to the superstitions and beliefs of the remote communities and perhaps made them even more introspective in their ways. However, as urbanization began to erode and change, many of the established mountain communities, although even today certain aspects of the old mountain ways, still flourish in some of the remoter mountain areas.

It is not hard to make a connection between places like Dogtown, areas of the region around Rutherford Mountain and the Great Smokies, and also the remote and reclusive communities, which characterize Lovecraft's fiction. With regard to Dogtown especially, it is easy to conjure up visions of the decaying settlements of Dunwich or Innsmouth. The notion of ancient families, stretching back to Settlement and Revolutionary times, together with the tales of inbreeding amongst the mountain clans, also provided fodder for his dark imagination.

In parts of rural Rhode Island, too, many communities were scattered, particularly around the south of the state. The isolation of such communities had allowed some queer beliefs to proliferate there, too. The area was mainly for apple growing and the communities were largely rural and centred around apple orchards. As well as that, Rhode Island had seen some military action, particularly during the War of 1812, and tiny country cemeteries lay tucked away at the end of some narrow road where the Revolutionary dead lay. Grand old houses, which had been abandoned during wartime, lay tucked away in secluded hollows, full of ghosts and emptiness. Here too, queer stone monoliths, left over from Indian days, bore witness to a prehistoric past, which in the sometimes insular climate of Rhode Island seemed incredibly imminent. It was the perfect place for the growth of strange beliefs and ancient fears. Indeed, between the late 18th and late 19th centuries, the South end of the State had suffered a minor vampire hysteria. There were also tales of phantoms along the lonely roads that stretched between the villages, of headless Revolutionary horsemen, and of things from the forest that lurked close to the overgrown graveyards tucked away in remote hollows. Here, too were stories of spots, which were to be avoided, and that held threats of dire consequences for the unwary. All of these fused together into a rich tapestry that underscored Lovecraft's tales.

The idea of an ancient civilization perhaps based in Rhode Island was given something of a boost when in the late 18th century, a skeleton dressed in armour of a peculiar construction and design was unearthed at Fall River. The dead body had been placed in a sitting position—in the style of the Hopewell and some instances of the Mississippi cultures—and was surrounded by curiously-shaped stones. At first, it was suggested that this might be the grave of some early explorer—possibly Vikings or Normans—but many also asserted that this was evidence of a developed but forgotten civilization that had flourished in Rhode Island in prehistoric times. Later, it was said that the stones (which were subsequently lost) had been inscribed with queer characters, which might have been a forgotten language. Such discoveries might well have excited Lovecaft's imagination and influenced his work.

Edward "John" Dimond

Lovecraft might also have been aware some "characters" who had lived in New England many years before. Two in particular might have greatly interested him. The first was Edward "John" Dimond, the famed "Magician of Marblehead," Massachusetts. A tall, thin, moody man, Dimond, who lived during the 18th century in a large, old Colonial-style house at Little Harbour,

Marblehead, could have stepped out of a Lovecraft story. Little about his personal history is known although he is thought to have been born around the time of the Salem Witch Trials in 1692. As a young man, he would enter curious trances during which he would neither eat nor sleep but from which he emerged strangely refreshed and with a foreknowledge of future events. His parents were worried about him and were indeed slightly scared of him and his odd powers. When his father died, Dimond inherited a small amount of money (his father was not a wealthy man) which he used to buy some land which curiously lay on the edge of the town's Old Burying Hill.

Old Burying Hill

This was particularly undesirable property as it had a certain sinister aspect to it and Dimond was suspected of having specifically occult reasons for the purchase—just twenty-eight years after the Salem Witch Trials, people were still superstitious enough to believe this. It was imagined that Dimond was a wizard and that he was practicing Black Magic in the tangled thicket beside the old cemetery. Certain people claimed to have heard him speaking with the Devil along the lonely tracks that ran down the side of the old Burying Hill. However, despite such a fearsome reputation, Dimond's eccentric ways were tolerated by the Marblehead community. New Englanders are nothing if not circumspect and the wizard's alleged "gifts" were proving useful to many of the locals. For example, when things went missing or were stolen, he could—when in a trance—usually identify where they had gone or offer some clues as to who the thief might be. However, he had his darker side as well and this was often experienced by those who crossed him. He would make his way to the centre of the cemetery where his presence would alert his neighbours to the approach of a squall or a storm. There he would call upon the elements to take revenge upon his enemies. Many ships were said to have been lost at sea simply because their captains had fallen out with Dimond. The Magician could also aid mariners as well. Sometimes as he stood there amongst the tombstones, neighbours would hear him call out to the captains of certain vessels as if giving them directions in a storm. "Captain Jasper McClelland of the *Elizabeth Anne*, do you hear me?" he would roar to the leaden skies above the old cemetery. "Keep four degrees to starboard, run true until you reach the Halfway Rock." He would then look around him. "Captain Benjamin Rowe of the *Hetty,* hear my words. Move six degrees to port or you will founder on a shoal!" Then his mood would change and a shadow would creep across his face. "Captain William Orne of the *Plymouth Lass,* hear what I have to say! I curse you from this appointed spot, both you and your brother Jacob, master of the *Charlotte Rose.* May neither of you ever see port again! May both of you perish with your ships in the storm that is coming! This is my earnest wish and my most fervent prayer." None of those boats whom he had cursed, nor their captains, ever returned to port.

Captain Micah Taylor

A famous row broke out between Dimond and a certain Captain Micah Taylor, master of the *Kestrel,* during which the seaman called upon the wizard to "do his worst as he had no fear of him." On a clear, calm morning, the *Kestrel* sailed out of Marblehead harbour. There was not even the slightest hint of bad weather but, all the same, Dimond climbed up to the top of the Old Burial Hill and began his chant amongst the gravestones. Slowly the sky started to blacken and dark clouds began to gather from the west. A gale suddenly blew out of nowhere and lashed the New England coast. The *Kestrel* never returned to Marblehead harbour—she was lost at sea with all hands including Micah Taylor. This incident made other captains extremely wary of crossing the gaunt, thin man. Besides seeing what was happening at sea, the Marblehead wizard also seemed able to view, from his cemetery vantage point, what was happening on the land. For instance, whilst sitting on top of his Burying Hill, he was apparently able to witness a fire in Concord many miles away, through his alleged powers of telepathy. He was also said to talk directly to the dead as they lay in their coffins beneath the gravestones.

No one actually knows when John Dimond died and no date is given for his demise. He had left a legend behind him but that legend was to be augmented by his granddaughter, Molly.

Molly Pitcher

Molly Pitcher was born at 42 Orne Street, Marblehead in 1738 in a timber-frame house that stood directly opposite an old overgrown path that led up to the summit of the Old Burying Hill. Shortly after her birth, her parents suspected that she had inherited certain "abilities" from her peculiar grandfather. As soon as she could talk, she could repeat almost verbatim, complicated conversations that she had overheard. When she went to school she could, upon returning home, repeat literally word for word conversations which her mother had been having with neighbours even though Molly had not been present. It was believed that she could read the thoughts of her family and of friends who came to visit—thoughts she would often repeat out loud much to the embarrassment of her parents. She is also credited with predicting the War of Independence and the American victory over the British. This made her deeply unpopular in Marblehead where the local traders supported British interests.

Molly grew up to be an extremely plain girl. Her head was large and much too big for her slender body and she had a hooked nose, thin lips, hooded eyes and a neck, which seemed to be permanently crooked or "wry." She had few suitors, many of whom were put off by her unprepossessing looks and her sinister reputation as a clairvoyant and mind reader. At the age of 22, however, she married Robert Pitcher, a tradesman in Marblehead, and, shortly afterwards, the couple moved to nearby Lynn around 1760. By the 1770s, her fame as a clairvoyant had spread throughout New England and people travelled long distances, from far beyond the borders of Massachusetts in order to consult her. Just how accurate her prophesies were is uncertain—some may have been no more than clever and educated guesses—but it is possible that she may have had at least some precognitive powers. Similar to her grandfather, Molly Pitcher could often tell which ships would or would not return to port, she could predict sudden and violent storms, and, in those days, when pirates prowled the New England coast, such knowledge was vital to the success of any enterprise. Moreover, similar to her grandfather again, Molly Pitcher was known to issue curses against those whom she did not like or who had crossed her in some way and many a mariner was said to have paid with his life in violent storms directly attributed by local people to his exchanging hot words with her.

Molly died in 1813, at the age of 75, and by this time her reputation as a "wise woman" or "witch" was well established all over the east coast of America. Her fame prompted the poet John Greenleaf Whittier to write a long poem dedicated to her amazing powers of prediction in 1832.

The idea of the thin, aesthetic "magician" making his way up to the ancient burying-ground to call down elemental powers or his misshapen and ill-proportioned granddaughter making predictions from her small house in Lynn must have appealed to Lovecraft's imagination. Both John Dimond and Molly Pitcher might well be characters from his tales and may indeed have formed the inspiration for some of the strange people who inhabit his fiction.

His imagination may also have been fired by the strange anomalies to be found in New England religious thinking. For many of the early settlers, primal America was an extremely frightening place. It was a land of deep, dark woods in which all manner of evils were waiting for God's people. There were creatures such as the colonists had never seen before and dark hellishly painted devils (as they took the Indians to be) who hid behind every bush, attempting to drag the righteous from the path that the Lord had set out for them. The only thing that these early settlers had to defend themselves with was their faith. And that faith could often take extreme forms, as the perceived evil grew stronger.

New Light Stir

One of the major religious occurrences in early New England life was the New Light Stir. The particularly unsettled time around the American Revolution saw a particularly strong evangelical revival that swept through the New England hill country and along the coast as far as maritime Canada between the years 1774 and 1783. This was described in many ways—a purification of the Faithful in a time of warfare and trouble or to elicit God's aid in the battle against the English. Radical Evangelism grew rapidly amongst the New England communities taking many forms—Shakers, Universalists, and

Freewill Baptists as well as the followers of many individual hill preachers who founded their own churches and sects. Many of the colonists believed that the war signalled the end of the world—that it was in fact, the Armageddon of which the Bible had spoken—and formed themselves into "belief groups" to await the Second Coming which must surely follow. This belief was strengthened by the famous Dark Day on 19th May 1780 when the entire New England coastline was plunged into darkness. The entire Hudson Valley was plunged into absolute blackness and the phenomenon extended as far east as Casco Bay. With the darkness came an eerie silence. No one could see even to read, except by candlelight and even the birds flew home to nest in trees, thinking it was night. All New England was affected and lay under a cloud of absolute gloom. The darkness was probably due to a solar eclipse, but occurring as it did roughly about halfway through the Stir, its effect on the hill country was electric. Even in sophisticated Newhaven, people were concerned and panicked that this indeed might mark the end of all things. For the Revivalists of the New Light Stir, however, this was the fulfilment of prophecy and a sure sign that the Lord was coming. Both their tone and worship took on more radical overtones and the hill preachers became much more fervent in their exhortations. Sects began to flourish as never before.

The Universal Friends

One of the more radical of them was the Universal Friends—the followers of the prophetess Jemima Wilkinson, who flourished in Rhode Island between 1776 and 1789. Wilkinson who had been born into a Quaker family in Cumberland, Rhode Island (she was the eighth child), was considered to be "touched by the spirit" which enabled her to see visions and make prophesies. By 1776, she had rejected the plain style of worship pursued by the Quakers and had joined a more "charismatic" Puritan congregation at nearby Abbott Run. In the year of the Revolution, Jemima's elder sister, Patience, bore an illegitimate child and was expelled from the Quaker congregation as were her two brothers who had volunteered for military service in the American army. They joined her and shortly after began to experience ecstatic visions themselves.

Later they would be joined by other members of the family including her father. In the latter half of that same year, Jemima contracted an "illness" during which her visions increased. She claimed to have been visited by two archangels who revealed "wonderful secrets" to her and also announced that the End of the World was fast approaching. She also claimed to have seen her own soul ascending into Heaven. This made her a "seeress" and a "prophet of the Last Days" and gained her a good number of converts. New branches of her sect appeared in South Kensington and New Millford in the early-to-mid 1780s. The prophetess herself urged celibacy and drew up rules for day-to-day living such as the preparation of food, dress, personal hygiene, and demarcation between the sexes in indoor and outdoor labour. Her influence grew steadily, bringing with it a tradition of seeing visions and of hearing voices, extending even beyond the borders of Massachusetts. Her sect drew the "spiritually lost" (a title in which she revelled), people who didn't really fit into any other religion but who gloried in visions and "miracles." Some even claimed to have "esoteric knowledge" granted to them by angels. By the time Jemima Wilkinson died in 1819, her visionary church was well established with congregations operating as far away as Philadelphia. There was even a small settlement of them in the Seneca Lake region of New York State. However, the Universal Friends did not long survive the prophetess's death and split in acrimony and division to be absorbed by other religions. Even the Seneca Lake settlement collapsed and was gone within a decade. The church that she had founded and which had briefly flourished in New England had nevertheless left behind a tradition of mysticism and supernatural experiences that tinged the fundamentals of religion in Rhode Island and many other New England colonies, and it is this aspect of which Lovecraft may well have been aware.

Samuel Sewell

Following in the tradition of Jemima Wilkinson were the followers of Samuel Sewell, a cobbler from Concord, who shared his name with one of the judges in the Salem Witch Trials over fifty years earlier. "The Sewellites," who flourished briefly in the 1780s, also saw visions and claimed to hear voices and sounds in the remote forest areas, which they interpreted as being the work of either angels of the Devil. They made reference to earlier civilizations that had brought down "great evil" upon America that the righteous must cleanse. Again after Sewell's death at the end of the 1700s, the sect seems to have folded and nothing further is heard of it. Even so, it had established a tradition of ancient and malignant powers living in the deep woodlands, an idea which was to give Lovecraft one of his most persistent themes.

The Brethren of the New Light

Possibly the most bizarre of all the New England sects around this time was that headed by a pipe fitter from Charlestown—the Brethren of the New Light. In the days before the Stir, the Brethren had been influenced by the message of an itinerant Freewill Baptist preacher, Isaiah Parker, who would afterward become their minister. In the meantime the pipe fitter, Shadrach Ireland, answered their call and in 1755 organized a congregation in Charlestown, Massachusetts. However, his increasingly eccentric message began to alienate many of his followers who deserted to become Baptists under Parker. In response, Ireland's message and behaviour became more and more bizarre. Around 1770, he abandoned his wife and announced a doctrine of "spiritual wifery" ("as the people of old") by which he could choose "wives" from amongst his female disciples. He made his followers build him a large brick dwelling called The Square House where he lived with several of his "spiritual wives" and a retinue of female disciples. He proclaimed himself to be immortal through a secret knowledge that he had obtained directly from God and assured his followers that they, too could live forever if they scrupulously obeyed his edicts. He declared all his followers "perfect" and stated that those who appeared to die were not dead at all but resting and awaiting the Call on the Last Day when they would wake up, walk out of their tombs, and meet the Lord. To this end, bodies were not to be buried in graves or cemeteries but were to be placed in specially sealed, stone-lined tombs, constructed under the New England hills, where they would lie awaiting the Final Trumpet. Such places (and it is said that some of these chambers were indeed constructed) must have been almost like "dormitories of the dead" where rows of cadavers lay together.

As Ireland's ministry grew more and more peculiar, many of his followers abandoned their own families and went to live with him in the Square House. Here they experienced ecstatic visions and heard the voices of angels and felt the touch of miraculous powers. In 1773, Ireland proclaimed himself blessed and immortal and shifted his church to a more apocalyptic vision, announcing that he was Christ's herald and that the End of All Things was fast approaching.

Ireland's congregation was to last roughly five more years. In 1777, exhausted by his prophetic visions, he began to "sicken" and took to his bed, stating that his earthly ministry was finished but that God had a far more glorious one waiting for him. He urged his disciples not to bury him, for the time was short. God was coming to take the Church. After his death in September 1778, his followers placed his body in a lime filled box where it reposed for six weeks before burial. His followers continued to occupy The Square House until around 1781 when the sect fell apart amid rancour and division. Many members were later absorbed into Mother Ann Lee's Shakers. The concept of uncoffined bodies, however, representing immortals, lying somewhere under the New England hills was the stuff of nightmares and must have added a rather sinister note to the region.

The idea of vanished civilizations that had worshipped monstrous gods; of dark and forbidden books containing ancient mysteries; of reclusive communities who held strange beliefs and might follow even stranger ways and of odd religious sects who carried out questionable practices all drew together in much of Lovecraft's fiction and in the stories of many of his adherents. Whilst charting the themes, which shaped his imagination, it is of course, easy to dismiss them all as mere superstition and as being without any real foundation. And yet the question remains—what if there was at least *some* grain of truth within them? What if Lovecraft *had* glimpsed some dark secret during his studies and what if there *is* something monstrous, lying just beyond the limits of the human mind—whose awful Presence is dimly suggested by various clues scattered across both history and folklore? The prospect is an unsettling one.

Perhaps the idea of Lovecraft and those similar to him is suggested by one of his earlier creations in his story *The Music of Erich Zann* (written in December

1921). In it the ancient, dumb musician sits alone in his garret room in the Rue d'Ausell, playing ceaselessly upon his viol whilst all around him great and inhuman shapes grow in the shadows and his narrow window reveals glimpses of strange and terrible other worlds. Perhaps this, more than any other is the abiding image of the strange recluse of Rhode Island and of those who would follow him.

Appendix
Miscellaneous Nightmares

From the shadow by the fireplace and the shape on the heath, from the Devil in the lone bush and the spirit lurking by the head of the bed, O Lord protect us all.

—Ancient prayer

Although we are all familiar with the traditional terrors of the Undead—vampires, werewolves, zombies, and so on, other, perhaps less well-known horrors also lurk in the deepest recesses of our minds. These are not necessarily the unquiet spirits of the departed but are creatures that hold a quality of menace and the supernatural. Arguably, these beings do not strictly qualify as members of the Undead, because they have never been truly alive, and yet they exude an air of fear, that is normally associated with unquiet spirits.

Mara

We often describe such imagined monsters and our deepest fears as nightmares, but where does the word come from? "Nightmare" has its origins in a night creature in Germanic and Scandinavian folklore that was known as the Mara. Such a creature was greatly feared by all sleepers as it had the power to draw energy from the body and to greatly disturb the mind, inducing wild fancies and imaginings. In many ways, the Mara resembled the ancient incubi and succubi that tormented Roman sleepers. It could enter a room through the tiniest aperture—through a keyhole or in the space under a door. It would then settle, astride, on the chest of the sleeper and commence to ride him or her like a horse. He or she would experience foul and exhausting dreams, awaking feeling badly rested and often soaking with sweat.

Nordic Lore

In Nordic lore, the Mara was invariably a female wraith that only attacked sleeping men, disturbing their sleep and interfering with their manhood. She committed lewd and strenuous sexual acts, which left them feeling weak and ill when they eventually woke. She tormented them with awful visions and made them toss and turn as if in the throes of passion. In fact, some of them could die with palpitations of the heart as a result of the Mara attack. There was no real defence against the attack of the Mara except to spend some time in deep and earnest prayer before going to bed. Some of the old Norse sagas from around the 8th or 9th centuries speak of the demon and she is sometimes depicted as having the upper torso of a horse and the lower body of a naked woman. Indeed, it was commonly believed in both Norway and Denmark, that the Mara was the spirit of an actual living woman who had lived a wanton life and was troubled by her memories as she slept. Her spirit therefore roamed the countryside, attacking men where she could find them.

Buddhism

The name also appears, as a dubious force, in the Indo-Aryan dialect and is thought to have come from the East. In fact, Mara appears in Buddhist folklore is the name of a demon who tempted the Gautama Buddha (563–483 B.C.) by assuming the shape of a beautiful woman. The Buddha resisted her temptations but other, lesser, men were not so fortunate. Her name is usually used in Buddhist literature to signify the "death" of the spiritual life. In Buddhist folklore, she is often portrayed as the Lord of Evil, desirous of destroying Mankind in lewd and lustful ways.

Latvia

The Mara is also featured in Latvian mythology. Here she is a goddess—one of the higher deities of Latvian folklore. She sometimes appeared as a beautiful young woman and at other times as an aged crone and, in either guise, not always sympathetic towards Humankind. Once again, she could enter a room through the tiniest crack in order to disturb the sleep of those who were resting within a house or room. She drew energies from them whilst they slept and troubled their minds with strange and frightening dreams. In many ways, she resembled what we would today describe as a vampire. In order to placate this rather wilful deity, a special day was set aside in her honour—August 15th. In Christian Latvia, as the Church grained a firmer hold on the popular mind, this became the Feast of Mary, the Mother of Christ, thus Christianising what was essentially a pagan entity.

Orkney and Shetland

The Mara was greatly feared on the islands of Orkney and Shetland. These islands had been colonized by the Vikings and much of the Old Norse tradition still remain in these parts to this day. In the folklore of Orkneys, the Mara was essentially female and closely resembled a form of vampire. In some cases, she also took the form of a large black horse, threatened the sleeper with its hooves. However, she could be driven away with charms, amulets, and incantations, that would protect the sleeper. A lengthy charm from Shetland had to be repeated in its entirety (and sometimes had to be said twice or three times) before retiring for the night. It said:

De man o' meicht,
He rode o' nicht,
Wi' nedder swird
Nor feard nor licht,

He socht da mare
He fund da mare,
He bund da mare,
Wi' her ain hair,
An' made her swear
By middin; meicht
Dat sho' was never bide a nicht
What he had rod, dat man o' meicht.

The notion of taking hairs from the hide or the tail of a supernatural creature is a very old one and appears in the folklore of a number of Celtic countries. In Ireland, the great hero-king Brian Boru (who was the only man even to ride the Pooka or Phouka a terrible horse-like creature with demonic powers) took three hairs from its tail and extracted a promise from it that it would never attack an Irish person again.

The Shetland Incantation was said over the cribs of newborn babies or over the beds of old people, both of whom were considered to be extremely susceptible to the Mara's attentions. In fact, strands of red thread were also placed amongst the bedclothes because these were protections against the Scottish fairy kind (the Mara was not strictly considered to be a fairy but was believed to have certain fairy attributes about her)—and fairies and fairy creatures feared the colour red.

Gradually, the idea of the Mara—the succubus-like woman, the old hag, and the threatening horse—visiting sleepers during the hours of darkness, became incorporated into psychological terminology and was given as a description of disturbed and troubled sleep (in German the *nacht mara* or nightmare). Nightmares, of course, have troubled us ever since and who is to say that they are not the work of demons of some sort?

VIking Tales

Amongst the Vikings it was common to bury the revered dead, such as chieftains or great warriors within little "houses" or mounds, surrounded by his wealth and weapons. From time to time, the corporeal body of the dead chieftain or warrior could leave his funeral mound or "house" and roam the countryside. Such creatures were either described as *hel-blar* (death black) or *na-foir* (corpse pale) and retained their human shape. They were also very violent and often went about carrying some sort of weapon in their hands, which they would use to assault any humans whom they encountered. The creature would also attack any individual who attempted to break into their tombs or mounds with the intention of stealing its treasure.

Hromunde saga Gropssonar

Draugrs appear in many old Viking folktales and also in the great Northern sagas. The most famous of these is the *Hromunde saga Gropssonar* (*The Saga of Hromond Gripsson*), an ancient saga from Iceland. This tells the story of Olaf konugr-lioli (warrior king) who fights (amongst other foes) with the Witch King (or draugr), Brainn, who is an Undead king of Gaul (France) and whom he managed to defeat. The Saga was well known throughout the Nordic world and may well have influenced many other such tales. Some of these come, not from the Scandinavian world but from England where the Vikings held large swathes of the country and serve to show a connection between Norse and Germanic beliefs. One of these was the story of Thorolf Halt-Foot, which was to be found in the Eyrbyggia Saga, written down in a monastery in Iceland, probably around the middle of the 13th century. This records the story of a berserker who rose from his tomb each night and, with several Undead companions, ravaged much of the countryside of Western Iceland, attacking flocks of sheep and, from time to time, people themselves. Indeed, such a menace did he become that his son was forced to erect a wall around his mound or barrow in order to keep him in. Variants of the story were retold in England where his exploits in the countryside were equated with the activities of the Wild Hunt. These creatures were simply violent and wandering corpses that seemed to rise at will from their tombs without any specific aim or purpose. However, with the advance of Christianity, a certain moral element began to creep in. The draugr was now a person who had led a sinful life or who had disobeyed some fundamental law of the Church and this was why he or she (most, of course, tended to be men) could not rest easily in the grave.

Historia Rerum Anglicarum

This is made plain by such English writers as William of Newburgh (1136–1198) in his *Historia Rerum Anglicarum—The History of the Events of England*—and particularly in his account of a ghost in Berwick. This was the corporeal revenant of a wealthy man who had died in sin and who each night rose from his tomb and wandered about, committing nuisances wherever he went. The country people feared to go out after dark for fear of meeting the lifeless thing on the road and being physically attacked by it. The creature also brought sickness and disease in its wake, which devastated most of the town of Berwick. The connection between draugrs and disease was a very strong and potent one. Similar tales also appear in the works of English writers such as Gervaise of Tilbury and fragmentary stories from the Abbey of Byland in Yorkshire.

There was really only one way to defeat a draugr and that was to cut off its head and consign its body to flames. The Church, however, argued that a Ritual of Absolution was just as effective but there were many who questioned that. Avoidance was probably the best resort and so, as the Nordic night darkened down, many people stayed close to their hearths, refusing to venture out for fear of meeting a draugr—that violent member of the restless dead—upon the road.

Baba Yaga

Whilst the Scandinavians and, to some extent, the English kept close to their houses, terrified by draugrs and the Mara—the Russians feared yet another type of visitor who came most (though not always) at night. This was the deadly Baba Yaga—an eternal Witch. In many respects Baba Yaga, embodied the evil hag or crone who terrified many societies all across the world. There are many descriptions of her—usually as a wizened, black-faced creature, stooped and with a thin, evil countenance. She was also credited with having iron teeth and hooked bird-like, razor-sharp claws. She was also said to have a taste for human flesh, particularly the flesh of young children. Indeed, she may well have been the prototype for the "cannibal hag" who appears in such stories as the Germanic tale of *Hansel and Gretel.* Although classed as an "undead Witch," she did not travel about on a broomstick as a conventional Witch is said to do. Rather she cruised about the skies in a giant mortar in which she squatted with her bony legs wrapped around her thin body, propelling it through the air with a great pestle. As she travelled, she was accompanied by fierce winds and tempests and by a throng of wailing spirits, which signalled her coming.

Chicken-leg house

As with the Mara, old people and young children were especially susceptible to her attentions and she could descend from the clouds and down the chimney of a cottage in the blink of an eye, to snatch them away. Only prayer warned the Church would keep the Baba Yaga away. She would then carry them away to her hut, deep in the Russian forests from which they would never escape. This, of course, was no ordinary hut but a magic dwelling, balanced on four thin chicken legs. When anyone approached it, it would turn away from them, emitting ear-splitting cries and shrieks. Its windows seemed to act as eyes. Sometimes the place was said to be surrounded by a fence of bone, topped by skulls with blazing eyes, which bit and snapped at those who tried to cross. No matter what sort of entry was sought, the chicken-leg house always managed to avoid it. The inside of the dwelling, however, was filled with horrors—mainly bodiless hands that grabbed, pulled, and pinched those who managed to enter. These were said to be the hands of the evil dead—those who had died without making a final confession. The house was also filled with the emaciated bodies of the dead that attacked those who came through the door.

White, Red, and Black

Baba Yaga was also surrounded by other supernatural beings. There were, for example, three horsemen who rode around the dwelling protecting it from intruders. These were known by their colours—white, red, and black. White represented Bright Morn, Red the colour of Blood and Fire, and Black deepest midnight. All were heavily armed and would slay any trespasser on the Baba Yaga's property.

Koschey the Deathless

Baba Yaga's most terrifying "servant," however, was her huntsman Koschey. He was sometimes known as Koschey the Deathless or Koschey Bassmerty (meaning lean or boneless) and he was well-known throughout the Caucus Mountains. He would gallop, completely naked, on his magical steed, through the frozen mountain wastes, carrying away those whom he encountered to be eaten by the Baba Yaga. Although he was described as "deathless" or immortal, it was possible to slay him but this could only be done by a hero who could find his soul. Koschey's spirit, it must be noted, did not reside with his body and this made him difficult to kill. His soul, or life force, resided within a large egg, which had been placed in a massive chest, bound with iron chains that had been buried amongst the roots of a tree in the middle of a dense forest that grew in the middle of an inaccessible island that lay in the centre of a subterranean ocean. If, after much searching, a hero were to find the egg, he should break it open and inside would be a pin upon which Koschey's soul was speared. The dread huntsman would then be in his power. If he were to destroy the pin then Koschey himself would be destroyed forever.

In some descriptions of the wild huntsman, he was described as wearing the flayed skin of some of his victims, which he cast off him as he rode. When naked, he was at the height of his magical powers and nothing could stand against him. He invariably fought naked because all along his hairy arms were a number of venom glands containing a deadly poison that would snap and bite at his attacker. One bite from them could cause intense pain and eventual death.

Koschey's voice might also be used as a kind of weapon because he could modulate it to imitate any other sound. Thus children, playing on the village edge at twilight might be lured away into the forest by what they assumed to be the voice of their mother or of some relative or friend. They would then be captured by the huntsman and delivered to the Baba Yaga. He was also a master of twisting words in order to gain his way over people, especially women and if necessary, could be particularly charming, However, he secretly despised women and, his favourite "put down" to the female gender ran thus: "Foolish woman, long of hair but short of wit."

His relationship towards the Baba Yaga (who was always considered to be female) was always ambiguous. Although officially described as her "servant," it was believed throughout the Caucuses that Koschy had powers and status in his own right. It is, of course, possible that both of these entities were folkloric remnants of ancient deities—undead and undying gods and goddesses—that were once worshipped in Eastern Europe. There was little formal protection against either of them but they could be repelled by love—particularly the love of a mother. This would strip both the Baba Yaga and Koschey of their powers and protect the person who was loved against their advances. Nevertheless, this did not stop the people of Russia and of the Caucuses from locking their doors late at night against the supernatural terrors that lurked outside in the snowy dark.

Yuki-Onna

Further east in Japan, the snow and gloom brought other terrors to the doors of isolated dwellings. In remote mountain areas, the Yuki-Onna or Snow Woman was greatly feared. The Yuki-Onna has become one of Japan's most famous demons, mainly through the works of the writer Lafacio Hearn (1850–1904) who portrayed her as a kind of ghost who appeared during storms and blizzards. In recent folklore, she was portrayed as a beautiful woman, always deathly pale, who appeared in a snowstorm and who lured travellers to their doom. In order to destroy her victims, the Yuki-Onna acted similar to a vampire, drawing the breath from them and into herself. Her touch was extremely cold, cold enough to freeze the blood in their veins. When she had feasted, the Woman of the Snows melted away like a white mist. Similar to other Japanese ghosts she is portrayed in art, without legs, simply drifting through the shows like a phantom in search of her victims and gliding up to the doors of mountain dwellings seeking to gain admission. Once she did so, she could change the temperature of the house and freeze the inhabitants to death. In fact, the Yuki-Onna became the embodiment of the mountain blizzard. Hearn depicts her as incredibly lovely and tells a story of two woodcutters in Mousashi district—one old and one very young—whom she attacked. She slew the elder of the two but her heart was moved by the handsome younger one and she spared him, making him promise that he would tell nobody of his escape. Later he grew up and married a beautiful girl from another Province and brought her to live with him. He was so comfortable with her that, one night, he broke his promise and told her of his encounter with the Yuki-Onna. To his horror, she became incredibly angry, even furious, and revealed herself as the Woman of the Snows and in her rage, killed him. In this way, she completed the task that she had begun many years before.

Tengu

Although Hearn described her as a type of ghost, the idea of the Snow Woman was probably much older than the folklore that he had heard. In some parts of Japan, the Yuki-Onna was usually described as a form of *tengu,* very ancient Japanese demons. She was specifically classed as one of the *marak-aykas*, a type of Japanese minor demon that sometimes preyed on humans. Similar to the Tengu, it had a red (not a pale) face, sharp, rending teeth, and a long nose and could be extremely vicious if provoked. This class of demon sometimes took the form of a *yamabushi* (hermit) or else as an attractive girl for the purposes of waylaying travellers on the road. Many of these creatures tended to inhabit the lands around Mount Takao, near Hachoiji City. There, they attacked pilgrims on their way to the shrines and prevented individuals from fulfilling their religious obligations.

Whether the Snow Woman was one of these monsters or whether she was an undying ghost as Lafcadio Hearn has suggested, is a matter that is open for debate, as is the question as to whether she is actually a vampire or a demonic monster. Whatever her nature and origins she is still greatly feared in the remoter areas of Japan when the wind starts to blow and the snow begins to fall.

The previous examples are only a few of the undead terrors that have frightened us across the ages and may still hold a certain horror for us all. Many more are lingering in the deepest recesses of our own minds and imaginations. Although it is easy to dismiss them in the full light of day or when we are surrounded by friends and companions; when the light starts to fail and we are alone with the darkness crowding around outside, it is a different matter. Who knows what inhuman things may lurk in the gloom—werewolves, vampires, zombies—a veritable carnival of the Undead. The things that have the power to horrify us may be closer than we imagine. Maybe they're waiting no further away than just beyond the outermost edge of the comforting lamplight, waiting to pounce! You have been warned!

Index

About the Author and Illustrator

DR. BOB CURRAN was born in a rural area of County Down, Northern Ireland. After leaving school he worked at many jobs, including journalism, music, truck driving, and grave-digging. He traveled to the United States, North Africa, and Holland before returning to Northern Ireland to settle down and obtain degrees in history and education and also a doctorate in educational psychology. From his early years, he has been interested in folktales and legends and has made a study of these, writing widely in books and magazines. His work has been printed in his native Ireland, Great Britain, France, Germany, and Japan. Still lecturing and teaching, he lives in County Derry with his wife and young family.

IAN DANIELS works professionally as a painter and illustrator. His works include themes of earth and spirit, nature, dreaming, memory, ghosts, and ancient mythology. His previous illustration projects range from children's fairytales to fantasy fiction, and gothic romance, including book covers for Edgar Allan Poe, Marion Zimmer Bradley, Orson Scott Card, and Poul Anderson. He has also illustrated two collections of fairytales, *Classic Celtic Fairytales* and *Tales of the Celtic Otherworld* that feature many of his visionary paintings. Ian lives in Kent, England.